how to
Teach
Vocabulary

Scott Thornbury

Longman

series editor:
Jeremy Harmer

Pearson Education Limited
Edinburgh Gate
Harlow
Essex
CM20 2JE
England
and Associated Companies throughout the world.

www.longman.com

Printed in Malaysia, PP
Seventh impression 2008

Produced for the publishers by Bluestone Press, Charlbury, Oxfordshire, UK. Text design by Keith Rigley. Copy-edited by Sue Harmes. Illustrations on pages 90 and 159 by Margaret Jones.

ISBN 978-0-582-42966-6

Acknowledgements

We are grateful to the following for permission to reproduce copyright material:

Cambridge University Press for extracts from the *Catalan Word Selector* and *English Vocabulary in Use* (Elementary) by McCarthy and O'Dell and *The New Cambridge English Course 2* by Swan and Walter; Carcarnet Press Limited and the family of Allen Curnow for his poem 'Wild Iron' published in *Collected Poems*; Cummington Press for the poem 'Silence' by William Carlos Williams published in *The Wedge*; EMI Music Publishing for the lyrics from *Wannabe* recorded by The Spice Girls; the poet, Ruth Fainlight, for her poem 'Handbag' published in *Selected Poems* by Random House Group Limited; Oxford University Press for an extract from *New Headway Intermediate* by Soars and Soars; and Pearson Education Limited for an extract from *Longman Language Activator* © Longman Group Limited 1993.

We are grateful to the following for permission to reproduce illustrative material:

Corbis Stock Market for page 166; Language Teaching Publications for page 118; Net Languages for page 43; Oxford University Press for page 97.

We regret that we have been unable to trace the copyright holder of the following and would welcome any information enabling us to do so:

pages 95, 150 and 165

Contents

Acknowledgements

Thanks, Jeremy, David and Hester once again. What a team! Thanks are also due to Guy Cook, for his very useful feedback and suggestions. I'd also like to thank the authors and publishers of the books listed in the Further Reading list, without which this present book could not have been written. (I should add, of course, that no blame must be attached to those books for any flaws in this one.) And thanks, P. It takes two to tandem, sorry, tangi, er tango …

Introduction

Who is this book for?

How to Teach Vocabulary has been written for all teachers of English who wish to improve their knowledge and to develop their classroom skills in this important area.

What is this book about?

There has been a revival of interest in vocabulary teaching in recent years. This is partly due to the recent availability of computerised databases of words (or *corpora*), and partly due to the development of new approaches to language teaching which are much more 'word-centred', such as the 'lexical approach'. This interest is reflected in the many recent titles you will find in the *Further Reading* list on page 183. However, these developments have been slow to reach teachers in a form that is easily transferable to the classroom. This book aims to bridge that gap: to sketch in the theoretical background while at the same time suggesting ways in which the teaching of vocabulary can be integrated into lessons.

Given the challenge involved in processing, storing and producing words in a second language, the book attempts to answer the question: what can teachers do to help?

Before looking at specific procedures and techniques, we will need first to define what a word is, and how words relate to one another (Chapter 1). Chapter 2 looks at the way this knowledge is acquired, organised, stored and retrieved, and includes a brief discussion of the nature and role of memory. Crucial to the success of a teaching sequence – whether a lesson or a whole course – is the selection of items to focus on. There are a number of sources from which to select words, and Chapters 3 and 4 survey these sources – including coursebooks, dictionaries, corpora and literature.

Classroom techniques for presenting vocabulary items, and for practising them (or 'putting them to work') are dealt with in Chapters 5 and 6 respectively. In Chapter 7, the concept of the word is expanded to include both the way individual words are formed from smaller components, and the way words themselves combine to form larger 'chunks', often with idiomatic meaning. In Chapter 8, the testing of vocabulary is dealt with, while Chapter 9 looks at ways of helping learners to take responsibility for their own learning, including ways of coping with gaps in their vocabulary knowledge.

Practical classroom applications are signalled throughout by this icon. Finally, the Task File consists of photocopiable task sheets, relevant to each chapter. They can be used for individual study and reflection, or for discussion and review in a training context. An answer key is provided.

1 What's in a word?

Introduction

'A word is a microcosm of human consciousness.' (Vygotsky)

All languages have words. Language emerges first as words, both historically, and in terms of the way each of us learned our first and any subsequent languages. The coining of new words never stops. Nor does the acquisition of words. Even in our first language we are continually learning new words, and learning new meanings for old words. Take, for example, this description of a wine, where familiar words are being used and adapted to express very specialised meanings:

> A deep rich red in colour. Lush and soft aroma with plums and blackberries, the oak is plentiful and adds vanilla to the mix, attractive black pepper undercurrents. The mouthfeel is plush and comfortable like an old pair of slippers, boysenberry and spicy plum fruit flavours with liquorice and well seasoned oak. The generous finish ends with fine grained tannins and a grippy earthy aftertaste.
>
> (from web page at www.ewinexchange.com.au)

If you are not familiar with wine-tasting terminology, you may have found this text heavy going, due to both the density and specialised nature of its vocabulary. For example, you may be familiar with *lush* and *plush* but uncertain as to what they mean, or how they differ in meaning, in this context. Some words may be entirely new to you – such as *grippy* and

1

mouthfeel. Learners of a second language experience a similar bewilderment even with much simpler texts. They may be confronted by words that are totally unfamiliar, or are being used in ways that for them are novel and possibly obscure. They may even be meeting concepts that are simply not represented by words in their first language.

Their problems are compounded when they need to produce language. Finding the right word to fit the intended meaning is frustrating when your store of words is limited. And when words get confused with each other, even within this limited store, the results can be disastrous, as in this example from a student's composition:

> I am writing to complain you about an unnecessary operation that I had at St Charles Hospital, last May 24. Two months ago, I went to visit Doctor Sánchez, who works at this Hospital, because I had adenoids that prevented me to breathe. He persuaded me to have a noise operation to get out the adenoids. I was worried with this idea, but finally I accepted his decision. Two weeks later I had been operated.
>
> The problem was when he removed the bandages of my noise. I gave a shout!!!! My noise had been changed by a small noise similar to the pig's noises ...

To sum up, learning the vocabulary of a second language presents the learner with the following challenges:

- making the correct connections, when understanding the second language, between the form and the meaning of words (e.g. *mouthfeel*, *grippy*), including discriminating the meanings of closely related words (e.g. *lush* and *plush*)
- when producing language, using the correct form of a word for the meaning intended (i.e. *nose* not *noise*)

To meet these challenges the learner needs to:

- acquire a critical mass of words for use in both understanding and producing language
- remember words over time, and be able to recall them readily
- develop strategies for coping with gaps in word knowledge, including coping with unknown words, or unfamiliar uses of known words

Identifying words

In order to address the above issues, it may pay to start at the beginning, and to attempt to define what exactly a word is. Here is a sentence that, at first glance, consists of twenty of them:

> I like looking for bits and pieces like old second-hand record players and doing them up to look like new.

Of course, there are not twenty *different* words in that sentence. At least two of those twenty words are repeated: *and* is repeated once, *like* three times: *I* **like** *looking for bits and pieces* **like** *... look* **like** *new.* On the other hand, the first *like* is a verb, and the other two are prepositions – so is this really a case of the same word being repeated? And then there's *looking* and *look*: are these two different words? Or two different **forms** of the same word? Then there's *second-hand*: two words joined to make one? Probably – the hyphen suggests we treat *second-hand* differently from, say, *I've got a second hand*. But what about *record player*? Two words but one concept, surely?

It gets worse. What about *bits and pieces*? Isn't this a self-contained unit? After all, we don't say *pieces and bits*. Or *things and pieces*. A case, perhaps, of three words forming one. (Like *bits and bobs*.) And *looking for*: my dictionary has an entry for *look*, another for *look for*, and yet another for *look after*. Three different meanings – three different words? And, finally, **doing them up**: although *doing* and *up* are separated by another word, they seem to be so closely linked as to form a word-like unit (*do up*) with a single meaning: *renovate*. One word or two?

The decision as to what counts as a word might seem rather academic, but there are important implications in terms of teaching. Is it enough, for example, to teach *to look* and assume that learning *to look for* and *to look after* will follow automatically? Do you teach *look, looks, looking* together? Should you teach *record* and *player* as separate items before introducing *record player*? And how do you go about teaching *to do something up* when not only is the meaning of the whole more than the sum of its parts, but the parts themselves are moveable? You can *do a flat up* or *do up a flat*. Finally, how do you assess how many words a learner knows? If they know *bits* and they know *pieces*, can we assume they know *bits and pieces*? Does the learner who knows *bits and pieces* know 'more' than the learner who knows only *bits* and *pieces*?

Let's take a closer look at these different aspects of what constitutes a word. In so doing, we will attempt to cover the main ways in which words are described and categorised. Knowing how words are described and categorised can help us understand the decisions that syllabus planners, materials writers and teachers make when it comes to the teaching of vocabulary.

Word classes

We can see from our example sentence that words play different roles in a text. They fall into one of eight different **word classes**:

nouns	bits, pieces, record, player
pronouns	I, them
verbs	like, looking, doing, to look
adjectives	old, second-hand, new
adverb	up
prepositions	for, like
conjunction	and
determiner	–

Like, like many words in English, can belong to two or more word classes. The unrepresented class are the determiners – words like *a, the, some, this, last*.

In terms of the meanings associated with these word classes, we can make a crude division into two groups. On the one hand, there are words like *for, and, them, to* that mainly contribute to the grammatical structure of the sentence. These are called **grammatical words** (or **function words**) and are generally prepositions, conjunctions, determiners and pronouns. On the other hand, there are the **content words**, those that carry a high information load. Content words are usually nouns, verbs, adjectives and adverbs. The sense of a text is more or less recoverable using these words alone:

> like looking bits pieces old second-hand record players doing up look new

Compare this with:

> I for and like and them to like

Typically, where space is at a premium, such as in text messages, newspaper headlines, and road signs, it is the content words alone that do the job: *RAIL STRIKE TALKS END*. Content words are an open set: that is, there is no limit to the number of content words that can be added to the language. Here are a few that have been added recently – *airbag, emoticon, carjacking, cybersex, quark*. Grammatical words, on the other hand, are a closed set. The last time a pronoun was added to the language was in the early sixteenth century. (It was *them*.)

Traditionally, grammatical words belonged to the domain of grammar teaching, while the teaching of vocabulary was more concerned with content words. However, the rigid division between grammar and vocabulary has become blurred recently. The interdependence of these two systems is a key tenet of what has been called the **lexical approach** (see page 112).

Word families

We've seen how words may share the same base or **root** (e.g. *look*) but take different endings: *looks, looking, looked*. This is a feature of the grammar of most languages: the use of add-ons (called **affixes**) to make a verb past (*looked*), for example, or a noun plural (*bits*). These different grammatical forms of a word are called **inflexions**. Adding affixes serves a grammatical purpose. It is also a fundamental principle of word formation generally – the adding of affixes to the roots of words (e.g. *play*) to fashion new words. A word that results from the addition of an affix to a root, and which has a different meaning from the root, is called a **derivative**:

> play
> play + er
> re + play
> play + ful

So, while *plays, played* and *playing* are inflexions of *play*, the words *player, replay* and *playful* are each derivatives of *play*. Inflexions and derivatives are both formed by the process of **affixation**. Note that -*er* and -*ful* are end-of-word affixes, or **suffixes**, while beginning-of-word affixes, like *re-, un-, pre-, de-*, etc. are called **prefixes**.

We can now talk about words as belonging to families. A **word family** comprises the base word plus its inflexions and its most common derivatives. To take another example, the base form *understand* includes the following members in its family:

understands
understanding
understood
understandable
misunderstand
misunderstood

Research suggests that the mind groups these different forms of the same word together. Therefore, rather than talk about the number of individual words a person knows, it makes more sense to talk about the number of word families.

Word formation

Affixation is one of the ways new words are formed from old. Another one is **compounding** – that is, the combining of two or more independent words, as in the case of *second-hand*, *word processor*, *paperback*, and so on. The fact that many compounds started life as two separate words is evident from their variant spellings. Thus: *dish washer*, *dish-washer*, *dishwasher*; and *wild flower*, *wild-flower*, *wildflower*. This is one reason why it is tempting to consider *record player* as one compounded word rather than two single words.

Another reason to consider *record player* a single word is that this kind of compound pattern – noun + verb + *-er* – is a very common, and highly productive, one in English: a *record player* is a machine that plays records. Likewise *dishwasher*, *hairdryer*, *bus driver*, *goalkeeper*, *typewriter*; they are all formed according to the same principle. New words that follow this pattern are constantly joining the language: *screensaver*, *trainspotter*, *particle accelerator*, *mail server*. Another common pattern is the noun + noun pattern, as in *matchbox*, *classroom*, *teapot*, *mousemat*, etc. Of course, the two patterns – noun + noun and noun + verb + *-er* – can re-combine to form even more complex compounds: *dumptruck-driver*, *candlestick-maker*, *windscreen-wiper*, and so on.

Two words can be **blended** to form one new one (called a **blend**): *breakfast* + *lunch* = *brunch*; *information* + *entertainment* = *infotainment*. Or a word can be co-opted from one part of speech and used as another, a process called **conversion**. Typically nouns are converted into verbs (or 'verbed') as in *The shell impacted against a brick wall*; *Let's brunch tomorrow*. But other parts of speech can be converted as well: *she upped and left* (preposition → verb); *a balloon flight is an absolute must* (verb → noun). Finally, new words can be coined by shortening or **clipping** longer words: *flu* (from *influenza*), *email* (from *electronic mail*) and *dorm* (from *dormitory*).

In the following text, [1] indicates words formed by affixation, [2] compounds, [3] conversion and [4] clipping:

> Weighed down by details? The 40MB Clik! PC Card Drive from Iomega, a lightweight[2], removeable[1] storage[1] drive for PC users, will soon sort that out. Designed with people on the go[3] in mind, the Clik! PC Card Drive removes the need for additional cables and cumbersome[1] storage back-up[2,3]. Each Clik! disc has the capacity to store 40 megas[4] of information quickly and conveniently. With packaging[1,3] akin to your

favourite pair of Cutler and Gross specs[4], this stream-lined[2] system is an essential lubricant[1] to life in the fast lane.

(from *Wallpaper* magazine, Time Life)

Multi-word units
Even when words are not joined to form compounds, we have seen that groups of more than one word, such as *bits and pieces*, *do up*, *look for*, can function as a meaningful unit with a fixed or semi-fixed form. Technically these are known as **multi-word units**, but they are often called simply **lexical chunks**. For example, in the following extract (in which two workers are discussing the Australian car industry – a Holden is an Australian car) the lexical chunks are in italics:

> KEITH: *It's amazing how* the bleeding car industry's *swung round*. It's Holdens *for years* and now Fords have got it. *Well and truly.* [...] *Year after year* they're *laying* more *off* towards *the end of the year* so they knew this was coming – it wasn't *out of the blue*.

> JO: I think that they shipped *a lot of* the accessory overseas too. Before they did *a lot of the bits and pieces* themselves.

(from Slade D, *The Texture of Casual Conversation*)

The chunks vary in terms of how fixed, and how idiomatic, they are. For example, *out of the blue* is both idiomatic (that is to say, its meaning is not easily recoverable from its individual components) and fixed – you can't say *from* the blue or out of the **green**, for example. *Well and truly* and *bits and pieces* (as we have seen) are also fixed, but less idiomatic. *Year after year*, on the other hand, is only semi-fixed. It allows a limited amount of manipulation: we can say *month after month* and *day after day*. Note that both *a lot of* and *for years* are typical of the enormous number of chunks that are used to express vague quantities and qualities: *loads of*, *that sort of thing*, *more or less*, *now and again*.

It's amazing how ... belongs to a set of semi-fixed multi-word units that function as **sentence frames**: they provide a structure on which to 'hang' a sentence, and are especially useful in reducing planning time in rapid speech.

Especially common in informal language are compounds of verb + adverb (like *swung round*), or verb + preposition (*look after*). These are known as either **phrasal verbs** or **multi-part verbs**. Because they are often idiomatic (like *lay off*) and can sometimes be separated (*laying more workers off* and *laying off more workers*), they present a formidable challenge to learners. (In Chapter 7 you will find more on chunks and phrasal verbs.)

To handle the fact that there are multi-word items that behave like single words, the term **lexeme** was coined. A lexeme is a word or group of words that function as a single meaning unit. So, to return to the sentence that started this chapter:

> I like looking for bits and pieces like old second-hand record players and doing them up to look like new.

we could count *looking for*, *bits and pieces*, *record players*, *doing ... up* and *to look* as single lexemes, along with *I*, *like*, *old*, *them*, etc.

Collocations
We have seen how words 'couple up' to form compounds, and how they 'hunt in packs' in the shape of multi-word units. There is a looser kind of association called **collocation**. Two words are collocates if they occur together with more than chance frequency, such that, when we see one, we can make a fairly safe bet that the other is in the neighbourhood. The availability of **corpus data** (i.e. databases of text – see page 68) now allows us to check the statistical probability of two words co-occurring. The most frequent collocate of *record*, for example, is *world*. Another is *set*. So we have no trouble filling in the blank when we hear someone say *She set a new world …*

Collocation is not as frozen a relationship as that of compounds or multi-word units, and two collocates may not even occur next to each other – they may be separated by one or more other words. *Set*, for example, is the second most frequent collocate of *record* but it seldom occurs right next to it: *He set the junior record in 1990*. Notice that *set* and *record* can also collocate in quite a different sense: *Just to set the record straight …* In fact *set the record straight* is such a strong collocation that it almost has the status of a chunk, and indeed it gets a separate entry (under *record*) in dictionaries, as do some other strong collocates with *record*, such as *for the record*, *off the record* and *on record*.

Collocation, then, is best seen as part of a continuum of strength of association: a continuum that moves from compound words (*second-hand*, *record player*), through multi-word units – or lexical chunks – (*bits and pieces*), including idioms (*out of the blue*) and phrasal verbs (*do up*), to collocations of more or less fixedness (*set the record straight*, *set a new world record*).

Here is a text with some of its more frequent collocations underlined, while the more fixed multi-word units are in italics:

A <u>record number</u> of 54 teams will be competing in three sections as the Bryants Carpets Intermediate Snooker League *gets underway* <u>this week</u>. <u>Once again</u> all three sections *are likely to* be very <u>closely contested</u>. In Section A, <u>defending champions</u> Mariner Automatics, captained <u>once again</u> by the most successful skipper in the league, John Stevens, will be *the team to beat*.

The <u>biggest threat</u> *is likely to* come from Grimsby Snooker Club A, and P and J Builders who will have Steve Singleton *at the helm* for the <u>first time</u>.

(from the *Grimsby Evening Telegraph*)

It should be clear from this passage the extent to which word choice is heavily constrained by what comes before and after. This is perhaps the single most elusive aspect of the lexical system and the hardest, therefore, for learners to acquire. Even the slightest adjustments to the collocations – by substituting one of its components for a near synonym (underlined) – turns the text into non-standard English:

A record <u>lot</u> of 54 teams will be competing in three sections as the Bryants Carpets Intermediate Snooker League <u>reaches</u> underway <u>that</u> week. <u>One time</u> again all three sections are <u>possibly</u> to be very <u>nearly</u> contested …

By way of an example, in the learner's text in the Introduction to this chapter (page 2) there are a number of collocations that are non-standard:

to get out the adenoids (for *to remove …*)
I was worried with this idea (for *The idea worried me*)
I gave a shout (for *I shouted*)

Taken individually, each of these 'mis-collocations' is perfectly intelligible and nowhere near as serious as the *nose–noise* confusion, but in combination they may have a negative effect on some readers.

Homonyms   We have seen how *like* and *like* can be two quite different words: *I **like** looking … look **like** new.* Words that share the same form but have unrelated meanings are called **homonyms**. For historical reasons, English is rich in homonyms: *well, bat, shed, left, fair,* etc. Thus, while *fair* in the sense of beautiful or pleasing comes from an Old English word (*fæger*), its homonym *fair,* as in *Skipton Fair,* comes from Latin *feria* by way of French *foire.* While homonyms provide a headache for the learner, their ambiguity is a rich source of humour. Like the joke about the duck who went to a chemist's to buy lip-salve. 'Will you be paying by cash or credit card?' asked the pharmacist. 'Just put it on my bill,' replied the duck.

Another potential source of confusion are the many words in English that sound the same but are spelt differently: *horse* and *hoarse, meet* and *meat, tail* and *tale, discrete* and *discreet, aloud* and *allowed.* These are called **homophones** (literally 'same sound'). There are also words that are pronounced differently but spelt the same: *a **windy** day,* but *a long and **windy** road; a **live** concert,* but *where do you **live**?; a **lead** pipe,* but *a **lead** singer.* These are called **homographs** (literally 'same writing').

Polysemes   As if homonyms, homophones and homographs weren't enough, another potential source of confusion for learners – and a challenge for teachers – is the fact that very many words in English have different but overlapping meanings. Take *fair,* for example. Clearly these two senses of *fair* are homonyms:

She had long *fair* hair.
My pig won first prize at Skipton *Fair*.

But what about these?

This isn't *fair* on anyone, but it does happen.
We have a *fair* size garden and we may as well make use of it.
She was only a *fair* cook.
The sun's rays can be very harmful, beating on unprotected *fair* skin.
This *fair* city of ours …
It will be *fair* and warm.

Although there appear to be six different senses of *fair* represented here, ranging from *reasonable* through *quite large, average, pale, beautiful* to *dry and pleasant,* there is an underlying sense that at least some if not all of these meanings are related. Try substituting *pleasing*, for example, and you'll find that it more or less fits most of these contexts. Dictionary writers (lexicographers) classify words like *fair* as being polysemous – that is, of having multiple but related meanings, each of which is called a **polyseme**. *Hold* is another good example of a polysemous word:

> I *held* the picture up to the light.
> I was *held* overnight in a cell.
> You need to *hold* a work permit.
> Mrs Smith is *holding* a party next week.
> Marxists *hold* that people are all naturally creative.
> He was finding it a strain to *hold* his students' attention.
> They'll probably *hold* the London train if we're late in.
> The theatre itself can *hold* only a limited number of people.
> Will you tell her the offer still *holds*.
> These books *hold* the bed up.

> (All examples of *fair* and *hold* are from the *Collins COBUILD English Dictionary*.)

If the polysemous nature of English vocabulary provides a challenge to dictionary compilers, it is a complete headache for learners. At what point can you be said to know a word such as *fair* or *hold* – when you know its most basic meaning, or when you know the different shades of meaning represented by all its polysemes? This is an issue we will return to when we look at the teaching of word meaning.

Synonyms and antonyms

Synonyms are words that share a similar meaning. Thus: *old, ancient, antique, aged, elderly* are all synonyms in that they share the common meaning of *not young/new*. However, there the similarity ends. We are more likely to talk about *an old record player* and even *an antique one* than *an elderly record player* or *an aged one*. Synonyms are similar, but seldom the same. Even between words that seem interchangeable, such as *taxi* and *cab*, or *aubergine* and *egg-plant*, one will be preferred over the other in certain contexts and by particular speakers.

Notice we were forced to define *old* in terms of what it is not: *not young/new*. Words with opposite meanings – like *old* and *new* – are called **antonyms**. Again, like synonyms, the relation between such opposites is not always black and white (to use two antonyms) and the very notion of 'oppositeness' is troublesome. The opposite of *an **old** woman* is *a **young** woman*, but the opposite of *an **old** record player* is *a **new** one*, not *a **young** one*. Your **old** boyfriend, however, could be either the boyfriend who is not *your **young** boyfriend* or the one who is not *your **new** boyfriend*. Nevertheless, like synonyms, antonyms have a useful defining function and are therefore a convenient teaching resource.

Hyponyms

Hyponym is another *-nym* word that is useful when talking about the way word meanings are related. A hyponymous relationship is a *kind of* relationship, as in *A hammer is a kind of tool* or *A kiwi is a kind of bird (and a* *kind of fruit).* Thus, *hammer* is a hyponym of *tool*; *kiwi* a hyponym of *bird* (and *fruit*). **Co-hyponyms** share the same ranking in a hierarchy: *hammer, saw, screwdriver* are all co-hyponyms; *tool* is the **superordinate** term. But *saw* also has a superordinate relation to different kinds of saw: *fretsaw, chainsaw, jigsaw,* etc. We can illustrate these relations like this:

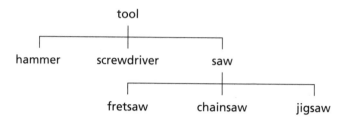

A similar kind of relationship is *a part of*: as in *a keyboard is part of a computer.* Notice that this is quite different from saying *a keyboard is a kind of computer.* In this poem by William Carlos Williams, the words that have this kind of relationship (called **meronymy)** are underlined, while co-hyponyms are in italics:

> Under a low sky
> this quiet morning
> of *red* and
> *yellow* <u>leaves</u> –
>
> A bird disturbs
> no more than one <u>twig</u>
> of the *green* leaved
> peach tree

Thus, *leaves* and *twigs* are parts of trees, while *red, yellow* and *green* are kinds of colours.

Lexical fields

In the following passage (from a short story by David Guterson) there are a number of words that are connected to the idea of Christmas (*Christmas Eve, the* [*Christmas*] *tree, lights* and *carols*):

> We were at my sister's house for Christmas Eve, fire in the fireplace, lights on the tree, Christmas carols playing on the stereo. Outside the window a light snow blew down. Icicles hung from the gutters and in the yard the grass looked sprinkled with powder. By morning everything would be white.

As Christmas-themed words, *snow, icicles* and *fireplace* could also be included, since they all belong to a mental scenario associated with northern hemisphere Christmas celebrations. Words that have this kind of thematic relationship are said to belong to the same **lexical field**. *Tree, carols, fireplace* and *lights* all belong to the lexical field of 'Christmas' – although all of them, with the possible exception of *carols* – belong to other lexical fields as well. Notice that the text also contains a lexical field of weather-related words that partly overlaps with the Christmas words (*snow, blew, icicles, powder, white*), as well as words connected with the *house* theme (*fireplace, stereo, window, gutters, yard, grass*).

Style and connotation

Here's an extract quoted earlier in this chapter:

KEITH: It's amazing how the bleeding car industry's swung round. It's Holdens for years and now Fords have got it. Well and truly. […] Year after year they're laying more off towards the end of the year so they knew this was coming – it wasn't out of the blue.

JO: I think that they shipped a lot of the accessory overseas too. Before they did a lot of the bits and pieces themselves.

Expressions like *the bleeding car industry, out of the blue* and *bits and pieces*, suggest a **style** of language that is closer to spoken, informal English than to a formal written style. Moreover, the use of *bleeding* suggests British or Australian English rather than North American English. British, Australian and North American are different **varieties** of English. More than anything, choice of words is an indicator of style and place of origin. Dictionaries typically indicate the style and variety of a word by conventions such as the following:

Am	North American English
Aus	Australian English
Br	British English
dated	
fml	formal
infml	informal
law	
literary	
poetic	
slang	
taboo	

(from *The Cambridge International Dictionary of English*, CUP)

A distinction is often made between style and **register**. A register of English is a variety of the language as used in specific contexts, such as legal English, academic English, or technical English. Discrepancies in style and register are as disconcerting as unusual collocations. Take, for example, this email I received (from somebody I had never met):

Dear Scott,
I have booked Diana to arrive in Barcelona at 22.25 (10.25pm) on Saturday 19th August. I hope the lateness of the hour doesn't discommode you too much. Di will be flying out of Barcelona on Friday 25th August at 1.25pm. Are you cool with these arrangements? If not, I can change them no probs.
Also, I'm still trying to track down the article you want.
Regards,
[…]

Note the difference in style between words and expressions like *lateness of the hour* and *discommode* (formal, and somewhat archaic, on the one hand) and *are you cool, no probs, track down* (colloquial and spoken, on the other).

Linked to style is the issue of **connotation**. Two words may be synonyms, but each may evoke quite different associations. *Famous* and *notorious* both have an underlying meaning of *well-known*, but only the latter has negative connotations. In this book, you will find the term *learners* used in preference to *students* or *pupils*, which have somewhat passive connotations. In the following newspaper text, the emotive connotations of the underlined words emphasise the writer's disapproval of an event that itself was triggered by a politician's use of the negative (or **pejorative**) term 'mongrel':

> EX-PRIME Minister Ted Heath last night <u>torpedoed</u> William Hague's <u>desperate</u> <u>bid</u> to <u>shut down</u> the Tory race <u>row</u>. He compared <u>maverick</u> MP John Townend – who described the British as a 'mongrel race' – to Enoch Powell and said he should be <u>kicked out</u> of the party. Sir Ted, who <u>booted</u> Powell out in 1968, warned 'many other' right-wing MPs shared Townend's <u>extreme</u> views.
>
> (from *The Sun* newspaper)

Conclusions

In this chapter the aim has been to show that a word is a more complex phenomenon than at first it might appear. For example:

- words have different functions, some carrying mainly grammatical meaning, while others bear a greater informational load
- the same word can have a variety of forms
- words can be added to, or combined, to form new words
- words can group together to form units that behave as if they were single words
- many words commonly co-occur with other words
- words may look and/or sound the same but have quite different meanings
- one word may have a variety of overlapping meanings
- different words may share similar meanings, or may have opposite meanings
- some words can be defined in terms of their relationship with other words – whether, for example, they belong to the same set, or co-occur in similar texts
- words can have the same or similar meanings but be used in different situations or for different effects

Looking ahead

Now that we have looked at some of the complexities of vocabulary, the next chapter will examine how words are learned, both in the first language and in a second language. We will also explore how theories of learning might impact on the teaching of vocabulary – a theme that will be developed in subsequent chapters.

2 How words are learned

- How important is vocabulary?
- What does it mean to 'know a word'?
- How is our word knowledge organised?
- How is vocabulary learned?
- How many words does a learner need to know?
- How are words remembered?
- Why do we forget words?
- What makes a word difficult?
- What kind of mistakes do learners make?
- What are the implications for teaching?

How important is vocabulary?

'Without grammar very little can be conveyed, without vocabulary *nothing* can be conveyed.' This is how the linguist David Wilkins summed up the importance of vocabulary learning. His view is echoed in this advice to students from a recent coursebook (Dellar H and Hocking D, *Innovations*, LTP): 'If you spend most of your time studying grammar, your English will not improve very much. You will see most improvement if you learn more words and expressions. You can say very little with grammar, but you can say almost anything with words!'

Most learners, too, acknowledge the importance of vocabulary acquisition. Here are some statements made by learners, in answer to the question *How would you like to improve your English?*

- Oral is my weakness and I can't speack a fluent sentence in English. Sometimes, I am lack of useful vocabularies to express my opinions.
- My problem is that I forget the words soon after I have looked in the dictionary. For example when I read a English book.
- I would like to improve my vocabulary. I have the feeling that I always use the same idiomatic expressions to express different sort of things.
- I'd like to enlarge my vocabulary (this word I also had to find in dictionary). Too often my speaking is hard caused by missing words.

However, vocabulary teaching has not always been very responsive to such problems, and teachers have not fully recognised the tremendous communicative advantage in developing an extensive vocabulary. For a long

13

time, teaching approaches such as the **Direct Method** and **audiolingualism** gave greater priority to the teaching of grammatical structures. In order not to distract from the learning of these structures, the number of words introduced in such courses was kept fairly low. Those words which were taught were often chosen either because they were easily demonstrated, or because they fitted neatly into the 'structure of the day'.

The advent of the **communicative approach** in the 1970s set the stage for a major re-think of the role of vocabulary. The communicative value of a core vocabulary has always been recognised, particularly by tourists. A phrase book or dictionary provides more communicative mileage than a grammar – in the short term at least. Recognition of the meaning-making potential of words meant that vocabulary became a learning objective in its own right. In 1984, for example, in the introduction to their *Cambridge English Course,* Swan and Walter wrote that 'vocabulary acquisition is the largest and most important task facing the language learner'. Coursebooks began to include activities that specifically targeted vocabulary.

Nevertheless, most language courses were (and still are) organised around grammar syllabuses. There are good grounds for retaining a grammatical organisation. While vocabulary is largely a collection of **items**, grammar is a system of **rules**. Since one rule can generate a great many sentences, the teaching of grammar is considered to be more productive. Grammar multiplies, while vocabulary merely adds. However, two key developments were to challenge the hegemony of grammar. One was the **lexical syllabus**, that is, a syllabus based on those words that appear with a high degree of frequency in spoken and written English. The other was recognition of the role of **lexical chunks** (see page 6) in the acquisition of language and in achieving fluency. Both these developments (which we will look at more closely in Chapter 7) were fuelled by discoveries arising from the new science of **corpus linguistics**.

The effect of these developments has been to raise awareness as to the key role vocabulary development plays in language learning. Even if most coursebooks still adopt a grammatical syllabus, vocabulary is no longer treated as an 'add-on'. Much more attention is given to the grammar of words, to collocation and to word frequency. This is reflected in the way coursebooks are now promoted. For example, the back covers of three recent courses claim:

> Strong emphasis on vocabulary, with a particular focus on high frequency, useful words and phrases. (from *Cutting Edge Intermediate*)

> Well-defined vocabulary syllabus plus dictionary training and pronunciation practice, including the use of phonetics. (from *New Headway English Course*)

> … a strongly lexical syllabus, presenting and practising hundreds of natural expressions which students will find immediately useful. (from *Innovations*)

What does it mean to 'know a word'?

We have been talking about the importance of having an extensive vocabulary – that is, knowing lots of words. But what does it mean to *know* a word?

At the most basic level, knowing a word involves knowing:

- its **form**, and
- its **meaning**

If I tell you that there is, in Maori, a word that takes the form *tangi*, you can not really claim to say you 'know *tangi*' since you don't know what *tangi* means. The form of the word tells you nothing about its meaning.

So, what does *tangi* mean? Well, it means *sound*. But is that *sound* the noun, or *sound* the verb, as in *to sound*? In fact, it can mean both – so part of knowing the meaning of *tangi* is knowing its grammatical function. But *tangi* doesn't mean only *sound*; it also means *lamentation*, *dirge* and *to weep*. In fact the *waiata tangi* (funeral lament) is an integral part of the *tangihanga*, or Maori funeral ceremony, so much so that *tangi* has come to mean (colloquially) simply *funeral*. But, of course, not a funeral in the European sense. A Maori *tangi* is a very different kind of ceremony. For a start … (and so on). In other words, knowing the meaning of a word is not just knowing its dictionary meaning (or meanings) – it also means knowing the words commonly associated with it (its collocations) as well as its connotations, including its register and its cultural accretions.

Finally, we need to distinguish between receptive knowledge and productive knowledge. Now that you know the meaning of *tangi* you can probably make sense of the opening passage from the short story 'Tangi' by Witi Ihimaera:

> Do not listen to the wailing, Tama. Do not listen to the women chanting their sorrows, the soaring waiata tangi which sings alone and disconsolate above the wailing. It is only the wind, Tama. Do not listen to the sorrows of the marae …

Assuming you understood *tangi* in this extract, you may still feel uncomfortable about working the word into a letter or dropping it into a conversation. (And so far you have only had its written form, not its spoken form.) In other words, you have receptive, but not productive, knowledge of the word. Receptive knowledge exceeds productive knowledge and generally – but not always – precedes it. That is, we understand more words than we utter, and we usually understand them *before* we are capable of uttering them.

To summarise, word knowledge can be represented as in this diagram for the word *tangi*:

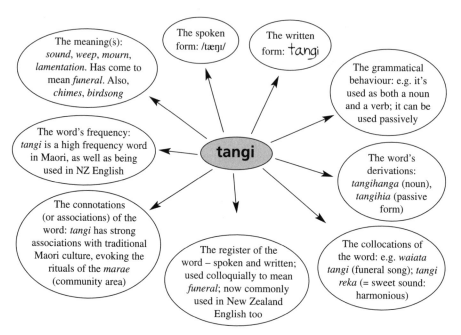

What is involved in knowing the word 'tangi'

Of course, even a proficient speaker of Maori may not 'know' all these aspects of the word *tangi*: word knowledge is incremental and takes time. What is sometimes called a state of **initial fuzziness** seems to be an inevitable part of vocabulary learning.

How is our word knowledge organised?

The above diagram for the word *tangi* suggests that the way words are stored in the mind resembles less a dictionary than a kind of network or web. This is an apt image: the mind seems to store words neither randomly nor in the form of a list, but in a highly organised and interconnected fashion – in what is often called the **mental lexicon**.

The mistakes we make offer an insight into the way the mental lexicon is organised. For example, the speaker who says 'I watched this Maori *tango* on television' is confusing two words that are similar in form, if quite different in meaning: *tangi* and *tango*. This suggests that words with similar sound structure are closely interconnected, so that the search for one may sometimes activate its near neighbour. The comic effect of this kind of mistake (called a **malapropism**) has not been lost on writers, including Shakespeare:

BOTTOM: 'Thisbe, the flowers of odious savours sweet –'
QUINCE: 'Odious' – odorous!

As in a dictionary, similar forms seem to be located adjacent to each other. But if every time we 'looked up' a word in the mental lexicon, we started with its form, we would have to scroll through a great many similar-sounding but totally unrelated words: *tandem, tangent, tangle, tango,* etc. This would be very time-consuming. To speed things up, words are also interconnected according to their shared meanings – all the *fruit* words being interconnected, and all the *clothing* words interconnected too. So, if I want to say *I had a delicious **mango** for breakfast,* the lexicon activates the fruit department before triggering a search of words beginning with *mang-*. This accounts for the fact that, in experiments, subjects find that answering the first of the following two questions is easier and quicker than answering the second:

1 Name a fruit that begins with *p*.
2 Name a word that begins with *p* that is a fruit.

In each case the word search simultaneously focuses on form and meaning, but it seems the brain is better disposed to begin the search via the meaning-based (thesaurus-like) lexicon than the form-based (dictionary-like) one. This also accounts for the fact that, once subjects have accessed the *fruit* category, they are able to find other fruits more quickly. All of this suggests a semantic (meaning-based) organisation, but one that also has a form-based (or what is called **morphological**) back-up. The two systems work in tango, sorry, in tandem. This explains why malapropisms (such as *odious/odorous*) are not only similar in sound to the intended word, but are almost always the same part of speech and often share aspects of their meaning. Hence, many learners of English confuse *chicken* and *kitchen*: not only do the two words sound alike, they are both nouns and they share elements of meaning in that they belong to the same lexical field.

We can think of the mental lexicon, therefore, as an overlapping system in which words are stored as 'double entries' – one entry containing information about meaning and the other about form. These individual word entries are then linked to words that share similar characteristics, whether of meaning (*mango/papaya*) or of form (*tangi/tango*) – or both (*chicken/kitchen*). The number of connections is enormous. Finding a word is like following a path through the network, or better, following several paths at once. For, in order to economise on processing time, several pathways will be activated simultaneously, fanning out across the network in a process called 'spreading activation'.

Linked to this system are other areas of cognition, such as world knowledge (like an encyclopedia) and memory (like a personal diary or autobiography), so that activation of a word like *tangi* or *mango* or *tango* also triggers general knowledge and personal experiences that extend beyond the simple 'dictionary' meanings of these words. Knowing a word, then, is the sum total of all these connections – semantic, syntactic, phonological, orthographic, morphological, cognitive, cultural and autobiographical. It is unlikely, therefore, that any two speakers will 'know' a word in exactly the same way.

How is vocabulary learned?

Knowing a word is one thing – but how is that knowledge acquired? In learning their first language the first words that children learn are typically those used for **labelling** – that is, mapping words on to concepts – so that the concept, for example, of dog has a name, *dog*. Or *doggie*. But not all four-legged animals are dogs: some may be cats, so the child then has to learn how far to extend the concept of *dog*, so as not to include cats, but to include other people's dogs, toy dogs, and even pictures of dogs. In other words, acquiring a vocabulary requires not only labelling but **categorising** skills.

Finally, the child needs to realise that common words like *apple* and *dog* can be replaced by superordinate terms like *fruit* and *animal*. And that *animal* can accommodate other lower order words such as *cat, horse* and *elephant*. This involves a process of **network building** – constructing a complex web of words, so that items like *black* and *white*, or *fingers* and *toes*, or *family* and *brother* are interconnected. Network building serves to link all the labels and packages, and lays the groundwork for a process that continues for as long as we are exposed to new words (and new meanings for old words) – that is, for the rest of our lives.

In what ways is the development of a second language (L2) lexicon any different from that of the first language (L1)? Perhaps the most obvious difference is the fact that, by definition, second language learners already have a first language. And not only do they have the words of their first language, but they have the conceptual system that these words encode, and the complex network of associations that link these words one with another. Learning a second language involves both learning a new conceptual system, and constructing a new vocabulary network – a second mental lexicon.

Consider, for example, the problems I faced when learning Maori kinship terms:

> The word *teina* is used by (1) a boy when speaking of his younger brother; (2) a girl when speaking of her younger sister. The word *tuakana* is used by (1) a boy when speaking of his older brother; (2) a girl when speaking of her older sister. The word *tuahine* is used by a boy when speaking of his sister. The word *tungane* is used by a girl when speaking of her brother.
>
> (from Harawira K, *Teach Yourself Maori*, Reed Books)

The cultural 'distance' between Maori and European conceptual systems is relatively large, but for most language learners there will be much more that is shared than is foreign. Even learning Maori, I did not have to relearn the concept of *hand*, for example, or of *horse*. The fact that the adult learner's concept system is already installed and up-and-running, means that he or she is saved a lot of the over- and under-generalising associated with first language learning. An adult learner is unlikely to confuse a dog with a cat, for example.

However, there is a downside to having a ready-made conceptual system with its associated lexicon. Faced with learning a new word, the second language learner is likely to short-cut the process of constructing a network of associations – and simply map the word directly onto the mother tongue equivalent. Thus, if a German-speaking learner learns the English word *table*, rather than creating a direct link from *table* to the concept of table, they are more likely to create a link to their L1 equivalent (*Tisch*). The L1 word acts as a stepping stone to the target concept.

Perhaps – in order to pre-empt an over-dependence on mental translation – learners should be advised to follow Christopher Isherwood's advice:

> When Christopher began giving English lessons, he would try to convey to his German pupils something of his own mystique about the German language. 'A table doesn't *mean* ein Tisch – when you're learning a new word, you must never say to yourself *it means*. That's altogether the wrong approach. What you must say to yourself is: Over there in England, they have a thing called a table. We may go to England and look at it and say "that's our Tisch". But it isn't. The resemblance is only on the surface. The two things are essentially different, because they've been thought about differently by two nations with two different cultures. If you can grasp the fact that that thing in England isn't merely *called* a table, it really *is* a table, then you'll begin to understand what the English themselves are like … Of course, if you cared to buy a table while you were in England and bring it back here, it would become ein Tisch. But not immediately. Germans would have to think about it as ein Tisch for quite a long while, first.'
>
> (from *Christopher and His Kind*, Eyre Methuen)

Isherwood is suggesting that the words *table* and *Tisch* are not synonymous – that their meanings do not map onto each other snugly. While this example may be a little far-fetched, it is true that the degree of semantic overlap between words in different languages can vary a lot. This is often a cause of lexical errors. A Spanish speaker who complains that her shoes make 'her fingers hurt' is over-generalising from Spanish *dedo* which means both *finger* and *toe*. Likewise, a German speaker who has left his 'clock' at home, may in fact mean his *watch*: *Uhr* stands for both *clock* and *watch*.

Many cross-language errors are due to what are known as **false friends**. False friends are words that may appear to be equivalent, but whose meanings do not in fact correspond. Examples of false English friends for speakers of Polish, for example, are:

actually   (*aktualnie* in Polish means 'at present', 'currently')
apartment (*apartament* in Polish is a 'hotel suite')
chef   (*szef* is Polish for 'chief' or 'boss')
dress   (*dres* is Polish for 'tracksuit')
history   (*historia* in Polish means 'story')
lunatic   (*lunatyk* in Polish is a 'sleepwalker')
pupil   (*pupil* in Polish is a 'pet' or 'favourite')

Over-reliance on transfer from L1 could, conceivably, result in a Pole saying: 'Tell the chef that actually there's a lunatic in a dress in my apartment!'

Generally speaking, however, languages that share words with similar forms (called **cognates**) have many more **real friends** than false friends. An

Italian learner of English, for example, need not feel suspicious of the English word *apartment* (*appartamento* in Italian), nor *garage* (the same in Italian), *garden* (*giardino*), or *balcony* (*balcone*) – among thousands of others.

As well as false friends and real friends, there are **strangers**: words that have no equivalent in the L1 at all, since the very concept does not exist in the learner's lexicon. Supposedly Chinese has no equivalent for the English words *privacy* or *community*. In this case, the Chinese learner of English is in a position not dissimilar to a child learning his or her L1; they are learning the concept and the word in tandem. The way colour terms are distributed in different cultures is also a possible source of conceptual strangeness. Russian, for example, distinguishes between two kinds of blue: *sinij* vs *goluboj,* for which English has no satisfactory equivalents. But one needs to be careful not to read too much into such reported differences; like the Inuit's one hundred different words for *snow,* they may in fact be language myths.

By analogy with false friends, real friends and strangers, it may be the case that, for a good many second language learners, most of the words in their L2 lexicon are simply **acquaintances**. They have met them, they know them by name, they even understand them, but they will never be quite as familiar to them as their mother tongue equivalents. This is because the associative links in the second language lexicon are usually less firmly established than mother tongue links. To extend the metaphor: learning a second language is like moving to a new town – it takes time to establish connections and turn acquaintances into friends. And what is the difference between an acquaintance and a friend? Well, we may forget an acquaintance, but we can never forget a friend. (For more on remembering and forgetting, see below.)

How many words does a learner need to know?

A further major difference between first and second language vocabulary learning is in the potential size of the lexicon in each case. An educated native speaker will probably have a vocabulary of around 20,000 words (or, more accurately, 20,000 word families – see page 4). This is the result of adding about a thousand words a year to the 5,000 he or she had acquired by the age of five. An English dictionary includes many more: the *Longman Dictionary of Contemporary English,* for example, boasts 'over 80,000 words and phrases', while the *Oxford English Dictionary* contains half a million entries. Most adult second language learners, however, will be lucky to have acquired 5,000 word families even after several years of study.

This relatively slow progress has less to do with aptitude than with exposure. The average classroom L2 learner will experience nothing like the quantity nor the quality of exposure that the L1 infant receives. It has been calculated that a classroom learner would need more than eighteen years of classroom exposure to supply the same amount of vocabulary input that occurs in just one year in natural settings. Moreover, the input that infants receive is tailored to their immediate needs – it is interactive, and it is often highly repetitive and patterned – all qualities that provide optimal conditions for learning. By comparison, the average L2 learner's input is, to say the least, impoverished. Given these constraints, how many words does the learner need to know?

The answer must depend to a large extent on the learner's needs. A holiday trip to an English-speaking country would obviously make different vocabulary demands than a year's study in a British university. But is there such a thing as a threshold level – a **core vocabulary** that will serve in most situations? One figure that is often quoted is 2,000. This is around the number of words that most native speakers use in their daily conversation. About 2,000 words, too, is the size of the **defining vocabulary** used in dictionaries for language learners. These are the words and suffixes that are used in the dictionary's definitions. Moreover, a passive knowledge of the 2,000 most frequent words in English would provide a reader with familiarity with nearly nine out of every ten words in most written texts. In this paragraph, for example, so far only the following words fall outside the top 2,000 words in written English: *vocabulary* (mentioned twice), *threshold, core, quoted, native, dictionaries/dictionary's, suffixes, definitions, moreover, passive, familiarity* and *paragraph*. In other words, fourteen out of 140 running words, or exactly ten per cent of the text, would be unfamiliar to the learner who had learned the top 2,000.

And very many of the words in the preceding paragraph – such as *the, to, a, on, would, in, but, is, there, that, will* and *one* – are extremely common indeed. In fact, it has been calculated that the most frequent 100 words in English make up almost fifty per cent of most texts. That is to say, a half of this book consists of merely 100 words!

Of course, the majority of these 100 high frequency words are grammar – or **function** – words, such as *has, to, did, she, were,* etc., and not **content** words like *answer, depend, large, extent, learner, needs,* etc. On their own, as we saw in Chapter 1, function words have very restricted usefulness: try having a conversation with the ten most frequent words in written English: *the, to, of, a, and, in, I, was, for, that*!

There is a strong argument, then, for equipping learners with a core vocabulary of 2,000 high frequency words as soon as possible. The researcher Paul Meara estimated that at the rate of 50 words a week (not unreasonable, especially if the emphasis is taken off grammar teaching) this target could be reached in 40 weeks, or one academic year, more or less. Of course, this is the minimum or threshold level. Most researchers nowadays recommend a basic vocabulary of at least 3,000 word families, while for more specialised needs, a working vocabulary of over 5,000 word families is probably desirable. Students aiming to pass the Cambridge First Certificate Examination (FCE), for example, should probably aim to understand at least 5,000 words even if their productive vocabulary is half that number.

On the other hand, students preparing for academic study might be better off working from a specialised academic word list. A recently published academic word list consists of just 570 word families, covering a variety of disciplines – arts, commerce, law and science – and includes such items as *analyse, concept, data* and *research*. These 570 word families account for one in every ten words in academic texts. For example, the following words occurring in the paragraph we analysed above are covered in this academic list: *core*, *quoted*, *passive* and *paragraph*. Knowledge of this academic list (on top of the 2,000 most frequent words in English) would have thus reduced the unfamiliar words in that paragraph to a mere ten.

A preoccupation with vocabulary size, however, overlooks the importance of vocabulary **depth**. Vocabulary knowledge is not an all-or-nothing phenomenon, that is, a case of either knowing a word or not knowing it. Consider, for example, these different degrees of 'knowing' in my own knowledge of Spanish, using words taken randomly from the *Q* section of the dictionary:

queso (cheese)	can understand and produce it (both in speaking and writing) without effort
querer (want)	can understand it and produce it, though need to think about past irregular forms
quedar (stay)	can understand it and produce it, but only in its main non-idiomatic senses
quirófano (operating theatre)	can understand it in context only, and can produce it if prompted (e.g. with first letter) but not confident about correct word stress
quiebra (bankruptcy)	can understand it in context only, and can't produce it even if prompted
quicio (hinge)	probably wouldn't understand it even in context, and certainly can't produce it

This suggests that, at the very least, estimates of vocabulary size must take into account **productive** and **receptive** knowledge. Then there is knowledge of spelling and pronunciation, of derivative forms and of different shades of meaning. Finally, there is the degree of control over word knowledge: is the word readily accessible, or does it require prompting? (Think of how you answer crossword clues: some words come only when several letters have been filled in; others require no prompting at all.) Again, these different aspects of 'knowing' suggest that the task of acquiring a functional lexicon is more complicated than simply memorising words from lists.

In the end, however, exactly which words a learner needs to know is a very personal matter. It is not easy either to predict learners' needs nor to ensure that the words that have been selected for teaching will be learned. Nor will there be time, especially in non-intensive language courses, for all the words that the learners need to be explicitly taught. A good part of vocabulary acquisition has to be incidental. Incidental learning is facilitated through exposure to language input, in the form of extensive reading, for example. Input from the teacher and from other learners is also an important resource for incidental learning (see Chapter 3).

Most important of all, perhaps, is that the teacher encourages an enthusiasm for vocabulary acquisition, and provides learners with the strategies for self-directed learning – strategies that will be discussed in Chapter 9.

How are words remembered? To achieve the kind of outcomes described in the last section, the learner needs not only to learn a lot of words, but to remember them. In fact, learning *is* remembering. Unlike the learning of grammar, which is essentially a rule-based system, vocabulary knowledge is largely a question of accumulating individual items. There are few short cuts in the form of generative rules: it is essentially a question of memory. How, then, does memory work? And what are the implications for teaching vocabulary?

Researchers into the workings of memory customarily distinguish between the following systems: the **short-term store, working memory**, and **long-term memory**.

The **short-term store (STS)** is the brain's capacity to hold a limited number of items of information for periods of time up to a few seconds. It is the kind of memory that is involved in holding in your head a telephone number for as long as it takes to be able to dial it. Or to repeat a word that you've just heard the teacher modelling. But successful vocabulary learning clearly involves more than simply holding words in your mind for a few seconds. For words to be integrated into long-term memory they need to be subjected to different kinds of operations.

Focussing on words long enough to perform operations on them is the function of **working memory**. Many cognitive tasks such as reasoning, learning and understanding depend on working memory. It can be thought of as a kind of work bench, where information is first placed, studied and moved about before being filed away for later retrieval. The information that is being manipulated can come from external sources via the senses, or it can be 'downloaded' from the long-term memory. Or both. For example, a learner can hear a word (like *tangi*), download a similar word from long-term memory (like *tango*), and compare the two in working memory, before deciding if they are the same or different. Material remains in working memory for about twenty seconds.

This capacity is made possible by the existence of the **articulatory loop**, a process of subvocal repetition, a bit like a loop of audio tape going round and round. It enables the short-term store to be kept refreshed. Having just heard a new word, for example, we can run it by as many times as we need in order to examine it (*tangi … tangi … tangi … tangi …*) – assuming that not too many other new words are competing for space on the loop. The holding capacity of the articulatory loop seems to be a determining factor in the ability to learn languages: the longer the loop, the better the learner. Or, to put it another way, the ability to hold a phonological representation of a word in working memory is a good predictor of language learning aptitude. Likewise, any interference in the processes of subvocal repetition – e.g. distracting background talk – is likely to disrupt the functioning of the loop and impair learning. Another significant feature of the articulatory loop is that it can hold fewer L2 words than L1 words. This has a bearing on the length of chunk a learner can process at any one time.

Also linked to working memory is a kind of mental sketch pad. Here images – such as visual **mnemonics** (or memory prompts) – can be placed and scanned in order to elicit words from long-term memory into working memory (see Chapter 9 for more on mnemonics).

Long-term memory can be thought of as a kind of filing system. Unlike working memory, which has a limited capacity and no permanent content, long-term memory has an enormous capacity, and its contents are durable over time. However, the fact that learners can retain new vocabulary items the length of a lesson (i.e. beyond the few seconds' duration of the short-term store) but have forgotten them by the next lesson suggests that long-term memory is not always as long-term as we would wish. Rather, it occupies a continuum from 'the quickly forgotten' to 'the never forgotten'. The great challenge for language learners is to transform material from the quickly forgotten to the never forgotten. Research into memory suggests that, in order to ensure that material moves into permanent long-term memory, a number of principles need to be observed. Here is a brief summary of some of the research findings that are relevant to the subject of word learning:

- **Repetition**: The time-honoured way of 'memorising' new material is through repeated rehearsal of the material while it is still in working memory – i.e. letting the articulatory loop just run and run. However, simply repeating an item (the basis of **rote learning**) seems to have little long-term effect unless some attempt is made to organise the material at the same time (see below). But one kind of repetition that *is* important is repetition of encounters with a word. It has been estimated that, when reading, words stand a good chance of being remembered if they have been met at least seven times over spaced intervals. (Are you still in any doubt, for instance, as to the meaning of *tangi*?)

- **Retrieval**: Another kind of repetition that is crucial is what is called the **retrieval practice effect**. This means, simply, that the act of retrieving a word from memory makes it more likely that the learner will be able to recall it again later. Activities which require retrieval, such as using the new word in written sentences, 'oil the path' for future recall.

- **Spacing**: It is better to distribute memory work across a period of time than to mass it together in a single block. This is known as the principle of **distributed practice**. This applies in both the short term and the long term. When teaching students a new set of words, for example, it is best to present the first two or three items, then go back and test these, then present some more, then backtrack again, and so on. As each word becomes better learned, the testing interval can gradually be extended. The aim is to test each item at the longest interval at which it can reliably be recalled. Similarly, over a sequence of lessons, newly presented vocabulary should be reviewed in the next lesson, but the interval between successive tests should gradually be increased.

- **Pacing**: Learners have different learning styles, and process data at different rates, so ideally they should be given the opportunity to pace their own rehearsal activities. This may mean the teacher allowing time during vocabulary learning for learners to do 'memory work' – such as organising or reviewing their vocabulary – silently and individually.

- **Use**: Putting words to use, preferably in some interesting way, is the best way of ensuring they are added to long-term memory. It is the principle popularly known as *Use it or lose it*. In Chapter 6 we will look at ways of putting words to work. Meanwhile, the following points all relate to ways of manipulating words in working memory.

- **Cognitive depth**: The more decisions the learner makes about a word, and the more cognitively demanding these decisions, the better the word is remembered. For example, a relatively superficial judgement might be simply to match it with a word that rhymes with it: e.g. *tango/mango*. A deeper level decision might be to decide on its part of speech (noun, adjective, verb, etc). Deeper still might be to use it to complete a sentence.

- **Personal organising**: The judgements that learners make about a word are most effective if they are personalised. In one study, subjects who had read a sentence aloud containing new words showed better recall than subjects who had simply silently rehearsed the words. But subjects who had made up their own sentences containing the words and read them aloud did better still.

- **Imaging**: Best of all were subjects who were given the task of silently visualising a mental picture to go with a new word. Other tests have shown that easily visualised words are more memorable than words that don't immediately evoke a picture. This suggests that – even for abstract words – it might help if learners associate them with some mental image. Interestingly, it doesn't seem to matter if the image is highly imaginative or even very vivid, so long as it is self-generated, rather than acquired 'second-hand'.

- **Mnemonics**: These are 'tricks' to help retrieve items or rules that are stored in memory and that are not yet automatically retrievable. Even native speakers rely on mnemonics to help with some spelling rules: e.g. *i* before *e* except after *c*. As the previous point suggests, the best kinds of mnemonics are often visual. The most well-attested memory technique is the **keyword technique**, which is described in Chapter 9.

- **Motivation**: Simply wanting to learn new words is no guarantee that words will be remembered. The only difference a strong motivation makes is that the learner is likely to spend more time on rehearsal and practice, which in the end will pay off in terms of memory. But even unmotivated learners remember words if they have been set tasks that require them to make decisions about them.

- **Attention/arousal**: Contrary to popular belief, you can't improve your vocabulary in your sleep, simply by listening to a tape. Some degree of conscious attention is required. A very high degree of attention (called arousal) seems to correlate with improved recall. Words that trigger a strong emotional response, for example, are more easily recalled than ones that don't. This may account for the fact that many learners seem to have a knack of remembering swear words, even if they've heard them only a couple of times.

- **Affective depth**: Related to the preceding point, affective (i.e. emotional) information is stored along with cognitive (i.e. intellectual) data, and may play an equally important role on how words are stored and recalled. Just as it is important for learners to make cognitive judgements about words, it may also be important to make affective judgements, such as *Do I like the sound and look of the word? Do I like the thing that the word represents? Does the word evoke any pleasant or unpleasant associations?* In this vein, Christopher Isherwood, continuing his discussion about *table* and *Tisch* (see page 19), makes the point that 'the difference between a table and ein Tisch was that a table was the dining-table in his mother's house and ein Tisch was ein Tisch in the Cosy Corner [a low-life bar in Berlin]'.

  Similarly, the reforming educationalist Sylvia Ashton-Warner, who taught reading and writing skills to underprivileged children in New Zealand in the 1960s, used the affective value of words as the basis of what she called her 'key vocabulary' approach. Her primary school children chose the words they wanted to learn. These often had a strong emotional charge, such as *Mummy, Daddy, kiss, frightened, ghost*. In teaching early literacy one of Ashton-Warner's basic principles was that 'First words must be made of the stuff of the child himself, whatever and wherever the child' (from Ashton-Warner S, *Teacher*, Virago).

Why do we forget words?

Even with the best will in the world, students forget words. As a rule, forgetting is rapid at first, but gradually slows down. This is true in both the short term (e.g. from lesson to lesson) and in the long term (e.g. after a whole course). It has been estimated that up to 80 per cent of material is lost within 24 hours of initial learning, but that then the rate of forgetting levels out. And a study of learners' retention of a foreign language (Spanish) over an extended period showed that – in the absence of opportunities to use the language – rapid forgetting occurred in the first three or four years after instruction, but then levelled out, with very little further loss, even up to 50 years later. Two factors seemed to determine retention. First, those words that were easy to learn were better retained. (See the following section for a discussion of what makes a word easy or difficult to learn.) Secondly, those words that were learned over spaced learning sessions were retained better than words that were learned in concentrated bursts – consistent with the principle of distributed practice (see page 24).

Forgetting may be caused both by interference from subsequent learning and by insufficient recycling. With regard to interference, most teachers will be familiar with the symptoms of 'overload', when the price for learning new language items is the forgetting of old ones. This seems to be particularly acute if words are taught that are very similar to recently acquired words. The new words have the effect of 'overwriting' the previously learned material. This is an argument *against* teaching words in lexical sets where words have very similar meanings (see Chapter 3).

More important, perhaps, as a remedy against forgetting, is **recycling**. Research shows that spaced review of learned material can dramatically reduce the rate of forgetting. But it's not enough simply to repeat words, or to re-encounter them in their original contexts. Much better is to recycle them in different ways, and, ideally, at successive levels of depth. Research suggests that if learners see or use a word in a way different from the way they first met it, then better learning is achieved. For example, study this sentence (in Maori), and its translation:

E Hōhepa e tangi, kāti ra te tangi!
(Joseph, you are crying, but you have cried enough!)

(from *The Penguin Book of New Zealand Verse*)

Even if you can't make much sense of the grammar, the novel encounter with *tangi*, in its sense of 'crying', is further reinforcement of *tangi* = funeral.

What makes a word difficult?

Anyone who has learned a second language will know that some words seem easier to learn than others. Easiest of all are those that are more or less identical, both in meaning and form, to their L1 equivalents. When this is due to the fact that they derive from a common origin, they are called **cognates**. Thus Catalan *vocabulari*, French *vocabulaire*, Italian *vocabolario* and English *vocabulary* are all cognates and hence relatively easily transferable from one language to the other. The global spread of English has also meant that many English words have been borrowed by other languages. Examples of such **loan words** in Japanese are *shanpu* (shampoo), *shoppingu* (shopping), and *sunakku* (snack). Cognates and loan words provide a useful 'way in' to the vocabulary of English, and are worth exploiting (see page 35). However, as we have seen, there are a number of traps for new players, in the form of **false friends**. Knowing that *actually* and *aktualnie* are false friends may make the learning of *actually* difficult for a Polish speaker (or a French or Spanish speaker, for that matter), since they may tend to avoid using it altogether.

Other factors that make some words more difficult than others are:

- **Pronunciation**: Research shows that words that are difficult to pronounce are more difficult to learn. Potentially difficult words will typically be those that contain sounds that are unfamiliar to some groups of learners – such as *regular* and *lorry* for Japanese speakers. Many learners find that words with clusters of consonants, such as *strength* or *crisps* or *breakfast*, are also problematic.

- **Spelling**: Sound–spelling mismatches are likely to be the cause of errors, either of pronunciation or of spelling, and can contribute to a word's difficulty. While most English spelling is fairly law-abiding, there are also some glaring irregularities. Words that contain silent letters are particularly problematic: *foreign*, *listen*, *headache*, *climbing*, *bored*, *honest*, *cupboard*, *muscle*, etc.

- **Length** and **complexity**: Long words seem to be no more difficult to learn than short ones. But, as a rule of thumb, high frequency words tend to be short in English, and therefore the learner is likely to meet them more often, a factor favouring their 'learnability'. Also, variable stress in polysyllabic words – such as in word families like *necessary*, *necessity* and *necessarily* – can add to their difficulty.

- **Grammar**: Also problematic is the grammar associated with the word, especially if this differs from that of its L1 equivalent. Spanish learners of English, for example, tend to assume that *explain* follows the same pattern as both Spanish *explicar* and English *tell*, and say *he explained me the lesson*. Remembering whether a verb like *enjoy*, *love*, or *hope* is followed by an infinitive (*to swim*) or an *-ing* form (*swimming*) can add to its difficulty. And the grammar of phrasal verbs is particularly troublesome: some phrasal verbs are separable (*she **looked** the word **up***) but others are not (*she **looked after** the children*).

- **Meaning**: When two words overlap in meaning, learners are likely to confuse them. *Make* and *do* are a case in point: you *make breakfast* and *make an appointment*, but you *do the housework* and *do a questionnaire*. Words with multiple meanings, such as *since* and *still*, can also be troublesome for learners. Having learned one meaning of the word, they may be reluctant to accept a second, totally different, meaning. Unfamiliar concepts may make a word difficult to learn. Thus, culture-specific items such as words and expressions associated with the game cricket (*a sticky wicket*, *a hat trick*, *a good innings*) will seem fairly opaque to most learners and are unlikely to be easily learned.

- **Range**, **connotation** and **idiomaticity**: Words that can be used in a wide range of contexts will generally be perceived as easier than their synonyms with a narrower range. Thus *put* is a very wide-ranging verb, compared to *impose*, *place*, *position*, etc. Likewise, *thin* is a safer bet than *skinny*, *slim*, *slender*. Words that have style constraints, such as very informal words (*chuck* for *throw*, *swap* for *exchange*), may cause problems. Uncertainty as to the connotations of some words may cause problems too. Thus, *propaganda* has negative connotations in English, but its equivalent may simply mean *publicity*. On the other hand, *eccentric* does not have negative connotations in English, but its nearest equivalent in other languages may mean *deviant*. Finally, words or expressions that are idiomatic (like *make up your mind*, *keep an eye on* …) will generally be more difficult than words whose meaning is transparent (*decide*, *watch*). It is their idiomaticity, as well as their syntactic complexity, that makes phrasal verbs so difficult.

What kind of mistakes do learners make?

Given the kinds of difficulty outlined above, it is not surprising that learners make mistakes with words. In fact, the researcher Paul Meara estimates that lexical errors outnumber other types of error by more than three to one. Here is a sample of lexical errors (underlined):

1 I <u>hope</u> after <u>biggening</u> English <u>studing</u> I <u>shell</u> not have a free time at all.
2 I'd like to spend a couple of week somewhere on a <u>peopleless</u> island.
3 I like <u>watching</u> flowers and <u>inhaling</u> their lovely smell.

All lexical errors are instances of a wrong choice of form – whether a spelling error (e.g. *biggening, shell*), or a suffix error (*peopleless*), or the wrong word altogether (*hope, watching, inhaling*). However, for convenience we can categorise errors into two major types:

- form-related
- meaning-related

Form-related errors include **mis-selections, misformations,** and **spelling** and **pronunciation errors**. A mis-selection is when an existing word form is selected that is similar in sound or spelling to the correct form – the equivalent to a native speaker's malapropism (see page 16). For example: *My girlfriend was very **hungry** with me* (for *angry*). Or, *He persuaded me to have a **noise** operation* (for *nose*).

Misformations often result from misapplying word formation rules (see page 5), producing non-existent words, as in *a **peopleless** island*, or *his **hopeness** of peace*. Sometimes these misformations will show a clear influence from the learner's mother tongue, as in *the people looked **emocionated*** – from the Spanish *emocionado* (*excited*). Whole words may be combined wrongly to form non-existent combinations: *Most of time I just **watch shops' window*** (for *go window-shopping*). Idioms and fixed expressions are vulnerable to this kind of mix up: *A strike could **kill the gold eggs goose** and cause the ruin of a country.*

Spelling mistakes result from the wrong choice of letter (*shell* for *shall*), the omission of letters (*studing* for *studying*), or the wrong order of letters (*littel* for *little*). Pronunciation errors may result from the wrong choice of sound (*leave* for *live*), addition of sounds (*eschool* for *school*), omission of sounds (*poduk* for *product*) or misplaced word stress (*comFORTable* for *comfortable*).

Meaning-related errors typically occur when words that have similar or related meanings are confused and the wrong choice is made. Thus: *I **hope** ... I shell not have a free time* (instead of *I expect ...*). And *I like **watching** flowers and **inhaling** their lovely smell*. While *watching* belongs to the set of verbs related to *seeing* it is inappropriate for relatively static objects like flowers. Similarly, *inhaling* tends to be used for smoke or gas, and not smell. That is to say, *inhaling* doesn't **collocate** with *smell*. Many 'wrong word' mistakes are in fact wrong collocates. For example: *I have fifteen years experience as a **particular professor*** (rather than *a private teacher*).

Meaning-related wrong-choice errors may derive from the learner's L1, where the meaning of an L1 word may not exactly match its L2 equivalent. A common example made by Spanish speakers is: *I'm live with my **fathers** in Mexico city*. In Spanish, the plural of *padre* (*father*) means *parents*.

Learners may also be unaware of the different **connotations** of related words, causing wrong-choice errors such as: *I have chosen to describe Stephen Hawking, a **notorious** scientific of our century*. Wrong choice may result in clashing styles, as in this letter by a Japanese student to the accommodation bureau at my place of work:

Dear Sirs/Madams,
I'm so harry because I may leave Japan at the end of January.
I'm gonna stop by NY and go to España. Please get busy!

Indiscriminate dictionary use may be the cause of this stylistic error by a Russian learner: *May be I'll stay here and keep on my **hodiernal** work* (where *hodiernal* is an archaic synonym for *day-to-day*).

Sometimes errors can be both form- *and* meaning-induced. That is, a similar-sounding form is selected because it has a similar meaning to the target one. For example: *I went to a party for see my friends. It was **very funny**.* (Instead of *It was a lot of fun*.) Or, *I have friends who speak English as their **nature** language* (for *native language*). The occurrence of this kind of error is not surprising, given the way words are stored and accessed in the mind, with form and meaning modules overlapping and interconnected.

What are the implications for teaching?

In this chapter we have looked at how the mental lexicon is structured and the way it develops, in both first and second languages. What then are the implications of these findings for the teaching of vocabulary?

- Learners need tasks and strategies to help them organise their mental lexicon by building networks of associations – the more the better.
- Teachers need to accept that the learning of new words involves a period of 'initial fuzziness'.
- Learners need to wean themselves off a reliance on direct translation from their mother tongue.
- Words need to be presented in their typical contexts, so that learners can get a feel for their meaning, their register, their collocations, and their syntactic environments.
- Teaching should direct attention to the sound of new words, particularly the way they are stressed.
- Learners should aim to build a threshold vocabulary as quickly as possible.
- Learners need to be actively involved in the learning of words.
- Learners need multiple exposures to words and they need to retrieve words from memory repeatedly.
- Learners need to make multiple decisions about words.
- Memory of new words can be reinforced if they are used to express personally relevant meanings.
- Not all the vocabulary that the learners need can be 'taught': learners will need plentiful exposure to talk and text as well as training for self-directed learning.

Conclusions

In this chapter we have surveyed the principles underlying the acquisition of vocabulary in a second language, and sketched some possible implications for teaching. Perhaps the most important points to be emphasised are these:

- learners need a critical mass of vocabulary to get them over the threshold of the second language

- achieving this critical mass requires both intentional and incidental learning
- the first language is a support but can also be a potential block to the development of a second language lexicon
- vocabulary learning is item learning, and it is also network building
- vocabulary learning is a memory task, but it also involves creative and personalised use, i.e. learning *and* using
- learners have to take responsibility themselves for vocabulary expansion

Looking ahead   Having sketched out some implications for teaching, the rest of the book will explore these implications in more detail. One key issue is the relation between teaching and learning. What is the teacher's role in vocabulary development? And how useful are other possible sources of vocabulary input? In the next two chapters we will review and evaluate some of the main potential sources of vocabulary input, including the teacher.

3 Classroom sources of words

- **Lists**
- **Coursebooks**
- **Vocabulary books**
- **The teacher**
- **Other students**

Lists In order to achieve the kinds of learning targets mentioned in the last chapter (i.e. a threshold of 2,000 to 3,000 words), vocabulary learning requires a rich and nourishing diet. Some of these words will be learned actively. Others will be picked up incidentally. So this diet will need to consist of words that have been selected for active study (i.e. for intentional learning) and it will also need to be a source for incidental learning through exposure. Where are learners going to find these words – and in sufficient quantity and with sufficient frequency?

Traditionally, words targeted for active study were supplied to learners in the form of lists. On the right, for example, is a list of words from

(from Girau L T, *Método de Inglés*, Colección Magister)

VOCABULARY			
glass	vidrio	*to dress*	vestir, vestirse
a student (stiúdent)	un estudiante	*daily* (déili)	diariamente, diario
healthy (jélzi)	saludable	*Arnold* (áarnold)	Arnaldo
a doll (dol)	una muñeca	*Albert* (æ'lbœrt)	Alberto
a safety razor (séifti réisœr)	una máquina de afeitar	*a looking-glass* (lúuking glas)	un espejo
a wood (úud)	un bosque		
those (thóus)	esos-as, aquellos-as	*probably* (próbabli)	probablemente
with (uíz)	con	*the way* (uéi)	el camino
George (Jóorj)	Jorge	*the police* (polís)	la policía
Arthur (áarzœr)	Arturo	*the bath-room* (baz rúum)	el cuarto de baño
Julia (júlia)	Julia	*a member* (mémbœr)	un miembro, un individuo
to copy (cópi)	copiar	*the soap* (sóup)	el jabón
the sister-in-law (sístœr in lóo)	la cuñada	*breakfast* (brékfast)	el almuerzo
to shave (shéiv)	afeitar, afeitarse	*dinner* (dínœr)	la comida
to wash (uósh)	lavar, lavarse	*supper* (sœ'pœr)	la cena

the thirteenth lesson of an English course published in 1925 for Spanish-speaking students.

Note that there seems to be no apparent rationale behind the choice and ordering of these words. Criteria of usefulness, frequency or lexical field membership don't seem to apply. Lists like this one have given list learning a bad name. As the character played by Hugh Grant in Woody Allen's *Small Time Crooks* says: 'I'm not a hundred per cent convinced that memorising the dictionary is the best way of improving your vocabulary …'.

However, the value of list learning may have been underestimated. Many students quite like learning words from lists – even such oddly assembled lists as the one above. One reason is that it is very economical: large numbers of words can be learned in a relatively short time (where learning is taken to mean the ability to recall items in subsequent tests). Some researchers estimate that up to thirty words an hour can be learned this way. Having the mother tongue translation alongside not only deals with the meaning conveniently, but allows learners to test themselves (from L1 to English, and from English to L1) as well as to test one another. Even the fact that the words are not related nor in alphabetical order may be a bonus because, as we will see below, this reduces the chance of getting words confused with each other. Better than lists, though, are **word cards** (see page 145). Having each word on an individual card means the sequence can be varied, as a precaution against what is called the 'serial effect'. This occurs when one word on a list triggers recall of the next word, and so on. This is not of much use for real life vocabulary use, when words must be recalled independently of the context in which they were learned.

Here are some ways of exploiting word lists in class:

- The teacher reads words from the list in a random order. Learners show they can match the sound with the written form by ticking the ones they hear. They can then do this with each other in pairs.

- Learners cover the L1 translation (if they have a bilingual list); the teacher gives translations and learners tick the English equivalents.

- Both the preceding activities can be turned into a form of *Bingo!* Ask learners each to write down, say, twelve words (from a list of twenty). Read out twelve words from the master list in random order, or read out their L1 translations. Alternatively, if the words can be illustrated, show pictures of the words. Learners tick off each word as it occurs – the first learner to have ticked all twelve of their words shouts out *Bingo!*

- From a random list of words, ask learners to make connections between words and explain them to their classmates: the more connections the better, no matter how far-fetched. For example, using the list on page 32 where the words *to copy* and *to shave* appear, a student might produce: *I learned to shave by copying my father.*

- Students construct a story from the list: they can do this by choosing twelve words from a list of twenty, and working them into a narrative. Or they take turns to make a sentence that includes the next word in the list so as to continue the story.

    📖 Ask learners to make their own list from the words that come up in the lesson (see below under *Other students*) and to bring their lists to class for the next lesson. At the beginning of the following lesson, pair students up to test each other on their word lists.

    📖 Learners can also make lists of words that have appeared in previous units of the coursebook, and test each other by, for example, asking *How do you say … in English?* or *What's the English for …?* Or, they could prepare gapped sentences to be completed by words from their lists.

Coursebooks   Coursebook treatment of vocabulary varies considerably. For example, one study of nine beginners' courses showed that the number of words introduced ranged from just over a thousand to nearly four thousand. Nowadays, it is customary to make explicit reference to the lexical content of a course in the syllabus description. Here, for example, is an extract from the syllabus of *Look Ahead*:

	UNIT TITLE	PAGE	VOCABULARY AREAS	GRAMMAR
	Welcome !	6	The topics in this book	
1	At the weekend	8	Interests and hobbies Leisure activities Housework	Present simple/present progressive Question: *How often?* Adverbs of frequency *Would like* + infinitive with *to* Stative verbs
2	Doing new things	16	Languages Countries Adult education classes Times, dates, days, months Money Life changes	*Going to* + infinitive *Can/can't, could/could(n't)* + infinitive Adverbs: *very well, a little, not at all* *Like/enjoy* + *ing* *Want/would like* + infinitive with *to* Past simple
3	Planning a trip	24	Means of transport Travel	Comparative adjectives (+ *er* and *more*) Comparative adjectives (irregular forms) *Prefer* + *ing* Modal: *will* for decisions *I'll* + infinitive for promises *Let's* + infinitive

(from Hopkins A and Potter J, *Look Ahead*, Longman)

What factors determine the choice of words for inclusion in the lexical strand of a coursebook syllabus? Briefly, they are: usefulness, frequency, learnability and teachability.

    Words are **useful** if they can be put to immediate use – a case for teaching classroom vocabulary (*pen, board, door, notebook*, etc.) very early in an elementary course. However, for learners studying the language but with few opportunities to put it to use, it becomes harder to predict what words they are likely to need. Accordingly, the notion of a **core vocabulary** was devised. Core words are those that – all things being equal – are likely to be more useful than non-core words. Core words are typically those words used when defining other words. For example, the definition of both *giggle* and *guffaw* involves using the word *laugh*: *A giggle is a kind of laugh*, etc. But the opposite is not true: we don't use *giggle* or *guffaw* to define *laugh*. *Laugh*, therefore, is more of a core word than *giggle*.

Another test of 'core-ness' is whether the word collocates widely. Thus, *bright* collocates with *sun, light, idea, smile* and *child*, whereas its synonym *radiant* has a much narrower range of collocates. *A radiant idea* and *a radiant child* are unlikely (although, of course, not impossible). Superordinate words (see page 10) are also good candidates for a core vocabulary: *flower* being more useful than either *rose* or *geranium*. And a word is less useful if it is used in a narrow register. Thus *spud* (colloquial) is less useful than *potato* (neither colloquial nor formal), *medical practitioner* (formal) less useful than *doctor* (neither colloquial nor formal).

The relative **frequency** of a word is another key factor in determining its inclusion in a syllabus. The argument for teaching the most frequent words in the language is a powerful one. It is claimed that the most frequent words express the most frequent meanings in the language – a view that will be explored in Chapter 7 (see page 112).

In Chapter 2 we looked at factors that make some words easier to learn than others – such as their similarity to words in the learner's mother tongue e.g. *telephone* and *teléfono*. This is a good indicator of how **learnable** they are. Choice of words to include in a syllabus, especially for beginner students, will be determined in part by their learnability. It is now common to find a section at the beginning of many courses which directs attention to English words (such as *taxi, cinema, restaurant*) that are likely to be loan words or cognates in the student's mother tongue, as in the example overleaf from *The Beginners' Choice*.

Learnability is not to be confused with **teachability**. Words are more easily teachable if they can be demonstrated or illustrated – by the use of pictures or real objects, for example (see page 78). It is easier to teach a word like *blackboard* than a word like *though*, even though *though* is much more frequent, and probably more useful, than *blackboard*. As a rule of thumb, nouns are more easily taught than verbs or adverbs, and concrete nouns are more easily taught than abstract nouns.

How, then, is the coursebook vocabulary syllabus realised in the actual content of the book? Normally, vocabulary input is incorporated in three ways:

- in segregated vocabulary sections
- integrated into text-based activities
- incidentally, as in grammar explanations and exercises, task instructions, etc.

In **segregated** vocabulary activities, words are often presented in the form of **lexical sets**. These are a group of words that share a relation of **hyponymy** (see page 9). For example, in the unit in *Look Ahead* called *Planning a trip* (shown in the table on the previous page) the general topic area is travel, and the following lexical set is provided:

boat	car	helicopter	balloon	bicycle (bike)
bus	coach	plane	ship	

from Mohamed S and Acklam R,
The Beginners' Choice, Longman

Introducing words in lexical sets would seem to make good sense. As we saw on page 17, it seems to reflect the way that words are stored in the mind. Moreover, the meanings of the words can be made clearer by contrasting them with closely related words in the same set. And, if the words are being introduced to support a specific grammar structure, words belonging to the same lexical set are more easily slotted into the structure than words chosen more randomly.

However, evidence suggests that words that are too closely associated tend to interfere with each other, and can actually make the learning task more difficult. Words that can fill the same slot in a sentence are particularly likely to be confused:

I took the	car	to Switzerland.
	train	
	bus	
	coach	
	plane	

One research study, by T Tinkham, compared the rate of learning of words organised into lexical sets (*apple, pear, nectarine, peach*, etc.) with sets of unrelated words (*mountain, shoe, flower, mouse, sky, television*). The study showed a better learning rate for the latter organisation than for the former. What's more, the learners themselves thought that the lexical sets were more difficult to learn. This suggests that the fact that words are stored together does not mean that they should be learned together. It also explains why learners often confuse the days of the week, colours, or such seemingly easy words as *hot* and *cold*.

Nevertheless, most coursebooks still favour a lexical set approach. It is important, therefore, to present the sets in such a way as to reduce the chances of confusion. One way of doing this is to emphasise the differences (rather than the similarities) of words in a set. This means avoiding using them interchangeably, as in *it's hot, it's cold*, or *hot water, cold water*. Better to introduce them along with their commonly associated collocates, such as *hot coffee, hot and dry*, and *hot summer*, but *cold beer, cold and wet* and *cold winter*.

Easier to learn are words that are **thematically** linked but have a looser relation than lexical sets. In the unit on leisure activities (in *Look Ahead*), the following words are introduced in order to talk about *bungee jumping*:

| to jump | bridge | rope | to hang | boat |
| to wear | harness | ankle | to help | river |

Because these words do not substitute for each other, there is less chance of interference. Moreover, because they can be threaded into a narrative they are more easily and naturally practised. Also, they may be more easily recalled. It is easier to remember a narrative with words embedded in it, than to recall a list of de-contextualised words. So, even if presenting words in lexical sets, it may pay to put them into some kind of context as quickly as possible:

Piet went to Geneva by *plane,* then he rented a *car* to drive to Meiringen. On the return journey he took the *train* to Geneva, flew back to Barcelona, and caught the airport *bus ...*

Perhaps more important, though, than the manner of presentation is the kind of follow-up practice that is provided. As we saw in Chapter 2, the more decisions the learner has to make about a word, the more chance there is of the words being remembered. Here is a sequence from a coursebook that requires students to make several decisions about both the meaning and form of a lexical set of 'character' words:

Character adjectives

What sort of person *are* You?

1 Are you usually smiling and happy? ☐
2 Do you enjoy the company of other people? ☐
3 Do you find it difficult to meet new people? ☐
4 Is it important to you to succeed in your career? ☐
5 Does your mood change often and suddenly for no reason? ☐
6 Do you notice other people's feelings? ☐
7 Do you think the future will be good? ☐
8 Can your friends depend on you? ☐
9 Is your room often in a mess? ☐

10 Do you get annoyed if you have to wait for anyone or anything? ☐
11 Do you put off until tomorrow what you could do today? ☐
12 Do you work hard? ☐
13 Do you keep your feelings and ideas to yourself? ☐
14 Do you often give presents? ☐
15 Do you talk a lot? ☐
16 Are you usually calm and not worried by things? ☐

Work in pairs.

1 Do the personality quiz above to discover what type of person you are. Use a dictionary to check any new words. Write **Y** for Yes, **N** for No, and **S** for Sometimes.

2 Ask your partner to do the quiz about you. Look at your ideas and your partner's ideas about you. Are they the same?

3 Match these adjectives with the questions in the quiz.

a untidy   9
b optimistic
c sociable
d talkative
e reserved
f shy
g impatient
h ambitious
i lazy
j generous
k moody
l hard-working
m easy-going
n reliable
o cheerful
p sensitive

Which are *positive* qualities and which are *negative*? Which could be both?

4 What is the opposite of each of the sixteen adjectives in Exercise 3?
Remember that the prefixes *in-* and *un-* can sometimes be used to make negatives. Which of the adjectives above can use these?

5 Describe someone in the class to your partner but don't say who it is. Can your partner guess who it is?

from Soars L and J, *New Headway Intermediate*, OUP

Another way of dealing with vocabulary in segregated activities is to focus on the rules of **word formation** (see page 5). Rather than grouping words together because of similarities in meaning, the focus here is on their formal properties, such as **affixation** or the way that words combine to form **compounds**. Here, for example, is a section on adjective formation:

VOCABULARY

Adjectives

Adjectives formed with -ed describe our reaction to someone or something. Example:
*I was **terrified** when I saw that film.*

Adjectives formed with -ing describe the person or thing that causes the reaction. Example:
*The film was **terrifying**.*

1 Match the adjectives in the box with the pictures below, and then make a sentence using each of the adjectives.

amused annoyed bored tired disappointed
interested

2 Complete the sentences below using the verbs in the box to make adjectives with -ing or -ed.

amuse annoy bore tire disappoint
interest

a) The film was very _____ and I fell asleep.
b) His jokes weren't very _____ and nobody laughed.
c) Andy said he was very _____ in hearing about your trip abroad.
d) My sister was very _____ with her exam results. She had expected better.
e) I fell asleep early. It had been a _____ day.
f) He was _____ with me for not telling him about Jasper's birthday.

3 Adjectives can also be formed from verbs and nouns by using suffixes. Recognising a suffix often helps when you are trying to work out the meaning of a new word in context. Use the suffixes to form adjectives from the nouns and verbs. Example:
attract → *attractive*

SUFFIXES

-y -ous -ic -ful -able -al -ive

NOUNS/VERBS

attract colour religion sympathy
romance crime dirt hope imagine

> from Bell J and Gower R,
> *Intermediate Matters*,
> Longman

Coursebooks nowadays take seriously the need to recycle vocabulary regularly, and often build into their content periodic review stages. Similarly, testing activities are often included; in Chapter 8 we will look at some examples of both recycling and testing tasks.

Finally, segregated vocabulary tasks can be aimed at developing particular vocabulary learning **strategies**, such as guessing words from context. In Chapter 9 we will look more closely at some examples of strategy training tasks.

Vocabulary work in coursebooks is often **integrated** into text-based activities. This can take the form of **pre-teaching** of vocabulary in preparation for a text-based task, whether for understanding (as in listening and reading) or for production (as in speaking and writing). Words selected for pre-teaching are those that are likely to be both unfamiliar to learners and crucial for the performance of the task. Note that this means that not all unfamiliar words in a text need to be pre-taught. Often coursebooks leave it up to the teacher to decide which words to pre-teach, on the assumption that the teacher's familiarity with the students will be the best guide. Research has shown that, in fact, teachers generally have fairly reliable intuitions as to which words will cause their learners difficulty. Sometimes, however, particular words are singled out by the coursebook writers and included in the instructions in the Teacher's Book or in the coursebook itself. For example:

You are going to read an extract from a book of fascinating facts. First check the meaning of the following words and phrases in your mini-dictionary:

to ban	a jury
plumbing and drains	a slave
smelly	traffic congestion
a vehicle	welfare

(from Cunningham S and Moor P, *Cutting Edge Intermediate*, Longman)

The value of extensive pre-teaching of vocabulary is debatable. It is obviously difficult to make an accurate prediction as to which words students won't know, or even which ones will be essential for understanding the text. One way is to use concordancing software to identify the **keywords** in the text – that is the words that occur with a significant degree of frequency (see the next chapter under *Corpus data*). And teaching isolated words out of context is time-consuming work. It may often be a better idea to get into the text as soon as possible, and either encourage learners to guess the meaning from context, or to explain words as the need arises.

Another way of preparing learners for a text-based task is to begin with some discussion on the general theme of the text. This can have two purposes: to trigger recall of known words, and to create the need for learning new, theme-related, words. The assumption is that at least some of the words elicited from such a task will help in the processing of the text. On the page opposite, for example, are two tasks (also from *Cutting Edge Intermediate*) designed to prepare learners for a listening activity:

Television

1 Discuss the following questions in groups.

- How much television do you watch?
- What are your favourite programmes?
- Are there any programmes that you particularly dislike?

2 Below is a list of things we can watch on television. If necessary, check the meaning of the words and phrases in **bold** in your mini-dictionary. Then mark them as follows:

XX if you think there are too many of these on television in your country.

✓✓ if you think there are about the right amount of these.

✓ if you think there should be more of these.

X if you don't have these in your country at all.

a **advertisements** that use attractive people to sell products like cars or perfume ☐

b government **advertising campaigns** against things like drink-driving ☐

c programmes with live **sports coverage** ☐

d children's programmes which include violence ☐

e long complicated **murder mysteries** or **thrillers** ☐

f **interviews** with politicians ☐

g **chat shows** ☐

h **game shows** ☐

i **soap operas** ☐

Follow-up text-based vocabulary tasks typically include such things as searching the text for words that match selected definitions or for words that complete gapped sentences. On the right, for example, is a reading text from Unit 3 of *Look Ahead* and its follow-up tasks:

from Hopkins A and Potter J, *Look Ahead 2*, Longman

4 Look at the title of the magazine article. What do you think the writer's main points are? Now read the article. Were you right? Do you agree with her?

FEAR OF FLYING

How can anyone like flying? It's a crazy thing to do. Birds fly; people don't. I hate flying. You wait for hours for the plane to take off, and it's often late. The plane's always crowded. You can't walk around and there's nothing to do. You can't open the windows and you can't get off. The seats are uncomfortable, there's no choice of food and there are never enough toilets. Then after the plane lands, it's even worse. It takes hours to get out of the airport and into the city.

I prefer travelling by train. Trains are much better than planes; they're cheaper, safer, and more comfortable. You can walk around in a train and open the windows. Stations are more convenient than airports, because you can get on and off in the middle of cities. If you miss a train, you can always catch another one later. Yes, trains are slower, but speed isn't everything. Staying alive and enjoying yourself is more important!

5 Read the article again and answer these questions.

1 How does the writer prefer travelling?
2 For the writer, which of these adjectives describe travelling by train? Which adjectives describe travelling by plane?

dangerous   fast   safe   bad   slow
expensive   comfortable   good
uncomfortable   convenient

6 Now match these verbs from the text and their definitions.

1 to land
2 to catch
3 to miss
4 to take off

a) to leave the ground and go up in the air
b) to arrive at an airport in a plane
c) to arrive too late for a plane, train, etc.
d) to get on or into public transport

Finally, coursebooks provide learners with a lot of incidental vocabulary embedded in task instructions, grammar explanations, and so on. This often takes the form of **metalanguage** – that is, the language that is used to talk about language. Grammatical terms such as *verb*, *preposition*, *present tense* and *linker* are examples of metalanguage. So, too, are functional terms, such as *inviting*, *refusing*, *apologising* and *complaining*. Understanding task instruction language (sometimes called **process language**) is particularly important for learners working without the assistance of a teacher. Here, for example, is an activity designed to introduce distance learners to the language they will meet in an Internet-mediated course:

from the Introductory Unit of *Net Languages*, International House, Barcelona

Vocabulary books   There is a wide selection of supplementary vocabulary books now available. This reflects the revival of interest in vocabulary teaching over the last twenty years or so – coupled with the need to supplement the often unsystematic treatment given to words in coursebooks. Sometimes vocabulary books are targeted at specific needs, such as business or technical English, or are designed as preparation for public examinations. Books on phrasal verbs have been particularly popular. More often, vocabulary books cover a wide range of general English needs.

Of course, books aimed specifically at vocabulary development are not an entirely new thing. The tourist's **phrase book** is as much a collection of words as it is a collection of phrases. In fact, the recent recognition of the important role of **chunk** learning (see page 115) suggests that the combination of phrases and words, organised semantically – i.e. according to meanings – may be an ideal learning aid.

Typically, supplementary vocabulary books are organised thematically, as in this extract from the contents page of *The Heinemann English Wordbuilder*:

Names
Age
Family relationships
Marital status
Countries, Nationalities
Location

Build
From the neck up
From shoulder to fingertips
From the bottom down
Inside and outside the torso
Compound adjectives about the body
etc.

Sometimes a focus on word formation (such as compounding) or on lexical relations (such as antonyms) is interwoven into this thematic organisation, often creating an apparently haphazard effect:

1	Things in the home 1	6	Phrases 1
2	Synonyms – adjectives	7	Things in the home 3
3	Countries and nationalities	8	Guess their jobs
4	Things in the home 2	9	Synonyms – verbs
5	Quantities	10	Name the sport

(from Watcyn-Jones P, *Test your Vocabulary 1*, Penguin)

Nevertheless, such books are very popular, not least because they allow learners to work independently on vocabulary areas that they are interested in. As the title of this last example implies, many of these books are designed to *test* vocabulary knowledge, rather than to *teach* it. The first unit in *Test your Vocabulary 1*, for example, looks like this:

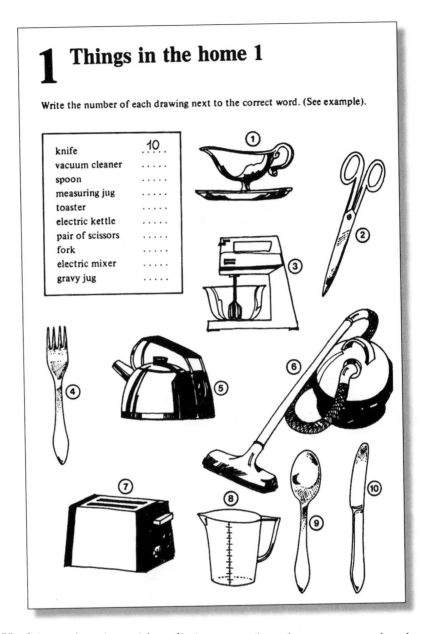

1 Things in the home 1

Write the number of each drawing next to the correct word. (See example).

knife	10
vacuum cleaner	. . . . .
spoon	. . . . .
measuring jug	. . . . .
toaster	. . . . .
electric kettle	. . . . .
pair of scissors	. . . . .
fork	. . . . .
electric mixer	. . . . .
gravy jug	. . . . .

Used in conjunction with a dictionary, or in pair or group work, where learners can pool their knowledge, even testing activities like this one can have a learning outcome. Or they can be used as diagnostic exercises, to find out what students already know in advance of their being taught a lexical area. (A logical follow-up task for the material above might be to ask learners to **brainstorm** other words they know related to the theme of *things in the home*. For more on brainstorming, see page 49.)

More recently, vocabulary books with a teaching component alongside the testing component have begun to appear. Overleaf, for example, is a page from *English Vocabulary in Use (Elementary)*.

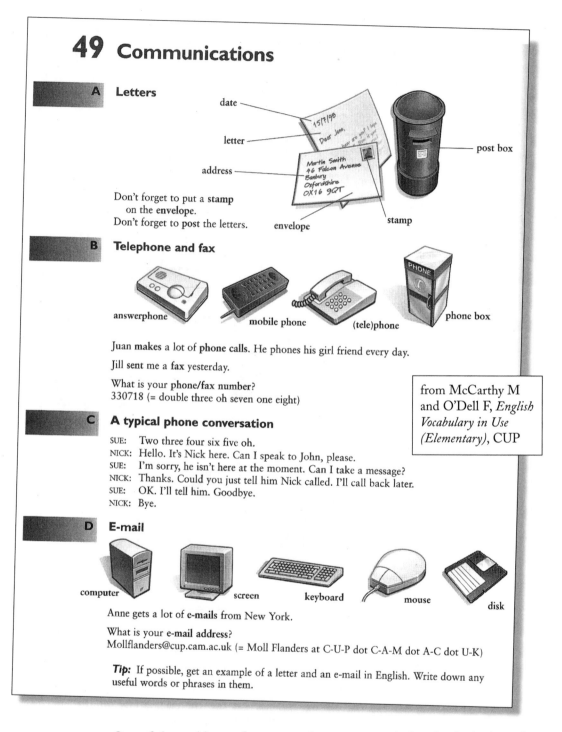

49 Communications

A **Letters**

date
letter
address

Don't forget to put a **stamp** on the **envelope**.
Don't forget to **post** the letters.

post box
envelope
stamp

B **Telephone and fax**

answerphone
mobile phone
(tele)phone
phone box

Juan **makes** a lot of **phone calls**. He phones his girl friend every day.

Jill sent me a **fax** yesterday.

What is your **phone/fax number**?
330718 (= double three oh seven one eight)

from McCarthy M and O'Dell F, *English Vocabulary in Use (Elementary)*, CUP

C **A typical phone conversation**

SUE: Two three four six five oh.
NICK: Hello. It's Nick here. Can I speak to John, please.
SUE: I'm sorry, he isn't here at the moment. Can I take a message?
NICK: Thanks. Could you just tell him Nick called. I'll call back later.
SUE: OK. I'll tell him. Goodbye.
NICK: Bye.

D **E-mail**

computer
screen
keyboard
mouse
disk

Anne gets a lot of **e-mails** from New York.

What is your **e-mail address**?
Mollflanders@cup.cam.ac.uk (= Moll Flanders at C-U-P dot C-A-M dot A-C dot U-K)

Tip: If possible, get an example of a letter and an e-mail in English. Write down any useful words or phrases in them.

One of the problems of many supplementary vocabulary books is that often lack of space prohibits a thorough development of a vocabulary area. Users aren't given more than one or two opportunities to make decisions about words. Thus, the principle of **cognitive depth** (see page 25) is sometimes missing. Teachers need to think of creative ways of developing an activity to ensure memorability. Here, for example, are some tasks that could accompany the unit on *Things in the home* (from *Test Your Vocabulary 1*) on page 45:

- Group the items into at least three different categories (of your own devising). With a neighbour compare and explain your categories.
- Use your dictionary to add different words to these categories. Teach your neighbour the words you have added.
- Who would you give these items to as birthday presents? Write a list of the items and names. Explain your list to a neighbour.
- Rank the items in terms of usefulness. Compare rankings.
- Imagine you and your classmate are sharing a flat. Decide which of the items you will buy, and in which order.
- Write definitions (or descriptions) of three of the items. Can your neighbour guess which ones they are?
- Write the first paragraph of a story. Include at least five items in your paragraph. Exchange with your partner. Continue your partner's story. Can you include more items?
- Tell the story behind any of the items that you yourself own. Where did you get it? How long have you had it? How often do you use it?

Of course, it would be a bit much to do *all* these activities, especially since the list of vocabulary items includes such low frequency words as *gravy jug*! Nor do all groups of words lend themselves to all these activities. But the extra speaking and writing practice students are getting justifies at least some of these activities, even if the targeted words are of a fairly low priority.

Some vocabulary books have imaginative tasks that are directed not so much at cognitive depth as at **affective depth** – that is, the emotional associations attached to words. As we saw on page 26, strong emotional associations can aid memory. Here, for example, is an activity from *Vocabulary* by Morgan and Rinvolucri:

E/4 Life keywords

LEVEL	Elementary to Advanced
TIME	25–40 minutes
IN CLASS	1 Ask the students what date it is today. Write it on the board. Ask them what the date was seven years ago. Put that on the board. Ask three or four people how old they were on that date, seven years ago.
	2 Now ask the students to write down ten key emotional or idea words and phrases that sum up their lives *now* and a further ten to sum up their lives *then*.
	3 Ask the students to pair off and explain the words and their significance to their partners. Have them change partners three or four times, not more, as this kind of talking is very tiring.

from Morgan J and Rinvolucri M, *Vocabulary*, OUP

The teacher

The teacher is a highly productive – although often undervalued – source of vocabulary input. Learners often pick up a lot of incidental language from their teachers, especially words and phrases associated with classroom processes, such as

> Let's see …
> Now then …
> Whose turn is it?
> Is that clear?
> What we're going to do now is …
> Have you finished yet?

The teacher is also the source of a lot of useful **interpersonal** language, especially in the more conversational stages of the lesson:

> Did you have a nice weekend?
> Oh really?
> That's amazing!
> Could you close the window?
> Nice tie.
> Whoops!
> Never mind.
> etc.

It is worth drawing learners' attention to this language from time to time. One way of doing this is simply to ask them: *What did I just say?* and *What other ways are there of saying the same thing?* And, if the class is a monolingual one, *How would you say that in (your language)?*

The teacher's own stories can also serve as a vehicle for vocabulary input. One way of doing this is for the teacher to tell the class a short anecdote while at the same time recording it on cassette. Having told the story, the teacher asks the learners to write down any words they remembered, comparing in pairs or small groups. The teacher then replays the recorded anecdote one or two times, each time letting the learners top up their list of words, and asking the meaning or spelling of any unfamiliar items. Using these words, the learners can then work in small groups to reconstruct the story as closely as possible to the original. The teacher then replays the cassette so that they can check, and edit, their written texts. This technique is a good way of introducing, in context, words that are often difficult to teach on their own – such as phrasal verbs (see page 6). Here, for example, is a story one teacher told her class (the phrasal verbs are underlined):

> 'I had to fly to Glasgow last week. As we were <u>taking off</u>, there was a loud bang in one of the engines. We had hit a bird. We had to <u>turn round</u> and <u>come back</u> to Barcelona. It <u>turned out</u> that the bird had damaged the engine. So we had to <u>get off</u>, and <u>hang around</u> for three hours, while another plane was <u>sent out</u> to <u>pick us up</u>. By this time I had missed my connecting flight, so I was <u>held up</u> another three hours in Luton. By the time I got to Glasgow, it had taken me fifteen hours!'

Other students

Other students in the class are a particularly fertile source of vocabulary input. Learners often pay more attention to what other learners say than they do to either the coursebook or their teacher. The researcher Assia Slimani who studied secondary school classrooms in Algeria found that, on the whole, the students remembered many more of the words related to the topics that other students had raised in the lesson, than words coming from any other source. Unfortunately, in many classrooms, the learners are not given many opportunities to raise their own topics. Apart from any other benefits, the vocabulary spin-off would seem to be justification enough for allowing learners more control of the topic agenda in the classroom.

It is easy to underestimate the combined strength of a class's shared 'lexicon'. It is the nature of vocabulary knowledge that no two learners' mental lexicons will correspond exactly. Between them they will have a surprising number of words. One way of sharing these words is by means of **brainstorming** activities. Here are a few ideas:

- Organise the class into groups of three or four, and set them a time limit to come up with as many words as they can that are related to the theme (e.g. school, cooking, crime). When they have finished, appoint a 'secretary' from each group to write their group's words on to the board (at the same time, if there is room). Alternatively, appoint a 'class secretary' to board all the words. You can make this a competition by allocating one point for each word that none of the other groups has. Allow groups to challenge any word that they think is 'off topic'.

- For a very large lexical field, such as food items, clothing, jobs, nationalities or animals, choose letters of the alphabet (B, S, A, M, etc.) for each 'round' of the game. In their groups students have to come up with only items that begin with that letter. Avoid infrequent letters of the alphabet (J, Q, K, X). Play several rounds, choosing different letters, allocating points to the group with the most words in each round.

- Set different topics (or different aspects of a topic) to different groups. For example, if the general theme is music – set one group the task of brainstorming musical instruments, another types of music, and another adjectives that collocate with music (*loud, soft*, etc). Re-group the students so that they can teach one another the words that they have brainstormed.

- Provide the class with pictures to prompt brainstorming activities. A collection of different magazine pictures (of, for example, people, interiors, landscapes or meals) distributed amongst groups can act as a productive focus for eliciting vocabulary. After learners have come up with sufficient words, a representative of each group can stick their picture on the board, and write their group's words underneath. Encourage other students to ask each group's representative the meaning of any unfamiliar words, using the formula *What does _____ mean?*

Any of the above activities can be done with or without the use of dictionaries (see page 60).

One way of giving learners at least temporary control of the topic agenda is to encourage them to prepare short class presentations on a topic of their choice. This is similar to the 'show-and-tell' type of activity common in primary classrooms. As they are giving their presentation, the teacher can keep a running record of new or interesting vocabulary that comes up. Or the students who are listening can note down words that they consider worth recording. After the presentation, this vocabulary can form the basis of a follow-up activity. For example, the teacher writes the topic-related words on the board, and students, in pairs or groups, write a summary of the presentation, incorporating the new vocabulary. Alternatively, the student giving the presentation can be asked to prepare a list of keywords which are distributed, or written up, in advance of the presentation itself.

Another way of 'capturing' classroom vocabulary as it occurs is to appoint 'word secretaries' during group work. When students are engaged on a group work task, the word secretary simply listens and notes down any new, unusual, or otherwise salient words, which are then shared with the class as a whole.

Many teachers keep an area of the board sectioned off in order to record words that crop up during classroom talk. It is relatively easy to write up words as they occur, without disturbing the flow of talk. At the end of the activity – or at the end of the lesson – time should be spent in running through these words. If the class is a monolingual one, the teacher can challenge students to provide translations of the words. Alternatively, they can attempt definitions, or at least try and recall the context in which the word emerged.

With experience, teachers are often able to 'pause' the classroom talk long enough to focus on words that arise naturally by means of an 'instructional aside'. In this example, at the points marked by an arrow, the teacher manages to intervene without interfering, as learners attempt to explain what 'barrancking' is – their ingenious coinage for 'canyoning', based on the Spanish word *barranquismo*:

    S1: What about going to mountains, we can do 'barrancking'. [Ss laugh]

    T: What's 'barrancking'?

    S2: Is a sport.

    T: Yes, but what do you do exactly?

    S3: You have a river, a small river and [gestures]

    T: Goes down?

    S3: Yes, as a cataract.

→   T: OK, a waterfall [writes it on board] What's a waterfall, Manel? Can you give me an example? A famous waterfall [draws]

    S1: Like Niagara?

    T: OK. So what do you do with the waterfall?

    S4: You go down.

    T: What? In a boat?

> S4: No, no, with a ... ¿como se dice cuerda? [How do you say *cuerda?*]
> S3: Cord.
> → T: No, rope, a cord is smaller, like at the window, look. [points]
> S4: Rope, rope, you go down rope in waterfall.

In order that this 'emergent class vocabulary' is not lost from one lesson to the next, some teachers keep a **word box** (or word bag) in their classrooms. New words are written on to small cards and added to the word box. At the beginning of the next lesson, these words can be used as the basis for a review activity. For example, the teacher can take words out of the box and ask learners to define them, provide a translation or put them into a sentence. The words can also form the basis for peer testing activities, in which learners take a number of word cards and test each other in pairs or small groups. (Further ideas for exploiting word cards can be found on page 147.) Periodically the word box should be 'purged' of words that the class agree no longer need recycling.

Conclusions

In this chapter:
• we have looked at five possible sources of vocabulary input for learners:
  – lists
  – coursebooks
  – vocabulary books
  – the teacher
  – other students

We noted that:
• lists are an economical way of organising vocabulary for learning, and that it doesn't matter a great deal if they are put together in a rather random way. It will help, though, if list learning activities are integrated into the lesson.
• coursebooks select vocabulary for active study on the grounds of:
  – usefulness
  – frequency
  – learnability
  – teachability
• coursebook content includes both segregated and integrated vocabulary work
• segregated activities typically present or practise lexical sets, or word formation rules, or recycle or test words introduced previously, or target specific vocabulary-learning strategies
• vocabulary is also integrated into skills work, typically in the form of a pre-task or post-task vocabulary focus
• some coursebook vocabulary is incidental, such as that included in instructions and grammar explanations
• supplementary vocabulary books are usually thematically organised, but cover a range of vocabulary skills

- coursebooks and vocabulary books cannot always provide sufficient practice of newly introduced words, in which case the teacher may need to devise 'multiple decision-making' tasks, to ensure an element of 'cognitive depth' in vocabulary learning
- the teacher is a potentially fruitful source of vocabulary input, not only in terms of incidental learning, but also as a means of introducing vocabulary through teacher talk
- in any one class, each learner can contribute to the shared class 'lexicon' through activities such as brainstorming, and research findings suggest that learner input is as powerful, if not more so, than other vocabulary sources. Productive use of this resource depends in part on allowing learners some control of the topic agenda.

Looking ahead   In the next chapter we will continue investigating sources of vocabulary input, with special reference to texts, dictionaries, and that more recent phenomenon, the corpus.

Texts, dictionaries and corpora

- **Short texts**
- **Books and readers**
- **Dictionaries**
- **Corpus data**

Short texts As we saw in the last chapter, vocabulary used to be offered to learners in the form of lists. Nowadays, the tendency is to present vocabulary in texts. For vocabulary building purposes, texts – whether spoken or written – have enormous advantages over learning words from lists. For a start, the fact that words are in context increases the chances of learners appreciating not only their meaning but their typical environments, such as their associated collocations or grammatical structures. Moreover, it is likely that the text will display topically connected sets of words (or **lexical fields** – see page 10). As we saw in the last chapter, evidence suggests that words loosely connected by topic may be easier to learn than more tightly connected lexical sets.

Short texts are ideal for classroom use, since they can be subjected to intensive grammatical and lexical study, without overtaxing learners' attention or memory, as may be the case with longer texts. Learning to cope with short texts is also good preparation for independent reading and listening, including dealing with longer texts. Moreover, short texts provide useful models for student production, in the form of speaking and writing.

A characteristic feature of cohesive texts is that they are threaded through with words that relate to the same topic – what are sometimes called **lexical chains**. This is even more likely if the text is **authentic** – that is, if it has not been especially written or doctored for the language classroom. Here, for example, is a short authentic text that contains a number of lexical chains, the main one being a *snake* chain. Words in this chain are underlined.

Snake sneaks into Auckland suburb

The hunt is on for a live snake which could be on the loose in Auckland. The reptile has left behind a freshly shed skin in the inner-city suburb of Freeman's Bay. Experts believe it has come from a boa or python nearly two metres long. Ten-year-old Victor McKenney found the skin near his home. 'I thought it was like fish scales and then my friend pointed out it looked like snake skin,' Victor said. The skin is now being tested at a site near Christchurch but experts believe it is a harmless variety and definitely still alive.

It is not the first <u>snake</u> to sneak into New Zealand this year. In March a poisonous <u>eastern brown snake</u> was found alive in Wellington and two others were discovered dead in Auckland and Wellington.

The Ministry of Agriculture and Forestry is worried. Although it is not a dangerous variety, MAF points out that all <u>reptiles</u> could be carriers of bacteria such as salmonella. The MAF <u>snakecatcher</u> team will be out again with dogs in a bid to find the <u>snake</u>. Meanwhile, MAF is urging anyone who spots the missing <u>snake</u> to call 0800-809 966.

(from web page at http://onenews.nzoom.com/national)

Intertwined with the *snake* chain is a *hunting* chain, which includes the words: *hunt, on the loose, snakecatcher, dogs, find/found, discovered, missing*. A *skin* chain includes *skin* (× 4), *shed* and *scales*. *Alive, dead* and *live* form a chain of their own, while *harmless, dangerous* and *poisonous* form a *danger* chain, to which could perhaps be added *carriers, bacteria* and *salmonella*. Notice how the dominant lexical chains provide a summary of the gist of the story: *The **hunt** is on for a **harmless live snake** after its **skin** was found.*

 Activities designed to exploit this characteristic of texts include setting the students the task of identifying the lexical chains for themselves – by, for example, underlining or circling associated words. They can then attempt to identify the type of relationship between words in a chain, such as collocations (*live snake; shed skin; snake skin; fish scales*); synonyms (*on the loose, missing; found, discovered*); antonyms (*harmless, dangerous*); and hyponyms and their superordinates: *reptile → snake → boa/python/eastern brown snake*. They may even note the juxtaposition of *snake* and *sneak* – this time a sound relationship, rather than a meaning one. Having done this 'lexical detective' work, learners can then attempt either to reconstruct the text from memory, or write a 50-word summary of it.

Lexical chain detection tasks offer another way of exploiting coursebook texts, even those written primarily for a grammatical purpose. In the text *Fear of Flying* on page 42, there are two dominant lexical chains: a *plane* chain, and a *train* chain. Setting the learners the task of extracting these linked items, and then using them to summarise the text, adds appreciably to the vocabulary learning potential of the text.

Different kinds of texts (or **genres**) are likely to display different lexical features. Academic writing, for example, is noted for having a higher proportion of nouns over verbs than non-academic texts. Not only that, but the nouns are often stacked together with adjectives or nouns (or both) to form relatively long sequences, as in this example, in which the compound noun phrases are underlined:

We investigate the suitability of deploying <u>speech technology</u> in <u>computer-based systems</u> that can be used to teach <u>foreign language skills</u>. In reviewing the <u>current state</u> of <u>speech recognition</u> and <u>speech processing technology</u> and by examining a number of <u>voice-interactive CALL applications</u>, we suggest how to create <u>robust interactive learning</u>

<u>environments</u> that exploit the strengths of <u>speech technology</u> while working around its limitations. In the conclusion, we draw on our review of these applications to identify directions of <u>future research</u> that might improve both the design and the <u>overall performance</u> of <u>voice-interactive CALL systems</u>.

(from web page at http://llt.msu.edu/vol2num1/article3/index.html)

On the other hand, less formal kinds of texts also have their own lexical characteristics. Horoscopes in magazines, for example, are typically rich in idiomatic language, including phrasal verbs. In this example, idioms and idiomatic phrasal verbs have been underlined:

LIBRA
23 September–22 October

LOVE A new man <u>on the scene</u> <u>sheds a fresh light</u> on a past relationship and you'll wonder if you can <u>make a fresh start</u> with him. <u>Give it a spin</u>. It won't be the same as the last one.

AMBITION <u>Nothing comes easy</u> now with a project, and your instinct is <u>to pack it in</u>. Don't! You'll get your inspiration back when Venus joins Neptune on the 22nd.

INSIGHT You <u>hang out</u> with so many people that <u>every now and again</u> you need <u>to hole up</u> and <u>take stock</u>. Deal with those jobs on your 'to do' list and you'll feel back in control.

(from *19* magazine)

There are a number of ways these lexical features can be exploited. Here, for example, is a procedure that can be applied to both the academic text and the horoscope text:

- Ask learners to skim the text and decide a) what kind of text it is, b) what its purpose is, c) who it is written for and d) what style it is written in (e.g. formal, informal).
- Learners read the text again and are asked to attempt a rough summary of its gist – e.g. 'what is it about?' (in the case of the academic text) or 'what three pieces of advice are offered?' (in the case of the horoscope).
- Ask learners to find all the examples of the lexical feature that is being targeted – e.g. long noun phrases (in the academic text) or idioms (in the horoscope). To ease the task, you can tell them how many to look for.
- Learners then work out the meanings of the phrases either from their components, or from their context, or both. At this point, they could be allowed to consult dictionaries.
- Alternatively, provide definitions, synonyms or L1 translations of the targeted words, and ask them to find the words in the text that match. For example: *Try it*. (For *Give it a spin*.)

- Ask learners to study the targeted items and analyse them in terms of their formal features – e.g. in the academic text, to separate the noun phrases into adjective + noun, or noun + noun combinations, or, in the horoscope, to distinguish between the phrasal verbs and other idiomatic phrases.
- Provide the learners with the same texts, but with the targeted items blanked out. See if they can complete the texts by replacing the items. Alternatively, provide them with a list of the items (including one or two extras, perhaps) to re-insert in the text.
- Ask learners to write their own texts, to include some of the items they have been studying.

So far, we have only been looking at written texts. But spoken language also comprises a wealth of exploitable material. Two lexical features of spoken language that are difficult to teach in isolation are **discourse markers** and **tags**. Discourse markers are words or phrases, such as *well, anyway, I mean, I'll tell you what*, that tend to occur at the onset of an utterance and indicate a change in the direction of the talk. Tags, on the other hand, occur at the end of an utterance, either to qualify what has been said (such as *I suppose, actually, really*), or to elicit the listener's involvement (such as *isn't it? you know, yeah?*). In this extract (between a driving instructor and his client), the discourse markers are underlined and the tags are in italics:

INSTRUCTOR: All right?
LEARNER: [Sighs] Yeah [laughs]
INSTRUCTOR: Well done, Maria, you did well on that lesson. You can switch off now.
LEARNER: Yeah, great, thank you very much.
INSTRUCTOR: <u>So</u> how d'you find it okay?
LEARNER: Yeah, it was great *actually*.
INSTRUCTOR: That's good.
LEARNER: I really enjoyed it. I thought I was more in control.
INSTRUCTOR: You've come on a lot on that lesson *actually*.
LEARNER: D'you think so?
INSTRUCTOR: Yeah. Since the last one even, *you know*.
LEARNER: I think the last one was a bad one *though*. <u>I mean</u>, I felt I wasn't patient *you know*.
INSTRUCTOR: <u>Yeah but</u>, <u>you see</u>, you had a gap before that.
LEARNER: That's why.
INSTRUCTOR: That's what was wrong *really*.

(after McCarthy M, in Coupland J, *Small Talk*, Longman)

Exactly the same identifying and categorising tasks, as suggested for the academic and horoscope texts, can be applied to a transcript of real talk such as this one. If the talk is recorded, so much the better, since learners can get the benefit of the prosodic features of the text – that is, the stress and intonation.

Finally, short **literary texts** offer multiple possibilities for vocabulary development. It goes without saying that writers and poets choose their words carefully, not only for their meanings but for their formal features as well. (Someone once defined poetry as 'the right words in the right order'.) Seeing how writers put words to use for their expressive function can only help enrich the network of word associations for the learner. Here, for example, is a poem that imbues rather mundane objects with special significance:

HANDBAG

My mother's old leather handbag,
crowded with letters she carried
all through the war. The smell
of my mother's handbag: mints
and lipstick and Coty powder.
The look of those letters, softened
and worn at the edges, opened,
read, and refolded so often.
Letters from my father. Odour
of leather and powder, which ever
since then has meant womanliness,
and love, and anguish, and war.

(from Fainlight R, *Selected Poems*, Cassell)

The following lexical features are worth drawing students' attention to (or helping them discover):

- The things in the text, and their relationships, i.e. *handbag* which contains *letters*, *mints*, *lipstick*, *powder*, and which is made of *leather*. Students could talk about the things they carry with them, or that they remember their mother or grandmother having.
- The complex noun phrases: *My mother's old leather handbag*; *The smell of my mother's handbag* … Students could construct complex noun phrases along similar lines to describe the things they have talked about previously.
- The describing function of participles: *softened, worn, opened, read, refolded*. Students could describe their own (or remembered) objects using sequences of participles.
- The sensations in the text: *the smell of … the look of …* Other expressions that follow this pattern are *the sound of* and *the feel of …* Students could apply these expressions to the objects they have been describing.
- The abstract nouns in the text: *womanliness, love, anguish* and the way these are connected to concrete objects and actions: *womanliness → lipstick, powder; love → letters; anguish → opened, read, refolded*. Students could search for abstract nouns which capture their own emotional associations with the objects they have been talking about.

- The pattern of two-syllable words ending in a *schwa* (unstressed central vowel sound): *mother, leather, powder, letter, father, odour, ever*. Students could add to this list, especially words that could fit the kind of loose associations created by the poem (*lover, brother, feather, lighter, never*, etc).
- Finally, students could attempt a 'personalised' version of the poem, following a similar pattern:

> an extended noun phrase
> +
> *the smell/look/feel/sound of …*
> +
> a list of items
> +
> *the smell/look/feel/sound of …*
> +
> single item from the list + sequence of participles
> +
> *odour/sound/appearance/feel of …*
> +
> *… which ever since then has meant* + abstract nouns

The patterned nature of many literary texts, especially poems, and the intricate 'web of words' that knits them together, means that the above approach can be generalised to almost any poem. (It is important, at some stage of the process, that learners *hear* the poem read aloud, in order to appreciate its formal characteristics, such as metre and rhyme.)

Books and readers

While coursebooks, vocabulary books and short texts are useful for focusing on specific words for active study, the point has been made that the learner needs plentiful opportunities for incidental learning to occur as well. The best way of providing the necessary exposure is through extensive reading – that is, the reading of long texts, and for pleasure rather than for information.

Extensive reading provides the opportunity to meet words in their context of use, and also supplies repeated encounters with many of these words. Research suggests that it takes six or more encounters with a word before learning is likely to take place. While coursebooks take the need to recycle vocabulary seriously, words are seldom repeated up to six times. This is partly due to the fact that, in the interests of variety and coverage, there is a high turnover of topics in a coursebook. This means that an area of vocabulary, such as food and drink, or clothing, or family relationships, or geographical terms, tends to be introduced just once, and then dropped. Simplified readers and 'real' books tend to follow a topic over a length of text, ensuring at least some repetition of key vocabulary.

Simplified readers are widely available, and at a variety of levels. They are graded both in terms of their grammar complexity and their vocabulary load. For example, the number of words used at each level of the Penguin series of graded readers is limited according to this scale:

Easystarts	200 words
Level One Beginner	300 words
Level Two Elementary	600 words
Level Three Pre-Intermediate	1,200 words
Level Four Intermediate	1,700 words
Level Five Upper-Intermediate	2,300 words
Level Six Advanced	3,000 words

Even if learners do not know all the words in a reader, the fact that the vocabulary range is restricted means that there should be enough familiar words to enable them to guess the meaning of the unfamiliar words from context. Researchers estimate that if 90 to 95 per cent of words in a text are familiar, then reading will not seem too much of a chore. Incidentally, this suggests a very simple test when recommending extensive reading to learners. Ask them to select any passage from the book and count out an extract with 100 words. If, in those 100 words, fewer than five are unfamiliar, then there is a good chance that the book will be within the learner's comfortable reading range. If more than ten words are unfamiliar, the learner is recommended to choose a reader from a lower level, or to look for authentic texts that do fall within the 95 per cent limit.

It is imperative that if learners are to enjoy, and get the most out of, extensive reading it should not be seen as hard work. Not only should texts be within their current competence, but, ideally, learners should have the opportunity to choose the kinds of texts they are going to read. This could mean having a class library of books to choose from. The teacher will need to exercise discretion, however, as to how learners' reading experiences are incorporated into the classroom. It may be counterproductive to insist on learners making formal reports or summaries of their reading, since this may turn reading into a chore not a pleasure. Nevertheless, some discussion of the value of free reading may help motivate those learners who do not normally read for pleasure, even in their own language.

Free reading, as we have seen, increases the chances of repeated encounters with words. Even better than free reading, from the point of view of recycling, is what is called **narrow reading**. (Its aural equivalent is **narrow listening**.) Narrow reading is reading around the same topic over the course of a number of texts. In this way learners become more familiar with the topic, which in turn makes reading easier. But more importantly, when you read a number of texts on the same theme, you will come across the same vocabulary used repeatedly. Narrow reading is in fact what most newspaper or magazine readers do on a daily basis. That is, they follow a particular news story over a period of time. Introducing narrow reading into the classroom therefore meets with little resistance. One student, who had recently been introduced to this technique, commented: 'I like reading one story because, after the first day, I don't have to use the dictionary as much, so it makes reading more enjoyable.'

As an example, here is a follow-up story to the story 'Snake sneaks into Auckland suburb' on page 53. Content words (i.e. not grammar words) that occurred in the previous story are underlined:

Snake shed from coat, not python

Auckland's snake hunt has ended after experts realised a skin found on a city street was shed from a fancy coat, and not a real live python.

The man who owns the coat has told the Ministry of Agriculture and Forestry a snakeskin sewn into his prized garment is missing.

He approached MAF last week after realising the skin was gone from the coat, last worn to a Halloween Ball just a couple of days before school children found the skin on a Freeman's Bay street.

The October finding prompted lengthy searches of the suburb by MAF tracker dogs and detector teams, after experts they consulted said the skin appeared to have been freshly shed.

Today MAF admitted those experts were probably wrong.

Spokeswoman Gita Parsot said New Zealand had little experience with snake skins, and experts were now reviewing how to identify the age of a skin.

Ms Parsot said experts in Australia, where there are a lot of snakes, might be consulted if skins were found in future. – NZPA

(from web page at http://www.stuff.co.nz)

Of the 108 or so content words (see page 4) in this text, 43, or nearly half, are repeated from the previous news story. If the story had run longer, the density of familiar vocabulary would probably have been even greater.

Both these snake stories were taken from Internet news sites, which are a useful source of narrow reading material. But conventional newspapers and magazines offer similar – if less conveniently accessible – material. Setting students the task of following a story that interests them – and reporting on it to their classmates – can be done using either electronic or print media, according to availability. For the latter, teachers may wish to collect sequences of news stories, filed according to topic, in order to build up a dossier of useful material. Narrow listening activities would require a collection of sequences of topic-based recordings, such as news stories, folk tales, or even just pop songs.

Dictionaries

For a long time the use of dictionaries in class was discouraged, generally on the grounds that dependence on a dictionary might inhibit the development of more useful skills, such as guessing from context. Also, it was argued that if the dictionary is a bilingual one, learners may over-rely on translation, at the expense of developing a separate L2 lexicon. Finally, indiscriminate dictionary use often results in the kind of errors where the wrong word has been selected for the meaning intended. A student of mine, for instance, wrote a recipe for *Close shave with pinenuts*: the Spanish word *rape* has two English equivalents in the dictionary: *monkfish* (the intended meaning) and *close shave* (the unintended outcome).

However, the role of dictionaries in vocabulary learning has been reassessed. As sources of words, and of information about words, they are unequalled. Nowadays, an excellent selection of learner dictionaries is available, and coursebooks regularly include activities designed to encourage resourceful and efficient dictionary use.

At this point, we need to distinguish between the different kinds of dictionary available. The first important distinction to make is between:

- bilingual dictionaries (e.g. a French–English, English–French dictionary), and
- monolingual dictionaries (e.g. English only)

On the whole, learners tend to favour bilingual dictionaries over monolingual ones. They are easy to understand, and the time taken to refer to them only minimally interrupts reading or listening. More importantly, they are also useful for production – for speaking and writing. For example, a German learner wanting to express the idea of *Schlange* but not knowing its English equivalent (*snake*), would have no trouble finding the right word in a German–English dictionary. But where would he start with an English-only dictionary? Even if he had a vague idea that it began with an *s,* there are a lot of words beginning with *s* to wade through before getting to *snake.*

Nevertheless, bilingual dictionaries, especially the pocket or electronic ones that most students have, can be misleading, as we saw with *close shave.* By suggesting a one-to-one match between L1 and L2 words, they often oversimplify matters. Here, for example, is how a pocket French–English dictionary deals with the word *shed* (which we met in the snake story on page 53):

shed[1] (ʃed) *n* hangar *m.* remise *f.*
shed[2] (ʃed) *vt* jeter, répandre

As it happens, if you consult the entries for *jeter* and *répandre* in the same dictionary, you will find that neither give *shed* as an equivalent. So, while the dictionary may be of some use in helping the learner understand *shed* when the word is encountered in a text, it gives no guidance that would help the same learner produce *shed* when engaged in a writing task, for example.

A further distinction can be made between

- native speakers' dictionaries, and
- learners' dictionaries

The latter use a restricted vocabulary for their definitions. They also include data that is of particular use for learners, such as grammar information – e.g. whether a noun is countable or not, or whether a verb is followed by the infinitive or the *-ing* form. The better learner dictionaries also include advice for learners that is based on an analysis of typical learner errors. On the right, for example, is a note on how *actually* is used:

from the *Longman Dictionary of Contemporary English*

> **USAGE NOTE: ACTUALLY**
> WORD CHOICE: **actually, currently, at present**
> **Actually** (and **actual**) does not mean 'at the present time' in English. Compare **currently** and **at present**: *"Have you ever met Simon?" "I actually met him two years ago"* (=in fact). *"Is the company doing well?" "Yes." "It's currently doing very well/ It's doing very well at present."*
> In conversation, especially in British English, **actually** can be used to make what you are saying softer, especially if you are correcting someone, disagreeing, or complaining: *"Great! I love French coffee!" "Er, it's German actually."* But it can be used with the opposite effect: *I didn't ask your opinion, actually.*

Another distinction is between dictionaries that are organised:

• alphabetically, or
• according to meaning categories

A reference book organised according to meaning categories is generally classed as a **thesaurus**. For example, in the *Cambridge Word Selector* series, words are organised not alphabetically but according to shared or similar meanings. Unlike a conventional thesaurus, only a limited number of words are included in each category, and definitions are provided in the learner's L1. Here, for example, is an entry from the Catalan version of the *Word Selector*:

---

202 Modern Modern

modern *adj* modern *the most modern equipment* l'equipament més modern [usades actualment] *modern languages* llengües modernes [habit. fa referència al segle passat] *modern history/literature/art* art/història/literatura moderna

modernize, TAMBÉ **-ise** (*brit*) *vti* [obj: p. ex. un mètode, un equip] modernitzar(-se) **modernization** *ni/c* modernització

up-to-date *adj* 1 [modern. Descriu: p. ex. un equip, un mètode] modern, actual 2 (sovint + **with**) [que coneix o conté l'última informació. Descriu: p. ex. un llistat, un mapa] al dia *to keep up-to-date with the latest developments* mantenir-se al dia de les últimes novetats *We must bring our records up-to-date.* Hem de posar al dia els nostres arxius.

update *vt* 1 [obj: p. ex. uns arxius, una informació, un model] actualitzar *We're.updating all our office equipment.* Estem actualitzant tot l'equipament de l'oficina. 2 (sovint + **on**) [donar l'última informació a] posar al dia *I'll just update you on the latest sales figures.* Em limitaré a posar-vos al dia de les últimes xifres de vendes. **update** *nc* actualització

newfangled *adj* [força informal i pej.] acabat d'inventar *I can't cope with this newfangled machinery.* No me'n surto amb aquesta maquinària tan moderna.

contemporary *adj* 1 [util. sobretot en la llengua escrita i en la parla més seriosa o intel·lectual] contemporani, coetani 2 (sovint + **with**) [que viu en una mateixa època o temps] coetani, contemporani **contemporary** *nc* contemporani -ània

current *adj* (habit. davant de *n*) [que succeeix o existeix en aquest moment] actual, corrent *current affairs* actualitat *the current economic climate* el clima econòmic actual *the current issue of the magazine* l'últim número de la revista [més aviat formal quan es fa servir darrere de v] corrent *These ideas are current in certain sections of the community.* Aquestes idees són corrents en alguns sectors de la comunitat. **currently** *adv* actualment

topical *adj* [relacionat amb esdeveniments actuals]. Descriu: p. ex. una pregunta, un problema, una al·lusió] d'actualitat, d'interès *topical talk* conversa sobre afers d'actualitat

202.1 Moda

fashion *nc/i* 1 moda *to be* **in/out of fashion** estar/no estar de moda *Pointed shoes are coming back into fashion.* Les sabates amb punta tornen a estar de moda. *Roller-skating is the latest fashion here.* Aquí l'última moda és el patinatge sobre rodes. 2 [roba] moda *men's/ladies' fashions* moda d'home/de dona (davant de *n*) *fashion designer* dissenyadora de moda *fashion model* model *fashion show* desfilada de models

fashionable *adj* [descriu: p. ex. una roba, una persona, una opinió, un restaurant] de moda, de bon gust *It's fashionable to live in a converted warehouse.* Està de moda viure en magatzems rehabilitats. **fashionably** *adv* (molt) a la moda

trend *nc* (sovint + **in, towards**) tendència *The present trend is towards products which are environment-friendly.* La tendència actual afavoreix els productes respectuosos amb el medi ambient. *to set a/the trend* imposar una/la tendència

trendy *adj* [força informal i sovint pej.] a l'última moda *trendy left-wing ideas* idees esquerranes de moda

be with-it *vi* [informal i més aviat obsolet] estar al dia, ser l'últim crit *a with-it vicar* un mossèn amb idees modernes

---

from the *Catalan Word Selector*, CUP

A meaning-based organisation is particularly useful for production, that is, for preparation for speaking or writing tasks, since it allows the learner to search for the exact word to represent an intended meaning. For example, a learner wanting to find an appropriately idiomatic expression to express the general idea that 'Teachers should "be modern" in their knowledge of teaching methods' would first look up *modern* (English) or *modern* (Catalan) in the book's index. This leads to the appropriate section where the student would not have to look far to find the expression *keep up-to-date*, so as to produce 'Teachers should keep up-to-date with teaching methods'.

A similar principle governs the organisation of both the *Oxford Learner's Wordfinder Dictionary* and the *Longman Language Activator*. For example, the *Activator* (dubbed 'the world's first production dictionary') is based on around 1,000 'key words', which together comprise 'the basic meanings of the core of English' (or a **core vocabulary** – see page 21). Organised under each key word is a 'menu' of words and phrases with related meanings. Unlike the *Word Selector*, the *Activator* is monolingual. Here, for example, is how the *Activator* deals with *modern*:

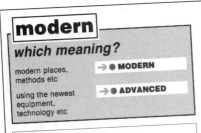

modern

which meaning?

| modern places, methods etc | → ● MODERN |
| using the newest equipment, technology etc | → ● ADVANCED |

● MODERN

1 words for describing machines, systems, processes etc that have been developed using the most recent ideas and equipment

2 using, or willing to use, the most recent ideas and ways of thinking

3 words for describing modern art, literature, music etc

4 to change something in order to make it modern

---

1 words for describing machines, systems, processes etc that have been developed using the most recent ideas and equipment

modern
up-to-date

modern /ˈmɒdn ‖ ˈmɑːdərn/ [adj]
There is a modern rail system to take passengers to and from the city. | *In Japanese car factories they have all the most modern machinery.* | *A sophisticated modern air-defence system can be very expensive.*

up-to-date /ˌʌp tə ˈdeɪt◂/ **up-to-date methods/machinery/equipment/facilities etc** (=based on the most recent knowledge or ideas) [adj]
Our athletes are trained on the most up-to-date facilities in Europe. | *All the equipment in the hospital is the most up-to-date there is.* | *What we need is a computer system that is up-to-date and flexible.*

---

2 using, or willing to use, the most recent ideas and ways of thinking

modern   forward-looking
progressive   move with the times
innovative   go-ahead

modern /ˈmɒdn ‖ ˈmɑːdərn/ [adj]
She wants a hospital that uses the most modern childbirth techniques. | *They're a very modern couple – he stays at home with the kids and she goes out to work.* | *The school is very modern in its approach to sex education.*

progressive /prəˈgresɪv/ keen to change and improve what you do by trying completely new methods and ideas [adj]
Even with the most progressive methods in agriculture you still can't do anything about the weather. | *He has a reputation as a social and industrial reformer with progressive views.*

innovative /ˈɪnəˌveɪtɪv/ using new methods and ideas that are clever and original [adj]
She has been praised for her innovative techniques in helping deaf people to speak. | *'Time' magazine called the mobile phone one of the ten most innovative products of the year.*
innovation /ˌɪnəˈveɪʃən/ [n U] *We have a career structure that rewards innovation and good ideas.*

---

forward-looking /ˈfɔːrwərd lʊkɪŋ/ willing to use new and recently developed methods and ideas in order to do your job better [adj]
The training methods in this school are very forward-looking. | *We like to think we're one of those forward-looking companies that isn't afraid to use new ideas.*

move with the times /ˌmuːv wɪð ðə ˈtaɪmz/ to change your way of living or working so that you are using modern ideas, methods etc, even though you may not want to [v phrase]
I'm not keen on all these electronic gadgets, but I suppose we must move with the times. | *Whereas Japanese industry has moved with the times our production methods have scarcely changed in 20 years.*

go-ahead /ˈgəʊ əˌhed/ always keen to use modern ideas and methods because you want to be successful [adj only before noun]
Fortuna is a young, go-ahead computer company based in Düsseldorf.

---

3 words for describing modern art, literature, music etc

modern   avant-garde
contemporary   futuristic

modern /ˈmɒdn ‖ ˈmɑːdərn/ using styles that are different from the existing styles of art, literature, music etc [adj]
Charles is a collector of modern art. | *Modern music can be difficult to get used to.* | *The dance was modern and quite interesting but I think I prefer a traditional ballet.*

contemporary /kənˈtempərəri, -pəri ‖ -pəreri/ produced or written recently rather than a long time ago, using a style different from the styles used in the past [adj]
Contemporary art is sometimes hard to understand and appreciate. | *The dancers performed to a contemporary arrangement of 'Swan Lake'.*

avant-garde /ˌævɒŋˈgɑːrd◂ ‖ ˌævɑŋ-/ extremely modern and strange or hard to understand because it is very different from existing ideas in art, music, literature etc [adj]
Although she likes avant-garde music, Lydia also plays classical guitar and piano. | *The Whitechapel Art Gallery usually displays the work of avant-garde sculptors and painters.*

futuristic /ˌfjuːtʃəˈrɪstɪk◂/ **futuristic design/building/film etc** (=one that appears so modern and strange that it seems to belong to the future and not to the present) [adj]
The futuristic sports stadium is the pride of the city. | *We think your designs are a little too futuristic for our factory.*

---

4 to change something in order to make it modern

modernize
bring sth up to date
update

modernize (also **-ise** British) /ˈmɒdənaɪz ‖ ˈmɑːdər-/ [v T]
The aviation authorities are attempting to modernize the air traffic control system. | *They bought a traditional farmhouse that had been modernized by the previous owners.*
modernization /ˌmɒdənaɪˈzeɪʃən ‖ ˌmɑːdərnə-/ [n U] *The company needs better staff training, computerization and general modernization of equipment.*

bring sth up to date /ˌbrɪŋ (sth) ʌp tə ˈdeɪt/ to make something modern by getting rid of any old-fashioned details or features that it has and adding the newest ones that are available [v phrase usually in passive]
All the old encyclopedias have been revised and brought up to date. | *The weathermen ought to bring their old-fashioned forecast models up to date.*

update /ˌʌpˈdeɪt/ to make something such as a design or system more modern by adding the most recent information or parts to it so that it does not become useless, old-fashioned etc [v T]

Picture dictionaries, because they are thematically organised, are another kind of meaning-based dictionary, and are particularly useful in that they group together words of the same lexical field. Their limitation is, of course, that they are restricted to things or actions that can be illustrated. But for younger learners they are ideal.

Finally, there are those learner dictionaries that have specialised functions, such as dictionaries of business English, dictionaries of idioms, of collocations, of phrasal verbs, and pronunciation dictionaries. (See the further reading list on page 183 for specific titles.)

What sort of information does a dictionary provide? Below, for example, is the entry for *shed* from the *Longman Dictionary of Contemporary English*.

Note, first of all, that there are two homonyms that have the form *shed* (see page 8), and that these two different meanings are listed separately as **shed¹** and **shed²**. Pronunciation is supplied, using phonemic script ($\int$ed). Grammatical information follows, including part of speech (*n*, *v*), the fact that the noun is countable [C] and the verb is transitive [T], as well as the verb's inflexions (*shed, shedding*). Both entries are further sub-divided into their different polysemes, e.g. **shed¹** *1 a small building* ... and *2 a large industrial building* ... In the case of

> **shed¹** /$\int$ed/ *n* [C] **1** a small building, often made of wood, used especially for storing things: *We had a tool shed in our back yard.*|*a cattle shed*|*a garden shed* **2** a large industrial building where work is done, large vehicles are kept or machinery is stored etc
>
> **shed²** *v* [T] *past tense and past participle* **shed** *present participle* **shedding**
> **1** ▶LIGHT◀ if something sheds light, it lights the area around it: *The lamp shed a yellow glow onto the desk.*
> **2** ▶DROP/FALL OFF◀ **a)** to drop something or allow it to fall: *He strode across the bathroom, shedding wet clothes as he went.* **b)** if an animal sheds skin or hair or a plant sheds leaves etc, they fall off as part of a natural process: *Deciduous trees shed their leaves in autumn.*|*As it grows, a snake will regularly shed its skin.*
> **3** ▶GET RID OF◀ to get rid of something that you no longer need or want: *The company is planning to shed about a quarter of its workforce.*|*I shed my inhibitions and joined the dancing.*|**shed pounds/stones** (=get thinner by losing several pounds etc) *I'd like to shed a few pounds.*
> **4 shed light on** to make something easier to understand, by providing new or better information: *We're hoping his letter will shed some light on the mystery.*
> **5** ▶WATER◀ if something sheds water, the water flows off its surface, instead of sinking into it
> **6 shed blood** to kill or injure people, especially during a war or a fight: *Too much blood has already been shed in this conflict.* —see also BLOODSHED
> **7 shed tears** *especially literary* to cry: *She had not shed a single tear during the funeral.*
> **8 shed its load** *BrE* if a vehicle sheds its load, the goods it is carrying accidentally fall off
>
> S 3

the verb *shed*, different meanings are signposted in capital letters for ease of reference. Definitions are written in easy-to-understand language, and examples are included that are chosen to display the word's meaning as well as its grammatical behaviour. Common collocations are included: *shed light on, shed blood*, etc. Links to derived forms are also signalled, as in *see also* BLOODSHED. Register and style information is also included, where relevant. Thus, *shed tears* is marked as being *literary* while *shed its load* is British usage. Finally, frequency information is added in the margin: S 3 means that the noun *shed* is in the 2,000–3,000 band in terms of frequency in spoken English (S = spoken). A word marked as W 1 , on the other hand, would be in the top thousand words of written English (W = written). A word marked W 2 would be in the next thousand, and so on.

If we compare this information with the map of what is involved in knowing the word *tangi* (see page 16), it is clear that all the relevant linguistic information is supplied by the dictionary. Of course, the less linguistic, more encyclopedic, information is missing: the iconic role of the *garden shed* in suburban British culture is not even hinted at. For this kind of information we would need to consult a dictionary of culture. For example:

> … In Britain people generally choose to sit in the back garden, out of view of other people. The back garden usually also has a lawn and **flower beds**, and sometimes a vegetable plot or fruit trees. There is often a **bird table** (= a raised platform on which food is put for birds) and a **shed** in which garden tools are kept.

(from the *Oxford Guide to British and American Culture*, OUP)

What kind of use can learners make of dictionary information? This will depend on how well trained they are in using dictionaries. Ideas for training learners to become effective dictionary users are found in Chapter 9.

Meanwhile, in this section the focus will be on the use of dictionaries not so much as reference aids (for reading or writing, for example) than as *learning* aids. How can the information in dictionaries be exploited to promote vocabulary acquisition? On the right, for example, is a coursebook activity (from Greenall S, *Reward Pre-Intermediate*, Macmillan Heinemann) that requires the use of a dictionary.

In this activity, learners are using their dictionaries to make at least two decisions about the targeted words: they are identifying their word classes, and they are discriminating between their different

> **2** Some words can be more than one part of speech. For example:
> *cook: A* **cook** (noun) *is someone who* **cooks** (verb) *food.*
> *orange: An* **orange** (noun) *is an* **orange** (adjective) *fruit.*
>
> Use your dictionary to find out what parts of speech these words can be.
>
> talk   head   drink   flat   start
> rent   slice   heat
>
> Write sentences showing their different parts of speech.
> *He talks all the time.*
> *There's a talk on insects tonight.*

meanings, both of which are necessary if they are to write coherent sentences. This two-step process reflects a key principle underlying the classroom use of dictionaries: **cognitive depth** (see page 25). The more decisions the learner makes about a word, the greater the degree of cognitive processing, and hence the greater the likelihood of retention in memory. Every time learners consult a dictionary they have initiated a decision-making process. And the fact that dictionaries contain such a wealth of information makes them ideal for use in multiple decision-making tasks. Dictionary-based activities can be designed that require students to make decisions about a word's spelling, its pronunciation, its meaning, its grammar, its collocations, its derivatives, the style and connotations of the word, and its frequency.

Here, for example, are two tasks that focus on spelling and pronunciation:

- Dictate a selection of words that share the same sounds, but may be spelt according to different rules, such as *date, great, wait, fate, eight, late, straight, bait, hate*, etc. Students use dictionaries to check spelling and organise words into spelling groups (e.g. all the *-ai-* words together). They can then draw conclusions as to which are the more frequent spellings, and which are exceptional.

- Students are given words on cards that share the same spelling features but may be pronounced differently. For example, the letter *g* in *guess, magic, gaol, fog, gym, gift, gene, logic, large*, etc. As in the preceding activity, dictionaries are used to sort words according to pronunciation, and to help discern patterns.

The following two tasks target word meaning:

- Students are dictated words or given words on cards, and must sort them into meaning categories, using the dictionary. The title of the category can be given, or, to make the task more difficult, left to the learners to work out. For example, the following twelve words can be grouped into three groups of four words each: *board, club, piece, net, hole, tee, racket, queen, umpire, check, green, court*. Note that many of these words are polysemous (i.e. they have more than one meaning) so learners will need to use their dictionaries intelligently in order to locate the correct meaning area (in this case, meanings connected with games).

- Students find the odd one out in sets of three or four words (*duck, pigeon, python, stork*); matching synonyms (*poisonous – venomous*), antonyms (*harmless – dangerous*); organising words into hierarchy ranks (e.g. *reptile, snake, python; fruit, apple, Granny Smith*).

Here are two tasks that involve researching the grammar of words:

- Students organise words into parts of speech, according to dictionary information, or into countable/uncountable (nouns), transitive/intransitive (verbs), etc.

- Students use dictionaries to check the grammatical correctness of sentences such as:

> I'd like some informations about Italy.
> How much potato would you like?
> I prefer Californian wines to French ones.
> The flat was full of furnitures.
>
> or
>
> I suggested him to see a dentist.
> She recommended the film.
> He explained me the lesson.
> The doctor advised me to rest.
> They apologised that they were late.

Dictionaries can also be used to raise awareness about collocation:

 Students match words on cards to form collocations, checking with the dictionary. For example:

densely	injured
fatally	enforced
narrowly	defeated
sorely	outnumbered
strictly	tempted
hopelessly	populated

Word derivation can also form the focus of dictionary tasks:

 Students use dictionaries to complete grids or 'spidergrams' of word families, to show common derived forms:

person	crime	verb
robber	robbery	rob
		murder
_____	_____	
hijacker	_____	_____
_____	rape	_____
_____	_____	smuggling

etc.

The following three tasks focus on style, connotation and frequency, respectively:

 Students use dictionaries to decide which word or expression in a group is the odd one out, in terms of style:

flee	run away	retreat	turn tail
occur	crop up	happen	take place
supervise	monitor	keep an eye on	oversee
bump off	murder	kill	assassinate

etc.

 Students use dictionary information to group words according to whether they have neutral or negative connotations. For example:

notorious	famous
publicity	propaganda
skinny	slim
chat	gossip
childish	childlike
queer	gay
officious	official
collaborator	ally
bachelor	spinster

Students use frequency information in the dictionary to rank words in terms of frequency. For example:

1	sick	unwell	ill
2	grill	cook	fry
3	ship	yacht	boat

(Answers: 1 sick, ill, unwell; 2 cook, fry, grill; 3 boat, ship, yacht)

Or, students underline words in a text that fall within the 2,000 (or 3,000) top most frequent words band.

Note that any of the above activities can be used in combination with others, thereby increasing the number of decisions about a selected set of words. For example, a set of words can first be dictated (decisions about spelling), then categorised (decisions about meaning), then sorted into neutral and negative (decisions about connotation). Alternatively, a set of words can be grouped according to part of speech (decisions about grammar) and then matched according to collocation. (See Chapter 6 for more discussion of multiple decision tasks.)

Corpus data Today's dictionaries provide accurate information about a word's frequency and its typical collocations, as well as supplying authentic examples of the word in context. This information is largely due to the development of **corpus linguistics**. A **corpus** (plural *corpora*) is a collection of texts that has been assembled for the purposes of language study. Modern corpora are stored electronically and consist of many millions of words of text, both spoken and written. They range from academic texts through newspaper articles to casual conversation, and include American, British, Australian, teenager and even learner varieties of English.

The benefit for teachers and learners of corpus data is that it provides them with easily accessible information about real language use, frequency and collocation. Before the advent of corpora, teachers had to rely largely on intuitions about the way words are actually used. To take one example: coursebooks give the impression that adverbs of frequency (*usually, never, sometimes, always*, etc.) cannot occupy two adjacent slots in a sentence. Thus: *I **usually** come home early on Fridays, I **always** come home early on Fridays*, but not *I **usually always** come home early on Fridays*. However, a search of two corpus websites (British National Corpus: http://sara.natcorp.ox.ac.uk/lookup.html and COBUILD Corpus: http://titania.cobuild.collins.co.uk/form.html) shows that, while not common, such combinations do occur:

Suede's imperturbable drummer *never usually* says a single word in interviews.
… the convent where we *usually never* set foot
Tickets are *normally always* available on the continent
Do you *normally usually* have sugar?

etc.

Because corpora consist of 'used' language, they can claim a certain authority over invented or imagined language. This does not deny the value of intuitions. In fact, it was an intuition that prompted me to check for *usually + always* type combinations in the first place. But access to corpora now means that we can provide learners with attested, rather than invented, examples of words in context. By this means, we can show learners not what someone thinks they *should* say, but what users of the language actually *do* say.

This does not mean, though, that corpus information should be used uncritically. Corpus information is only as good as the corpus it comes from. A corpus of teenage slang, for example, would not be of much use for teaching business English. Likewise, a corpus of written English may not be much use for teaching spoken English. Furthermore, just because an instance of language use is attested (such as *Do you normally usually have sugar?*) does not mean that it should be taught. In order to facilitate learning, teachers must do as they have always done, that is, select, adapt and supplement raw data so that it is optimally useful for the learner. Corpora have simply provided another source of data – one that, admittedly, reduces the need to rely on hunches.

Before the advent of corpora, **frequency** information was also largely guesswork – or involved a great deal of pen-and-paper counting. Now, learner dictionaries are able to provide statistically accurate data about frequency. High frequency words are flagged (as we saw in the case of *shed*). Sometimes, more specific information is provided. Here, for example, is a graph showing the relative frequencies of the verbs *let, allow* and *permit*.

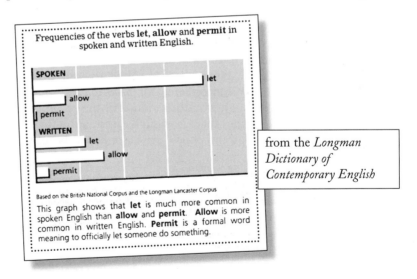

Frequencies of the verbs **let, allow** and **permit** in spoken and written English.

SPOKEN
let
allow
permit
WRITTEN
let
allow
permit

Based on the British National Corpus and the Longman Lancaster Corpus

This graph shows that **let** is much more common in spoken English than **allow** and **permit**. **Allow** is more common in written English. **Permit** is a formal word meaning to officially let someone do something.

from the *Longman Dictionary of Contemporary English*

Given that one aspect of knowing a word is knowing how frequently used it is, this kind of information is potentially useful to the learner. It is even more useful to the teacher and coursebook writer, as it can inform their decisions as to what words to select for active study. For example, the following adjectives are often presented together:

| beautiful | handsome | ugly | attractive |
| good-looking | pretty | unattractive | |

According to the *Longman Dictionary of Contemporary English*, only *beautiful, attractive* and *pretty* fall within the top 3,000 words band (and in that order). The absence of negative adjectives (*ugly, unattractive*) in the high frequency bands suggests that speakers use other means to express the idea of unattractiveness e.g. *not very pretty, not terribly attractive*, and that maybe these constructions should be taught in preference.

A closer examination of the kinds of words that **collocate** with these adjectives narrows the choice further. *Ugly*, for example, is used less to describe people than in the context of *ugly scenes* or *an ugly situation*, or in the expression *X rears its ugly head*. *Handsome*, which is relatively infrequent, collocates on the whole with male subjects. *Beautiful* collocates with *woman* and *girl*, but also frequently with *people, world, day, things* and *place*. *Pretty* and *attractive*, when used to describe people, also have mainly feminine collocates. Of all these adjectives, *good-looking* is the only one that applies equally to both sexes, and, what's more, is used almost exclusively for people. So, despite its lower frequency, as an all-purpose adjective for describing appearance, it may be the one to teach.

This kind of information (on frequency and collocation), to which only dictionary writers used to have access, is now freely available. I was able to assemble the above data simply by using a learners' dictionary and the Collins COBUILD English Collocations on CD-ROM. Collocational information is also available on the Internet – for example, the COBUILD corpus at http://titania.cobuild.collins.co.uk/form.html. With a little training, and perhaps some guidance in the form of a task sheet, learners themselves can access this kind of information.

Corpus information is typically presented in the form of **concordances**. A concordance displays the results of a word search as individual lines of text, with the targeted word (or words) aligned in the centre. Here, for example, is a concordance for *beautiful* (from the COBUILD website). Despite the slightly mutilated look of the sentences (necessary if they are to fit onto one line) there is enough information for students to work out what kinds of things and people are described as beautiful.

```
          as much as connoisseurs: it is a beautiful abstract painting. But it is
      was worn by, amongst others, the beautiful American actress Ruth Ford. This
             dweller alike. We know that a beautiful and living countryside requires
          inspiration for the bride-to-be. Beautiful fine bone china is not only a
              In addition to being a very beautiful garden, it has great historical
   in the Thirties. Now there are some beautiful houses on the outskirts, I reckon
       amid the forests and lakes of the beautiful Jels countryside. He brought in
              I have never forgotten this beautiful part of the world. I've not just
      living in what is arguably the most beautiful place in the United States, as
        arguably the most interesting and beautiful small city in the United States.
        which we ate at a very solitary and beautiful spot in the Harz Mountains.
             of primitive pine pews inside, a beautiful stained glass window faced into
        other, that Arzfeld girl is really beautiful, with those eyes, that skin, that
   was very simply a charming and very beautiful woman. A year later, Elizabeth
         who dated some of the world's most beautiful women. In 1951 Hanson Sr even
```

Concordances are a convenient way of presenting learners with data for analysis, from which they can work out the regularities and patterns associated with selected words. But they are not easy. The minimal contexts, truncated sentences, and ungraded vocabulary, can be off-putting for all but quite advanced learners.

However, if the concordance has been compiled from a text that the learners are already familiar with, it may be less intimidating. Here, for example, is the transcript of a coursebook recording from the *Collins COBUILD English Course 1*, in which two people talk about the busiest day they've had recently.

'Right. So the busiest day I've had recently was last Monday when I had to teach. I taught in three different schools. So, on Monday morning I taught in one school from nine thirty to twelve thirty. Then I went home, and on the way home I had to do a lot of shopping. Then I had lunch. I just had time to have lunch. Then I went out again. I went to another school, the other side of London, where I taught from four to six. Then I had half an hour to get from that school down to another school in the centre of London for six thirty to eight thirty. Then I got home and I went out for supper afterwards with friends. So that was quite a busy day.'

'The busiest day I've had recently was probably on Saturday, because I drove down from London to Sussex on Saturday morning. And, when I got home - I got home at about lunchtime. And I had lunch, and then after lunch my cousins came over. And I took them shopping. And then we went to visit an aunt of mine who lives nearby because they hadn't seen her for a long time. And then I came home, and I went out to supper. And then I went home again.'

In advance of the language-focused tasks, the teacher plays the class the cassette recording, and checks their general understanding by asking questions such as: *Which one is a teacher? Who left London on Saturday?* The teacher can then distribute the transcript of the recording, for more detailed question-and-answer work (*How many schools did the first speaker teach in? Did the second speaker visit his cousins, or did they visit him?* etc).

Now comes the language focus. A **keyword** search (see below) shows that among the significantly frequent words in this short text are: *went, then, home, school* and *had*. Using a concordancer (a program that searches for words in a text and sorts them into lines), any of these words can become the focus of a concordance. For example, here is the concordance for *home*:

```
1    ne thirty to twelve thirty. Then I went home, and on the way home I had to do a
2        Then I went home, and on the way home I had to do a lot of shopping. Then
3        six thirty to eight thirty. Then I got home and I went out for supper afterward
4        Saturday morning. And, when I got home - I got home at about lunchtime. An
5    morning. And, when I got home - I got home at about lunchtime. And I had lunch
6    en her for a long time. And then I came home, and I went out to supper. And then
7    d I went out to supper. And then I went home again.
```

Displayed like this, *home* is available for more focused study than when buried in a text. For example, learners can list the verbs that collocate with home (*go, get, come*), notice that no prepositions are used in these combinations, and find any other expressions that include *home* (*on the way home*). Moreover, it doesn't need a computer to display this information. Learners can make their own concordance lines by simply writing out all the sentences, or parts of sentences, that include the word *home*, and aligning them accordingly. For example:

> Then I went home, and on the way home
> on the way home I had to do a lot of shopping
> Then I got home
> when I got home
> I got home at about lunchtime
> And then I came home
> And then I went home again

The extra effort involved in compiling their own concordance may help draw learners' attention to salient features of the text. Alternatively, the teacher can provide the learners with a concordance with the target word (called the **node**) blanked out. The learners' task is to work out what the missing word is – i.e. what one word would fit all of the displayed contexts?

Concordances are starting to appear in coursebooks. Here, for example, is an activity from *The Intermediate Choice*:

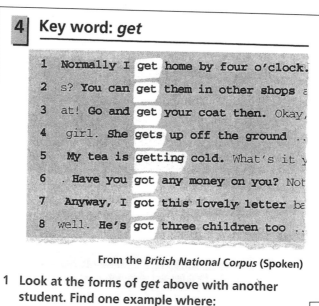

4 Key word: *get*

1 Normally I get home by four o'clock.
2 s? You can get them in other shops
3 at! Go and get your coat then. Okay,
4 girl. She gets up off the ground ..
5 My tea is getting cold. What's it y
6 . Have you got any money on you? Not
7 Anyway, I got this lovely letter ba
8 well. He's got three children too ..

From the *British National Corpus* (Spoken)

1 **Look at the forms of *get* above with another student. Find one example where:**

a) *get* means
- to buy
- to arrive
- to receive
- to collect/fetch
- to become

b) *get + preposition* shows movement.

c) *have + got* is used to talk about
- possessions
- family relations

d) *got* is the Past Simple form of *get*.

from Mohamed S, and Acklam R, *The Intermediate Choice*, Longman

Another useful tool when dealing with corpus material is a **keyword** program. (Note that this is a different sense of keyword from that used in Chapter 9 to describe a memory technique.) Keywords are words in the text that are not just frequent, but significantly so. For example, the fact that the most frequent word in a given text is *the* is of little significance. *The* is the most frequent word in almost *any* text. A keyword, on the other hand, is a word in a text that occurs more often in that particular text than it does across a whole range of texts. A keyword program is able to plot the keywords in a text simply by comparing the text with a large corpus of text. For example, in the two snake stories quoted earlier in this chapter on pages 53 and 60, the word *snake* occurs ten times (and thirteen times if we include *snakeskin, snakecatcher* and *snakes*). In the *British National Corpus (BNC) Sampler*, a corpus of one million words of spoken English and one million words of written English, *snake* occurs only eleven times. This means that the ten occurrences of *snake* in the two newspaper texts is highly significant. Even if you hadn't read them, it would be safe to assume from this one fact that the topic of the texts was something to do with snakes. Here are all the keywords in the two articles, in order of significance (I used WordSmith Tools from OUP): *snake, MAF, skin, experts, python, Auckland, shed, suburb, coat, found.*

Notice how the keywords tend to be nouns. Notice also that they provide a kind of very condensed summary of the story. Understanding the keywords of a text is a large part of understanding the text itself. So, when choosing words to pre-teach in advance of reading, a teacher need look no farther than the keywords. Also, giving learners the keywords of a text in advance of their reading the text is an excellent way of activating their knowledge of the topic of the text. Once activated, this knowledge allows them to make better sense of the text.

 These are some of the questions a teacher could ask, using the keywords:

'Where is Auckland?' (New Zealand)

'Do you associate snakes with New Zealand?'

'Why/Why not?'

'What is a *python?*'

'What do you know about snakes' skin?'

'What is the possible connection between *snake, skin* and *coat?*'

'What is the possible connection between *suburb, Auckland* and *found?*'

'What is the possible connection between *experts* and the rest of the story?'

'What could the letters *MAF* stand for?'

And, when the learners have read the text in order to confirm their predictions, they can then use the keywords to write a summary of the story.

Also, as we saw with the example using *home*, keywords can become the focus for a concordance search, especially those words that have particular collocational or grammatical characteristics.

Conclusions   In this chapter:
- we continued looking at sources, both direct and indirect, of vocabulary input
- the value of providing contextualised vocabulary input was emphasised, since texts display words in loose association and also in ways that are typical of their particular text type

We noted that:
- authentic texts (including literary texts), in particular, are rich in vocabulary learning potential, since a large part of their coherence is due to their lexical patterning
- extensive reading of, for example, simplified readers, is a good source of incidental vocabulary learning, particularly because of the repeated encounters readers have with words. Narrow reading – reading about one topic over a series of texts – offers even more opportunities for repetition.
- dictionaries are both a tool and a resource for vocabulary learning, since they contain a wealth of information about words, information that can be tapped through classroom activities involving multiple decision-making
- corpora are the latest addition to the resources available for vocabulary input. Corpora are particularly useful for providing attested examples of language in use, as well as frequency and collocational information. Concordancing and keyword programs are two of the tools that make corpus data available for classroom use.

Looking ahead   So far we have looked at sources of words. But vocabulary learning is not just a question of finding words. It also requires active mediation on the part of the teacher. In the next chapter we will look at ways the teacher can make the presentation of vocabulary maximally effective, both in terms of word form and word meaning.

5 How to present vocabulary

- **Presenting vocabulary**
- **Using translation**
- **How to illustrate meaning**
- **How to explain meaning**
- **How to highlight the form**
- **How to involve the learners**

Presenting vocabulary

In the last two chapters we looked at possible sources of vocabulary input, including vocabulary books, readers, dictionaries and corpora. A motivated and self-directed learner might be able to acquire a large vocabulary simply by using these resources. However, many learners sign up for language courses in the expectation that, at least some of the time, they will be **presented** with language, rather than having to go out and find it for themselves. By presentation, we mean those pre-planned lesson stages in which learners are taught pre-selected vocabulary items. Of course, incidental vocabulary teaching can occur at other times of the lesson, as when a text or a discussion throws up unfamiliar vocabulary. In this chapter, however, we will be mainly concerned with ways vocabulary can be formally presented in the classroom. But many of the issues are relevant to the informal teaching of vocabulary as well.

As we saw in Chapter 2, at the very least learners need to learn both the meaning and the form of a new word. We shall deal with each of these components in turn. But it's worth pointing out that both these aspects of a word should be presented in close conjunction in order to ensure a tight meaning-and-form fit. The greater the gap between the presentation of a word's form and its meaning, the less likely that the learner will make a mental connection between the two.

Let's say the teacher has decided to teach a related set of words – for example, items of clothing: *shirt, trousers, jacket, socks, dress, jeans*. The teacher has a number of options available. First, there is the question of how many words to present. This will depend on the following factors:

- the level of the learners (whether beginners, intermediate, or advanced)
- the learners' likely familiarity with the words (learners may have met the words before even though they are not part of their active vocabulary)
- the difficulty of the items – whether, for example, they express abstract

rather than concrete meanings, or whether they are difficult to pronounce
* their 'teachability' – whether, for example, they can be easily explained or demonstrated
* whether items are being learned for production (in speaking and writing) or for recognition only (as in listening and reading). Since more time will be needed for the former, the number of items is likely to be fewer than if the aim is only recognition.

Furthermore, the number of new words presented should not overstretch the learners' capacity to remember them. Nor should the presentation extend so far into the lesson that no time is available to put the words to work (see the next chapter).

Coursebooks tend to operate on the principle that a vocabulary presentation should include at most about a dozen items. Here, for example, are the items listed in the presentation of clothes vocabulary in a currently popular elementary coursebook (from Soars L and J, *Headway Elementary*, OUP):

a jumper	a shirt	a T-shirt	a dress	a skirt
a jacket	a suit	a tie		
trousers	jeans	trainers	shoes	boots

However, claims for the desirability of much higher vocabulary learning targets have been made, especially by proponents of teaching methods that subscribe to 'whole person learning', such as **accelerated learning** and **suggestopedia** (a method first developed by Georgi Lozanov in Bulgaria). Teachers following these methods use techniques of relaxation and suggestion, in order to predispose the learner to massive amounts of input, including literally hundreds of words in a session. Some of these claims may be excessive, but it may also be a fact that conventional teaching methods underestimate the learner's capacity to retain new vocabulary. Incorporating into lessons some of the basic principles of human memory (as outlined in Chapter 2) may be a means of extending the somewhat conservative targets set in coursebooks.

Having decided on the number of items to teach, there is then the choice of the **sequence** of presentation, either:

* meaning first, then form, or
* form first, then meaning

In the first option the teacher could, for example, hold up a picture of a shirt (the meaning), and then say *It's a shirt* (the form). In a 'form first' presentation she could say *shirt* a number of times, have the students repeat the word, and only then point to the picture. Both approaches are valid. There is an argument that presenting the meaning first creates a need for the form, opening the appropriate mental 'files', and making the presentation both more efficient and more memorable. On the other hand, 'form first' presentation works best when the words are presented in some kind of context, so that the learners can work out the meaning for themselves.

The next set of choices relates to the **means** of presentation – whether to present the meaning through:

- translation
- real things
- pictures
- actions/gestures
- definitions
- situations

And whether to present the word in its:

- spoken form, or
- written form

and in what order (e.g. spoken before written) and how soon (e.g. delaying the written form until the spoken form has been thoroughly learned).

There are also decisions to be made concerning the degree of learner involvement. For example:

- should the teacher provide both the meaning and the form herself?
- should the teacher present the meaning and attempt to elicit the form?
- should the teacher present the form and attempt to elicit the meaning?
- should the learners repeat the form, and if so, when?

We will address all these issues in this chapter.

Using translation

Traditionally, translation has been the most widely used means of presenting the meaning of a word in monolingual classes. Translation has the advantage of being the most direct route to a word's meaning – assuming that there is a close match between the target word and its L1 equivalent. It is therefore very economical, and especially suitable for dealing with incidental vocabulary that may crop up in a lesson. However, as we have seen, an over-reliance on translation may mean that learners fail to develop an independent L2 lexicon, with the effect that they always access L2 words by means of their L1 equivalents, rather than directly. Also, because learners don't have to work very hard to access the meaning, it may mean that the word is less memorable. A case of 'no pain, no gain'.

However, there are a number of different ways of incorporating translation into the vocabulary presentation. Here, for example, are three imaginary extracts in which the Spanish-speaking teacher is teaching her Spanish-speaking students clothing vocabulary:

1 TEACHER: En inglés *pantalones* se llaman *trousers*. *Trousers*. Ahora, todos juntos ... [In English *pantalones* are called *trousers*. *Trousers*. Now, all together ...]
  STUDENTS: *Trousers*.

2 TEACHER: Does anyone know the English for *una camisa*? No? Listen, it's a *shirt*. *Shirt*. Repeat.
  STUDENTS: *Shirt*.

3 TEACHER: What's this? [pointing to picture of a dress] Do you know
what this is in English? No? Listen, it's a *dress*. *Dress*. Repeat.
STUDENTS: *Dress*.
TEACHER: How do you say *dress* in Spanish? Marta?
MARTA: *Falda*.
TEACHER: That's right.

In the first extract all the teacher's talk is in Spanish. This effectively
deprives learners of valuable L2 input. Moreover, not much attempt is made
to involve the learners, apart from simply getting them to repeat the word.
In the second extract, the teacher uses only English (the target language),
apart from when L1 words are used to introduce meaning. They are thus
exposed to a lot more English than simply the target vocabulary items. In
the third extract, the presentation is entirely in English. Spanish is used only
to check that learners have understood.

Opinion is very much divided as to the merits of each approach. Here for
example, is an exchange on the subject of translation, between teachers
participating on an Internet discussion group (IATEFL Teacher Trainers
Special Interest Group Mailing List: ttsig@listbot.com):

[Derrin] On the L1 question. I, a native English speaker, frequently find
myself using L1 to quickly clarify my Catalan students' doubts as to the
meaning of unknown lexis in texts they are exposed to. I see little point
in walking around a room acting like a chicken for half an hour when you
can say 'pollo'.

[Dennis] Well, half an hour would be overdoing it (and are your students
THAT slow on the uptake?). But although there are clearly occasions
when a short, sharp translation is the most effective method of conveying
meaning, is it necessarily the most effective method of encouraging
learning? I bet if you did walk around the room acting like a chicken, even
for five minutes, saying: 'I'm a chicken. I'm a chicken.' your students
would never forget the English word for 'pollo'. And if you acted laying
an egg, your fame would spread.

[Gulfem] Thanks to Dennis for his support ... Which reminds me of the
whole issue of teaching Young Learners. Surely L1 translation cannot be
acceptable in this case. I actually have become a chicken who lays golden
eggs (Jack and the Beanstalk) for the students' benefit and much to their
delight: but that's maybe because I'm female, middle-aged and well
rounded: call it type casting if you like!

How to illustrate meaning

An alternative to translation – and an obvious choice if presenting a set of
concrete objects such as clothes items – is to somehow illustrate or
demonstrate them. This can be done either by using real objects (called
realia) or pictures or mime. The use of realia, pictures and demonstration
was a defining technique of the **Direct Method**. The Direct Method, in
rejecting the use of translation, developed as a reaction to such highly
intellectual approaches to language learning as Grammar-Translation. Here,

for example, is advice for teachers from a popular Direct Method course of the 1940s:

HOW TO TEACH THE NAMES OF OBJECTS
The usual procedure is as follows.

The teacher first selects a number of objects, in batches of say from 10 to 20. [...] The objects may be
(a) those that are usually found in the place where the lesson is given, e.g. door, window, knife, match, book; or parts of the body or articles of clothing.
(b) those collected specially for the purposes of the lesson, e.g. a stick, a stone, a nail, a piece of wire, a piece of string etc.
(c) those represented by pictures, such as those printed on picture cards or wall charts, or by rough drawings on the blackboard.
The teacher shows or points to each object in turn and names it. He says the name clearly (but naturally) three or four times. [...] When the pupils have had sufficient opportunity to *hear* the words and sentences (and to grasp their meaning) they are called upon to *say* them. In the first instance they may *repeat* them after the teacher ...

(from Palmer H, *The Teaching of Oral English*, Longman)

Such an approach is especially appropriate if teaching beginners, and with mixed nationality classes, where translation is not an option. It is also a technique that has been reclaimed by practitioners of **Total Physical Response** (TPR), a method that promotes initial immersion in a high quantity of comprehensible input. In making use of the immediate environment of the classroom, and of things that can be brought into the classroom, the intention is to replicate the experience of learning one's mother tongue. A TPR lesson typically involves the teacher demonstrating actions, using real objects, and then getting the learners to perform the same or similar actions in response to commands. Typical classroom commands might be:

Point to the apple.
Put the banana next to the apple.
Give the apple to Natasha.
Offer the banana to Maxim.
etc.
(Plastic fruit and vegetables are ideal for this kind of activity.)

Visual aids take many forms: flashcards (published and home-made), wall charts, transparencies projected on to the board or wall using the overhead projector, and board drawings. Many teachers collect their own sets of flashcards from magazines, calendars, etc. Especially useful are pictures of items belonging to the following sets: *food and drink, clothing, house interiors and furniture, landscapes/exteriors, forms of transport* plus a wide selection of pictures of people, sub-divided into sets such as *jobs, nationalities, sports, activities* and *appearance* (*tall, strong, sad, healthy, old,* etc). Not only can such pictures be used to present new vocabulary items, but they can be used to practise them.

The use of pictures or objects as prompts for vocabulary teaching can be enhanced if some basic principles of memory are taken into account, including the principle of distributed practice (see page 24). In teaching a set of, say, ten clothing items, it is important to keep reviewing the previously introduced items, preferably in a varying order – something like this:

present *shirt*
present *jacket*
present *trousers*
review *shirt*
review *trousers*
present *dress*
review *jacket*
present *sweater*
review *dress*
review *shirt*
present *socks*
etc.

Another principle underlying effective memorisation is, as much as is possible, to allow learners to work at their own pace. In this way they can form associations and think of mnemonic devices that are personally relevant, and appropriate to the degree of difficulty the word is causing them. This is more likely to happen if they are working on their own or in small groups. But by building pauses into a teacher-led presentation, the teacher can provide learners with time to 'catch up' and to reflect.

Here, by way of example, are some activities using flashcards:

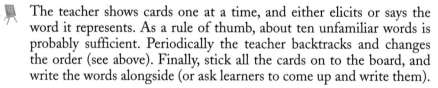 The teacher shows cards one at a time, and either elicits or says the word it represents. As a rule of thumb, about ten unfamiliar words is probably sufficient. Periodically the teacher backtracks and changes the order (see above). Finally, stick all the cards on to the board, and write the words alongside (or ask learners to come up and write them).

Stick a collection of picture cards (e.g. clothes) on the board and number them. (If you are working round a large table, place the cards face up on the table.) Invite learners to ask you about the words they are unfamiliar with. For example: *What's number 6?* Check to see if someone else knows before giving the answer. When students are sufficiently familiar go through them all, asking, *What's number 8?* etc. As a check, turn the cards around, one at a time, so that they can't be seen, and again ask *What's number 8?* Finally, write the words on the board alongside each picture.

Stick a selection of cards on the board and allow learners to use bilingual dictionaries to find the words they represent. They can then write the words adjacent to the pictures.

Give pairs or groups of three a selection of cards each. They can use bilingual dictionaries to find out the word for each picture. Then, representatives from each group can 'teach' the rest of the class the words they have discovered, using the visual aids.

Show the class a wall chart or a large picture containing many different items (e.g. a street scene or an airport) for a short period of time, say ten seconds. Individually or in pairs, the learners then have to write down as many words – in English – as they can remember having seen represented in the picture. Allow them to use dictionaries. Show the picture again for another few seconds, to let them extend their lists of words. Reveal the picture for the checking stage: the individual or pair with the most correct words is the winner.

How to explain meaning

Of course, reliance on real objects, illustration, or demonstration, is limited. It is one thing to mime a chicken, but quite another to physically represent the meaning of a word like *intuition* or *become* or *trustworthy*. Also, words frequently come up incidentally, words for which the teacher won't have visual aids or realia at hand. An alternative way of conveying the meaning of a new word is simply to use words – other words. This is the principle behind dictionary definitions. Non-visual, verbal means of clarifying meaning include:

- providing an example situation
- giving several example sentences
- giving synonyms, antonyms, or superordinate terms
- giving a full definition

All of the above procedures can be used in conjunction, and also in combination with visual means such as board drawings or mime. Although a verbal explanation may take a little longer than using translation, or visuals or mime, the advantages are that the learners are getting extra 'free' listening practice, and, by being made to work a little harder to get to the meaning of a word, they may be more cognitively engaged. Obviously, it is important, when using words in order to define other words, that the defining words themselves are within the learners' current range. Doctor Johnson's definition of a *net* in his famous dictionary is an example of what *not* to say in the classroom: *Anything reticulated or decussated at equal distances with interstices between the intersections!*

A **situational** presentation involves providing a scenario which clearly contextualises the target word (or words). Here, for example, is a situation for teaching *embarrassed/embarrassing*:

Catherine saw a man at the bus stop. His back was turned but she was sure it was her brother, so she tapped him on the shoulder with her umbrella and shouted 'Look out! The police are after you!' The man turned around. He was a complete stranger.
SHE WAS TERRIBLY EMBARRASSED. IT WAS A VERY EMBARRASSING EXPERIENCE.

(from O'Neill R, *English in Situations*, OUP)

Reinforcing a situational presentation with pictures, board drawings, or gesture makes it more intelligible, and perhaps more memorable. More memorable still is the situation that comes directly from the experience of the people in the room – whether the teacher or students. In other words, the teacher could tell her own story of when she was embarrassed, and then invite the students to tell their own. Again, the extra 'free' speaking and listening practice justifies the relatively long time spent on just one or two items of vocabulary.

An alternative to the situational approach is to provide students with **example sentences**, each one being a typical instance of the target word in context. This is not dissimilar to the way concordances can be used (see page 70). From the cumulative effect of the sentences the students should be able to hypothesise the meaning of the target word – using **induction**: the mental process of hypothesising from examples. Here is a teacher giving sentence examples for the word *fancy*:

> T: Listen to these sentences and see if you can work out what the verb *fancy* means: Number one: *He's really nice, but I don't fancy him.* [pause] Two: *I fancy eating out tonight. Don't you?* [pause] Three: *Do you fancy a cup of coffee?* [pause] Four: *Fancy a drink?* [pause] Five: *That guy on the dance floor – he really fancies himself.* [pause] And six: *I never really fancied package holidays much.* [pause] OK, talk to your neighbour and then I'll read them again …

Allow the students as many hearings of the sentences as they think they need before they are confident enough to venture an answer. (For particularly difficult words, it may help if the learners write the sentences down.) Depending on whether the class is monolingual or not, the teacher can then elicit a mother tongue translation of the target word, or, alternatively, a synonym or definition.

One advantage of this approach is that the learners hear the word several times, increasing the likelihood of retention in memory. Another advantage is that they hear the word in a variety of typical contexts (rather than just one) so they can start to get a feel for its range of uses as well as its typical collocations (e.g. **fancy a drink**). Finally, they get information on the word's form and grammar – whether, for example, it is irregular or transitive (if a verb), or countable (if a noun). It may seem to involve quite a lot of preparation for the teacher, but consulting dictionaries and corpora for examples of the target words in context can help reduce planning time.

Very often a quick explanation, using a synonym (*'fancy' – it means 'like'*), antonym (*'outgoing'* – *it's the opposite of 'shy, introverted'*) or a superordinate term (*a 'herring' is a kind of fish*), will serve, especially in incidental vocabulary work. This is particularly useful when **glossing** (explaining) words that come up in texts.

More elaborate **definitions**, such as those in dictionaries, require more effort on the part of both teacher and learner. Lexicographers (dictionary writers) spend a great deal of time agonising over definitions, so there is no reason to think that teachers will find them any easier. Fortunately, learners' dictionaries phrase their definitions in language that offers teachers a reliable model, should they need one. Here, for example, is the definition for *petrify* from two dictionaries – first, a conventional dictionary and, second, a learners' dictionary:

> **pĕ'trifȳ** *v.* **1.** *v.t.* change into stone; (fig.) paralyse or
> stupefy with astonishment, terror, etc., (*petrified with*
> *fear* etc.); deprive (mind, doctrine, etc.) of vitality. **2.**
> *v.i.* turn into stone (lit. or fig.). [f. F *pétrifier* f. med. L
> *petrificare* f. L f. Gk *petra* rock; see -FY]

(from the *Concise Oxford Dictionary*)

> **petrify** /pɛtrɪfaɪ/, **petrifies, petrifying, petri-**
> **fied. 1** If something **petrifies** you, it makes you feel   v+o
> very frightened indeed, perhaps so frightened that   ‡ scare
> you cannot move. ʙɢ *The warning whistle started to*   = terrify
> *blow. The sound petrified him.* ◊ **petrified.** ʙɢ *If I*   ◊ ADJ QUALIT
> *hadn't been alone I wouldn't have been nearly so*   = terrified
> *petrified.*
> **2** When something dead **petrifies**, it gradually   v·ERɢ
> changes into stone. ◊ **petrified.** ʙɢ *The mountain*   ◊ ADJ CLASSIF :
> *range loomed menacingly like some petrified prehis-*   ATTRIB
> *toric monster.* ◊ **petrification** /pɛtrɪfɪkeɪʃəⁿn/.   ◊ N UNCOUNT
> **3** If something such as a society or institution   v·ERɢ
> **petrifies** or if something else **petrifies** it, it ceases to   = stagnate
> change and develop; a formal use. ʙɢ *Militarism and*
> *xenophobia petrified the social order... ...if civiliza-*
> *tion was not to wither or petrify.* ◊ **petrification.** ʙɢ   ◊ N UNCOUNT
> *These statements, taken too literally, lead to the*   = stagnation
> *petrification of meaning.*

(from the *Collins COBUILD English Dictionary*)

A variant of the definition approach is to present a layered definition – that is, one that is segmented into several short statements, each one including the target word. This is similar to the example sentences approach mentioned above, but in this case the sentences are discrete components of a larger definition. For example:

> ᴛ: If you feel *petrified* you are very very frightened. Someone can be *petrified* by fear. *Petrified* literally means turned to stone. *Petrified* wood is wood that has become stone. In some places you can see *petrified* forests.

In this way, the meaning – and shades of meaning – of a word are built up piece by piece, with the added advantage that the learners hear the target word not only in context, but repeated (in the above example five times).

In reality, most teachers draw on a range of techniques – situations, synonyms, example sentences, etc. – in their presentations of word meaning. Here, for example, is an extract from a lesson in which the teacher uses a variety of means – including words that the students are already familiar with – to introduce *petrified*:

T: OK is anyone very frightened of ghosts? Would you be frightened if you saw a ghost? *Frightened*. OK, I know if I saw, for example, if I saw a ghost, there is one feeling I would feel. I would feel *frightened*. [writes] But even more than *frightened*, how would you feel if you saw a ghost? More than *frightened*, stronger, than *frightened*.

S: *Terrified*.

T: Good, *terrified*. [writes] *Terrified*. Anything even stronger than *terrified?* A word in English. Even, really, you're so *frightened* you're ...

S: *Scared?*

T: That's not, that's the same as *frightened*. There's something that's stronger.

S: *Astonished*.

T: *Astonished. Astonished* is a little bit more like *surprised*. I think – *terrified*; there's an even stronger word, which would be *petrified*. [writes] And it means when you are so *frightened* that you can't speak, you can't think, and you can't move. You're absolutely *petrified*. And I think if I saw a ghost I would probably be [laughs] probably be *petrified*, being the rather pathetic soul that I am.

Finally, it's worth emphasising that learning the meaning of a word – or learning anything, for that matter – is a process of gradual approximation. Even in our first language, it may take a long period of 'fuzziness' before we feel comfortable about using certain words. It is probably asking too much of teachers to expect them to clarify every nuance of a word's meaning at first encounter. Better that they orientate their learners in the general direction of a word's meaning, while equipping them with the skills and the motivation to continue exploring the further reaches of that word's 'semantic space'.

How to highlight the form

In Chapter 2 we noted the fact that the sound of words, as much as their meaning, determines the way they are stored in the mental lexicon. The fact that like-sounding words are often confused (*tambourines* for *trampolines*, or *chicken* for *kitchen*, for example) is evidence of this. This suggests that highlighting the spoken form of a word is very important in terms of ensuring it is appropriately stored. This in turn means drawing learners' attention to the way the word *sounds*.

Words seem to be stored and accessed primarily according to their overall syllable structure and stress. Hence it is easy to confuse *tambourine* and *trampoline* because they have the same general shape, despite some differences of individual sounds. This suggests that highlighting the stress and general shape of the word is a useful aid to retention and deserves as much attention as the individual sounds.

There are a number of ways of highlighting the spoken form of the word. Essentially these are:

- listening drills
- oral drills
- boardwork

Having established the meaning of a new word, the teacher can model it using **listening drills**. A drill is any repetition of a short chunk of language. In this case, it is the teacher who does the repeating, so as to accustom the learners to the phonological features of the word. Customarily, this takes the form of a clear but natural enunciation of the word (or words), usually preceded by some sort of cue, such as 'Listen …'. This is repeated two or three times. To draw learners' attention to the syllable structure and stress of the word, this modelling process can be accompanied by some kind of visual stimulus, such as using the fingers of one hand to represent the different syllables.

The teacher can also ask the class to identify the stressed syllable. The question *Where's the stress?* is a good one for learners to get used to. One way of introducing the idea of stress – in the first lesson, for example – is to ask the learners to say how many syllables there are in their own names, and which of these syllables is stressed. (Of course, if it's a one-syllable name, the stress will be on that one syllable.)

In drill-and-repeat type methodologies, such as audiolingualism, it would then be customary for learners to repeat the new word, both in chorus and individually, in order to reinforce it in memory. More recently, the value of simply repeating newly introduced language – especially grammatical structures – has been questioned. Some writers argue that the requirement to 'get one's tongue round it' may distract from the cognitive work involved in 'getting one's mind round it'. As we saw in Chapter 2 (see page 23), we forget words quickly if there is any interference or interruption of the **articulatory loop** (the process of subvocal repetition on which working memory depends). This suggests that allowing learners two or three seconds' 'processing' time between hearing a new word and saying it might have benefits in terms of retention in memory. One way of encouraging subvocalisation is sometimes known as a **mumble drill**. At a cue from the teacher, learners mumble or mutter the word to themselves at their own pace. Evidence suggests that subvocalisation is a technique that successful learners use naturally (see page 161), so it may be one worth establishing as standard classroom practice.

However, to withhold production indefinitely is likely to frustrate learners, whose instinct is often to have a go at repeating a new word themselves. And nothing gives learners a better feel for the shape of a word than saying it – even if the teacher's intention is to teach the word for recognition only. It may be appropriate, therefore, to get learners to vocalise the new words, after they have first subvocalised them, by means of choral or individual repetition, i.e. **drilling**.

Features of the word's pronunciation can also be highlighted using the board. Many teachers use some kind of symbol – such as a small box – to indicate where the primary stress is placed.

$$\text{frightened} \quad \text{petrified}$$

Providing learners with a transcription of the word using **phonemic script** is another way of highlighting the pronunciation visually. The phonemic transcription of *frightened* is /fraɪtənd/.

Use of phonemic symbols also avoids the potentially negative effects of sound–spelling mismatches (but see below). Of course, this assumes learners are familiar with phonemic script. If they are not, they may find the extra learning load daunting, especially if they are still getting used to Roman script (as may be the case for learners whose mother tongue uses a different script). On the other hand, there is no great mystery to phonemic script, especially reading it (as opposed to writing it). Most of the consonant sounds are easily decipherable so it is mainly a task of getting to know how the many English vowel sounds are represented – a task that can be spread over a number of lessons, if necessary. Also, the fact that all good learner dictionaries use a standardised form of phonemic script means that further reinforcement can be provided by dictionary activities that focus on pronunciation (see page 66). (For a detailed reference chart of English sounds and the way they are produced, see Appendix A in Gerald Kelly's *How to Teach Pronunciation*, in this series.)

How soon should learners meet the written form of a new word? Traditionally, it was felt that meeting the written form too soon would interfere with correct pronunciation habits. This is specially the case in English (it was argued), where sound–spelling matches are notoriously unreliable. Learners who are pronouncing words like *cupboard*, *suit*, and *island* perfectly correctly, having only heard them, often regress to 'cup-board', 'sweet' and 'is-land', once exposed to the written form. On these grounds, presentation of the written form used to be delayed until learners were thoroughly familiar with the spoken form.

However, the counter argument runs that – since learners are going to meet the written form eventually – it may be better to deal with any sound–spelling mismatches head on, and get these difficulties out of the way sooner rather than later. After all, learners are likely to form a mental representation of the probable spelling of new words as soon as they first hear them, so it is better that this mental representation is an accurate one. Moreover, the sound–spelling irregularities in English are often overstated. It is true that there are some extremely unreliable spellings (the *–ough* family being the most commonly cited). But the vast majority of words in English conform to a fairly small set of rules. Avoiding the issue by withholding the written form may deprive learners of the opportunity of observing these regularities for themselves. A useful strategy, therefore, might be to ask learners, soon after hearing a new word, to attempt to spell it. (Or, if the first meeting is with the written form, to attempt to pronounce it.) If they are having trouble doing this, the teacher can prompt them by reminding them of familiar words with a similar pronunciation or spelling. In Chapter 9 we will look at some useful spelling rules that can be taught to learners.

But there is an even more important reason for being introduced to the written form as soon as possible. Crucial clues to meaning are often much easier to identify in the written form than in the spoken form of the word. In speaking, sounds tend to merge, or are even dropped entirely, such that even in carefully articulated speech a word like *handbag* sounds like *hambag*, and *police station* comes out as *plee station*. In the absence of key morphological information (like *hand-* and *police*) learners have nothing to attach the new word to – or nowhere to 'file' it – and therefore find it difficult to understand and remember. So the effort involved in learning it is that much greater. Many experienced teachers will be familiar with the surprised look of recognition on students' faces once they see the written form of a word they have been labouring to make sense of. Depriving them of this form may be counterproductive.

How to involve the learners

The word 'presentation' has connotations of teacher as transmitter, and learners as passive recipients, of language facts. But, as was pointed out in Chapter 2 (page 30), 'learners need to be actively involved in the learning of words'. How can learners be given more involvement in the presentation phase of word learning?

One technique that has already been mentioned in this chapter is **elicitation**. A standard elicitation procedure is for the teacher to present the meaning of a word (e.g. by showing a picture) and asking learners to supply the form:

T: (showing picture of *waterfall*) What's this? Tomas?
S: Cataract?
T: Not exactly. Elena?
S: Waterfall?
T: Good.

Alternatively, the teacher can supply the word, and elicit a definition, synonym or example:

T: What's a waterfall? Anyone?
S: Like Niagara?
T: Yes, exactly.

This second procedure, going from form to meaning, is typical of text-based vocabulary work. It also occurs when words come up naturally in classroom talk (see, for example, the extract of classroom talk on page 50).

The rationale underlying elicitation is that:

• it actively involves the learners in the lesson
• it maximises speaking opportunities
• it keeps the learners alert and attentive

- it challenges better learners who might otherwise 'turn off'
- it acts as a way of checking the learners' developing understanding
- in the case of form-first presentations it encourages learners to use contextual clues

If overused, however, many of the advantages of elicitation may be lost. First of all, only the better learners may be involved in the process, while the others remain passive bystanders. The use of names (or **nominating**) when eliciting is one way round this: *What's a waterfall? Etsuko?* or *Sylvia, how do you say 'kolega' in English?*

Prolonged elicitation sequences can end up being very frustrating for learners if they simply don't know the answers the teacher is seeking – a cross between a quiz show and a police interrogation. Finally, if all or most of the teacher's questions are elicitation questions, the quality of teacher–student talk can become compromised. After all, in the outside world, we seldom spend a lot of conversational time asking questions for which we already know the answer (like *What's a waterfall?*) There are times when learners need exposure to 'real' questions, such as *What's the biggest waterfall you've ever seen?*

This suggests that another important way of involving learners is to have them **personalise** the new words. Personalisation is simply the process of using the new word in a context that is real for the learner personally. The point was made, in Chapter 2 (page 30), that 'memory of new words can be reinforced if they are used to express personally relevant meanings'. There are many ways of doing this. Here are some ideas:

Ask learners to write a true sentence using the new word, preferably applying it to themselves or someone they know – more easily done with words like *frightened* and *embarrassed* than perhaps words like *waterfall*. To help, provide a sentence frame, such as *The last time I felt frightened was when …* Or *The biggest waterfall I have ever seen …*

Learners write questions for other learners, incorporating the new word. For example: *What makes you embarrassed/frightened?* They exchange questions, write the answers, and then report to the rest of the class.

Ask learners to make an **association network** centred on the new word. That is, they connect the word to other words that they associate with it, however far-fetched, drawing a diagram in the manner of the example opposite. They then compare their networks with those of other students, asking about, and explaining, the associations. Here, for example, is the association network produced by one student for the word *iron*:

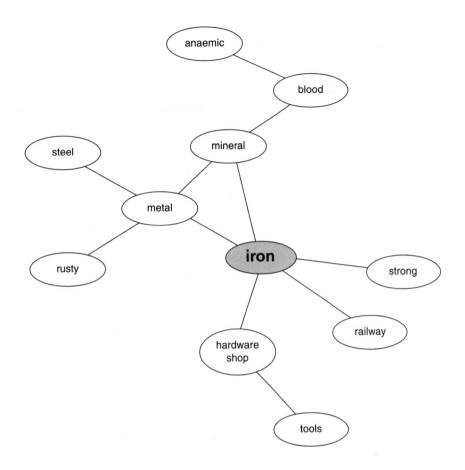

If teaching a lexical set such as food items, or forms of transport, or jobs, or kinds of film, ask the learners to rank the items in order of personal preference – from most preferred to least preferred. For example, *drama, thriller, musical, western, costume drama, horror movie* … Then, in pairs, they compare and explain their rankings.

Finally, an alternative to teacher presentation – and one that maximally involves learners – is **peer teaching**, i.e. learners teaching each other vocabulary. One way of doing this is through an **information gap** activity. This is an activity in which information is distributed between students in pairs or small groups. In order to complete a task, students must exchange information in order to 'fill the information gap'. If the information also includes words whose meaning is known only to individual members of the group, the information exchange will require members to teach each other those words.

For example, imagine each member of a pair has one of the following pictures:

The aim is to exchange information about the pictures in order to find the ten differences. At some stage this will involve students using the words that have been glossed at the bottom of their picture – for example *jug* in Picture A. Because their partner does not have the word for *jug*, (and in all likelihood will not know it) he or she will have to ask for an explanation. A probable sequence might go like this:

STUDENT 1: Is there a jug on the table in your picture?
STUDENT 2: A what?
STUDENT 1: A jug.
STUDENT 2: What is 'jug'?
STUDENT 1: A jug is a thing for keep water or milk.
STUDENT 2: Ah. Yes. I have one – what is called – judge?
STUDENT 1: Jug. J-U-G.
STUDENT 2: Yes, there is one jug on the table in my picture.
etc.

The extra effort put into negotiating the meaning and form of the unfamiliar words pays off in terms of learning. Note, for a start, how many times the word *jug* was used. Research suggests that negotiation of word meaning in this way is a very powerful learning tool, and is more memorable, on the whole, than teacher presentation. In order to maximise its usefulness, it may help if learners have been taught some simple defining expressions, such as *It's a thing you use for … It's made of … It looks like …*

Other ways of setting up peer teaching tasks include:

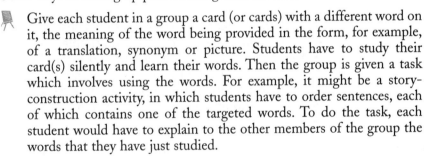

Give each student in a group a card (or cards) with a different word on it, the meaning of the word being provided in the form, for example, of a translation, synonym or picture. Students have to study their card(s) silently and learn their words. Then the group is given a task which involves using the words. For example, it might be a story-construction activity, in which students have to order sentences, each of which contains one of the targeted words. To do the task, each student would have to explain to the other members of the group the words that they have just studied.

Alternatively, they are asked to categorise the words on the cards into groups, or to rank them according to some criteria. They might, for example, be objects which are ranked according to their usefulness on a desert island. In order to do this task, students will first need to teach each other the words they have learned individually.

Each student is given a list of six to eight words, with their translations or definitions. For example, one student may get the following: *check in, boarding pass, duty free, luggage, security check, departure gate,* etc. Another may get: *camp fire, frying pan, pocket knife, matches, backpack,* etc. They have to work these words into a short narrative. They then tell each other their narrative, explaining any unfamiliar words as they go along.

Conclusions In this chapter we looked at techniques and procedures which involve direct teacher intervention in the teaching of pre-selected items of vocabulary. Among the choices available to the teacher when planning a vocabulary presentation are the following:

- how many words to present at a time
- whether to present the meaning of words first or the form first
- whether to use translation as the means of presenting meaning, or
- whether to use some form of illustration, such as realia, visual aids, or mime, or
- whether to use a verbal means of presentation, such as an example situation, example sentences, synonyms, or definitions
- how to present the spoken form and whether this should involve student repetition
- how soon to present the written form
- how, and to what extent, to involve the learners in the presentation, through the use of elicitation, personalisation, and peer teaching, for example

Some of the conclusions reached include the following:

- the number of words that can be learned is constrained by factors such as word difficulty, but need not be limited to only a few words
- establishing the meaning of a new word first and then presenting its form is a standard approach
- translation is an economical way of presenting meaning but may not be the most memorable
- illustrating meaning is effective, but is limited to certain kinds of words
- explaining meaning verbally is time-consuming but can be effective if explanations are kept clear and simple
- the spoken form can be highlighted through the giving of clear models, the use of phonemic script, and repetition
- the written form should not be withheld too long
- learners should be actively involved in the presentation

Looking ahead Presenting words is only the tip of the iceberg. To ensure that learners get to 'know' these words to the extent outlined in Chapter 2, they will need plentiful opportunities to engage with these words in a variety of contexts, and to 'put these words to work' – the theme of the chapter that follows.

How to put words to work

- **Integrating new knowledge into old**
- **Decision-making tasks**
- **Production tasks**
- **Games**

Integrating new knowledge into old

Traditionally, the presentation of new language items would swiftly be followed by the practice of these items. This practice would typically take the form of some of kind of oral repetition, such as a drill. This notion of mechanical practice underlies the popular belief that 'practice makes perfect'. However, as we saw in Chapter 2, simply repeating newly learned words is no guarantee that they will move from the short-term memory store into permanent memory. New knowledge – i.e. new words – needs to be integrated into existing knowledge – i.e. the learners' existing network of word associations, or what we called the **mental lexicon**. As we also saw in the discussion on memory, there is a greater likelihood of the word being integrated into this network if many 'deep' decisions have been made about it. In other words, to ensure long-term retention and recall, words need to be 'put to work'. They need to be placed in **working memory**, and subjected to different operations. Such operations might include: being taken apart and put back together again, being compared, combined, matched, sorted, visualised and re-shuffled, as well as being repeatedly filed away and recalled (since the more often a word is recalled, the easier recall becomes). In this chapter we will look at a range of activity types designed to do just that. They might best be thought of as **integration** activities, rather than 'practice activities' or 'reinforcement activities', since both these latter terms have associations with a more mechanical, less cognitive, approach to language teaching.

Decision-making tasks

There are many different kinds of tasks that teachers can set learners in order to help move words into long-term memory. Some of these tasks will require more brain work than others. That is to say, they will be more cognitively demanding. Tasks in which learners make decisions about words can be divided into the following types, roughly arranged in an order from least cognitively demanding to most demanding:

- identifying
- selecting
- matching

- sorting
- ranking and sequencing

The more of these task types that can be performed on a set of words the better. In other words, an identification task could be followed by a matching task, which in turn could be followed by a ranking task.

Identifying words simply means finding them where they may otherwise be 'hidden', such as in texts.

 Here, for example, are some identification tasks relating to the text *Fear of Flying* (on page 42). Give the learners the text and ask them to:

- Count the number of times *plane(s)* and *train(s)* occur in the text.
- Find four words connected with *flying* in the text.
- Find five phrasal verbs in the text.
- Find eight comparative adjectives in the text.
- Underline all the words ending in *-ing* in the text.

Ask them to read the text, then turn it over, and then ask:

- 'Did the following words occur in the text?'

  busy   crowded   fast   dangerous   uncomfortable
  dirty   convenient   inconvenient   noisy   .

- 'Now check the text to see if you were right.'

Listening out for particular words in a spoken or recorded text is also a form of identification activity. Below is a selection of identification tasks based on this text:

 OK, that's Mr Brown. He's wearing a jacket and trousers, no tie, and he's talking to the woman with the long dark hair – she's wearing a black dress. Now Mrs Brown is over there. She's wearing a skirt and a blouse, and she's talking to a tall man with fair hair. And their son, Richard ... yes, there he is, he's over in the corner. He's wearing jeans and a T-shirt – he's the one with very short hair.

(from Doff A and Jones C, *Language in Use (Beginner Workbook)*, CUP)

- List all the clothes items that you hear.
- Raise your hand when you hear a clothes item.
- Put these items in the order that you hear them:

  blouse   tie   skirt   jeans   jacket   T-shirt   dress   trousers

- Tick the items that you hear:

  blouse   shoes   tie   shorts   skirt   socks   jeans   jacket   hat
  T-shirt   dress   trousers   suit   shirt

- Listen for clothes words and write them in the correct column:

Mr Brown	Mrs Brown	Richard

Identification is also the process learners apply in tasks in which they have to unscramble anagrams (such as *utis, snaje, eti* – for *suit, jeans, tie*), or when they have to search for words in a 'word soup', such as the following (also from *Language in Use*):

1 **What are these clothes in English?**
   The answers are all in the wordsquare.

S	H	I	R	T	O	S	I
J	A	C	K	E	T	H	L
A	T	C	J	N	J	O	T
T	R	O	U	S	E	R	S
I	D	A	M	W	A	T	H
E	X	T	P	U	N	S	I
O	D	R	E	S	S	J	R
S	K	I	R	T	U	P	T
S	U	S	U	I	T	J	E

Selecting tasks are cognitively more complex than identification tasks, since they involve both recognising words and making choices amongst them. This may take the form of choosing the 'odd one out', as in this task (again, based on the lexical set of clothes):

Choose the odd one out in each group:

1	trousers	socks	jeans	T-shirt
2	blouse	skirt	tie	dress
3	T-shirt	suit	shorts	trainers

etc.

Note that with this kind of activity, there is no 'right' answer necessarily. What is important is that learners are able to justify their choice, whatever their answer. It is the cognitive work that counts – not getting the right answer.

Here is another open-ended selection task, with a personalised element:

---

1 Work in pairs. Choose five words to describe yourself. Use a dictionary if necessary.

> careful interesting clever cold confident fit funny imaginative intelligent kind lazy nervous optimistic patient pessimistic polite quiet calm rude sad sensitive nice serious tidy thoughtful

Think of other words you can use.
honest, friendly…

Discuss your choice of words with your partner.
I think I'm usually optimistic.
And I'm always polite!

Does he/she agree with you?

2 Think of three people you admire very much. They can be politicians, musicians, sports personalities etc. or people you know personally. Choose the person you admire most and think of three adjectives to describe this person.

Then choose the second and third person you admire and think of three more adjectives for each person to explain why.

from Greenall S, *Reward Pre-Intermediate*, Macmillan Heinemann

---

Another useful selecting task that can be applied to any vocabulary lesson is:

 Choose five (or ten or twenty) words from this lesson to learn. Think of how you will demonstrate – in the next class – that you have learned them.

The same kind of task can be applied to any text that the learners have read or listened to. And, as a way of recycling vocabulary items from previous lessons, learners can select words from their notebooks to 'test' their classmates at the beginning of each lesson.

A **matching** task involves first recognising words and then pairing them with – for example – a visual representation, a translation, a synonym, an antonym, a definition, or a collocate. As an example of this last type, here is a verb–noun matching task:

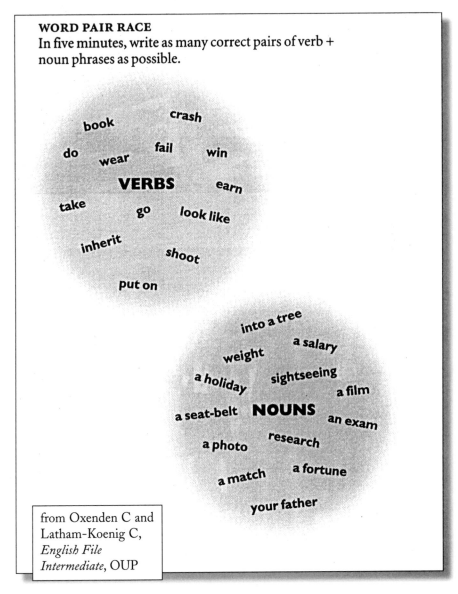

WORD PAIR RACE
In five minutes, write as many correct pairs of verb + noun phrases as possible.

VERBS

book   crash   do   wear   fail   win   earn   take   go   look like   inherit   shoot   put on

NOUNS

into a tree   weight   a salary   a holiday   sightseeing   a film   a seat-belt   an exam   a photo   research   a match   a fortune   your father

from Oxenden C and Latham-Koenig C, *English File Intermediate*, OUP

Pelmanism is a memory game which involves nothing but matching. Word pairs (or picture–word matches) are printed on individual cards which are placed face down in a random distribution. Players take turns to pick up a card and then search for its partner. If they correctly locate the partner (initially by guesswork, but, as the game progresses, by remembering where individual cards are located), they keep the pair, and have another turn. If not, they lay the cards face down where they found them, and the next player has a turn. The player with the most pairs at the end of the game is the winner. Typical pairs might be:

- antonyms (*tall – short, thick – thin, dark – light*, etc.)
- British and American equivalents (*bill – check, pharmacy – drugstore, lift – elevator*, etc.), or
- collocations (*wide + awake, stark + naked, fast + asleep*, etc.)

Sorting activities require learners to sort words into different categories. The categories can either be given, or guessed. Here is an example of the former (from Thornbury S, *Highlight Pre-Intermediate*, Heinemann):

Word field: characteristics

2 Put these adjectives into two groups – positive and negative.

emotional	friendly	good-humoured	outgoing
confident	ambitious	rude	self-centred
offensive	kind	selfish	nice

 Here is an activity in which learners (at a fairly advanced level) decide the categories themselves:

Put these words into four groups of three words each. Then, think of a title for each group.

goal	net	piece	club	racket	shoot	board	green
court	hole	pitch	referee	check	serve	tee	move

Now, can you add extra words to each group?

Finally, **ranking and sequencing** activities require learners to put the words into some kind of order. This may involve arranging the words on a cline: for example, adverbs of frequency (*always, sometimes, never, occasionally, often*, etc). Or learners may be asked to rank items according to preference:

 Imagine you have just moved into a completely empty flat. You can afford to buy one piece of furniture a week. Put the following items in the order in which you would buy them:

fridge	bed	desk	dining table	sofa
wardrobe	chair	dishwasher	bookcase	cooker
washing machine	chest of drawers			

Now, compare your list with another student and explain your order. If you were sharing the flat together, would you agree? If not, make a new list that you both agree about.

Here is an example of a ranking activity (from Morgan J and Rinvolucri M, *Vocabulary*, OUP) that can be adapted to different levels by changing the selected words:

D/13 Classifying knowledge

LEVEL	**Intermediate to Advanced**
TIME	**20–30 minutes**
IN CLASS	**1** Put the students in threes and ask them to rank the following types of skill/knowledge (a) for their usefulness in everyday life; (b) in terms of the value of qualifications that might be gained through acquiring such knowledge.

> *tooth care   soil chemistry   surgery   psychiatry   arithmetic*
> *micro-computing   knitting   geometry   plain cookery*
> *darning   league football   literary criticism   music*
> *nuclear physics   cordon bleu cookery   pop music*
> *servicing a motor car   ancient Greek   carpentry*
> *road safety   filling in tax forms*

2 Ask the threes to come together into nines and compare their rankings.

Ordering items chronologically is another way of getting students to make judgements about words. For example:

 Put the following words in the order in which they typically happen in your country:

> graduate   get married   be born   get divorced   get engaged
> die   retire   leave home   have children   re-marry   start school

Any sequence of activities – from starting a car to buying a home – lends itself to the same treatment. Here, for example, is a task that focuses on the language of air travel (from Garton-Sprenger J and Greenall S, *Flying Colours 2*, Heinemann):

Work in pairs. Think about what people do when they travel by plane. Put the actions below in the correct column.

before the flight	after the flight
check in	*leave the plane*

leave the plane	check in
land	collect your baggage
unfasten your seatbelt	go through passport control
go into the departure lounge	listen to the safety instructions
go to the departure gate	go through customs
fasten your seatbelt	board the plane
go through passport control	go into the arrivals hall

Number the actions in the order people do them.

Note that there may not be a 'right answer' in a ranking or sequencing task, but that the exercise of making the choices and – even better – comparing them with a classmate's choices, is good 'brain work'.

Production tasks

The decision-making tasks we have been looking at are principally receptive: learners make judgements about words, but don't necessarily produce them. (Of course, they can then become production tasks by the simple expedient of inviting the learners to talk about these judgements.) However, tasks that are productive from the outset are those in which the learners are required to incorporate the newly studied words into some kind of speaking or writing activity. These can be classified as being of two main types:

- completion – of sentences and texts
- creation – of sentences and texts

Sentence and text **completion** tasks are what are more generally known as **gap-fills**. They are usually writing tasks and they are often used in tests (see Chapter 8) as they are easy to design and mark. They have many different formats, but a basic distinction can be made between **open** and **closed** gap-fills. The open type is one where the learner fills the gaps by drawing on their mental lexicon. (There may be a clue, though, such as the first letter of the word.) In a closed gap-fill, on the other hand, the words are provided, in the form of a list at the beginning of the exercise, for example. It is simply a matter of deciding which word goes in which gap.

Here are some example instructions for open and closed gap-fill tasks:

- Complete the text by writing an appropriate word in each space: 'Greta Garbo, the Swedish-born film ____, was born in 1905. She won a scholarship to drama school, where she learned to ____. In 1924 a film director chose her for a ____ in a Swedish film called ...'

- Choose the best word from the list to complete each sentence. Use each word once ...

- Select words from the list to complete these sentences. Note that there are more words than sentences ...

- Choose words from the text you have just read to complete these sentences ...

- Choose the best word to complete each sentence:
  1 When I feel tired, I can't stop ____.
     a sneezing
     b yawning
     c coughing
     d weeping
     etc.

Note that the last example is a **multiple choice** task. These are very popular with designers of vocabulary tests (see Chapter 8).

In completion tasks, the context is provided, and it is simply a matter of slotting the right word in. Sentence and text **creation** tasks, however, require learners to create the contexts for given words. Here are some typical task instructions:

- Use each of these words to make a sentence which clearly shows the meaning of the word.
- Choose six words from the list and write a sentence using each one.
- Use each of these words to write a *true* sentence about yourself or someone you know.
- Write a short narrative (or dialogue) which includes at least five words from the list.

Tasks such as these lead naturally into speaking activities – either reading aloud or performing dialogues to the class, or comparing and explaining sentences in pairs or small groups. These activities involve many of the processes that serve to promote retention in long-term memory, such as rehearsal, repetition and explanation.

Not all creation activities need start as writing tasks. Here is a speaking task (also from *Flying Colours 2*) which requires learners to create sentences using pre-selected vocabulary:

Work in pairs. Ask and say how you feel about your town or village.

I love it.   It's all right.   I can't stand it.

Which of the following adjectives can you use to describe your town or village?

interesting boring annoying depressing frightening marvellous
beautiful peaceful noisy lively

Can you explain why?

I find it boring because there's nothing to do in the evenings.

The use of questionnaires is a good way of putting vocabulary to work in the form of question-and-answer exchanges. Many areas of vocabulary lend themselves to some kind of questionnaire or survey. The same vocabulary items in the preceding example could be used as the basis of a questionnaire or survey.

 Students can prepare a survey – using these examples as a model:

1 Is your hometown boring or interesting? Why?
2 Do you find big cities: depressing, interesting, lively or noisy? Why?
etc.

They then ask each other their prepared questions, and report the results to the class, using full sentences, such as *Mario thinks his hometown is interesting because it has a lot of historical monuments.*

Games While the title of this chapter is 'How to put words to work', it would be wrong to suggest that vocabulary learning has to be all work and no play. Language play, including word games, has a long history. Children of all cultures seem to enjoy games of the 'I spy ...' or 'Hangman' type, and there is a long tradition of adult word games, a number of which have been adapted for television. Most first-language word games transfer comfortably to the second-language classroom. The most useful will be those that are consistent with the principles of learning outlined on pages 24 and 25. For example, the more often a word is successfully retrieved from memory, the easier it becomes to recall it. Therefore, useful games are those that encourage learners to recall words and, preferably, at speed. Or, consistent with the principle that learners need to make multiple decisions about words, a useful game would be one like a 'dictionary race', where students first sort words into alphabetical order, then into parts of speech, and then into lexical sets – the first group to complete all three tasks correctly being the winner.

However, since many word games deal solely with isolated – rather than contextualised – words, and often require only shallow processing on the part of the learner, they should be used judiciously. The time spent on a single de-contextualised word in a game of 'Hangman', for example, has to be weighed up against the more productive, contextualised and cognitively deep activities outlined earlier in this chapter. Too often games are used to plug holes in lessons which could more usefully be filled with language-rich talk. Nevertheless, the fun factor may help make words more memorable, and, like it or not, a competitive element often serves to animate even the most lethargic students.

So, here are some word games to try:

 Word clap: Students stand or sit in a circle, and, following the teacher's lead, maintain a four-beat rhythm, clapping their hands on their thighs three times (one–two–three ...) and then both hands together (four!). The game should start slowly, but the pace of the clapping can gradually increase. The idea is to take turns, clockwise, to shout out a different word from a pre-selected lexical set (for example, fruit and vegetables) on every fourth beat. Players who either repeat a word already used, or break the rhythm – or say nothing – are 'out' and the game resumes without them, until only one player is left. The teacher can change the lexical set by shouting out the name of a new set at strategic points: *Furniture! Nationalities! Jobs!* etc.

 Categories: Learners work in pairs or small groups. On a piece of paper, they draw up a number of columns, according to a model on the board, each column labelled with the name of a lexical set: e.g. *fruit, transport, clothes, animals, sports*. The teacher calls out a letter of the alphabet (e.g. *B!*), and to a time limit (e.g. three minutes), students write down as many words as they can beginning with that letter in the separate columns (*banana, berry; bus; bikini, blouse; bear, bat; baseball, basketball* ...). The group with the most (correct) words wins.

Noughts and crosses: Draw two noughts and crosses grids on the board:

			Food and drink	clothes	the home
			jobs	colours	the weather
			sports	transport	parts of the body

One is blank. In the other each square is labelled with a category, or with nine different phrasal verb particles (*up, on, off, in, back*, etc), or nine different affixes (*un-, non-, -less, -tion*, etc). Prepare a number of questions relating to each category. For example (if the class is monolingual): *How do you say 'tamburo' in English?* Or, *What is the opposite of 'shy'?* Divide the class into two teams: noughts and crosses. The object is to take turns choosing a category and answering a question in this category correctly so as to earn the right to place their team's symbol in the corresponding position in the blank grid. The winning team is the first to create a line of three (noughts or crosses), either vertically, horizontally, or diagonally.

 Coffeepot: This is a guessing game. One learner answers yes/no questions from the rest of the class (or group) about a verb that she has thought of, or that the teacher has whispered to her. In the questions the word *coffeepot* is used in place of the mystery verb. So, for example, students might ask *Do you coffeepot indoors or outdoors? Is coffeepotting easy or difficult? Can you coffeepot with your hands?* etc. If the verb that the student has selected is *yawn* the answers would be: *Both indoors and outdoors; It's easy; No, you can't, but you might use your hands ...* To make the game easier a list of, say, twenty verbs can be put on the board and the person who is 'it' chooses one of them. This can also be played in pairs.

 Back to board: This is another guessing game, but this time the student who is 'it' has to guess a word by asking the rest of the class questions. The student sits facing the class, back to the board; the teacher writes a recently studied word or phrase or idiom on the board, out of sight of the student. The student asks different students yes/no or either/or questions in order to guess the word. For example: *Helga, is it a verb or a noun? (A verb.) Dittmar, is it an action? (No.) Karl-Heinz, is it something you do with your mind? (Yes.)* ... etc. To make the game easier, the words chosen can be limited in some way – e.g. all phrasal verbs; all character adjectives, and so on.

Pictionary®: Based on the commercialised game of the same name, this involves students guessing words or phrases from drawings. They work in teams, each member of the team taking turns to be the 'artist'. If there are three teams, for example, the three 'artists' go to the front of the class where the teacher shows them a word (or phrase) on a card. At a cue, they quickly return to their group and try to get their group to correctly guess the word by drawing it with pen and paper. The first team to guess correctly earns a point, and three new 'artists' have a turn with another word. This is good for reviewing idiomatic expressions, such as *green with envy, down in the dumps, under the weather, in the dark, over the moon*. At the end of the game, groups can use the pictures as memory prompts in order to recall and write down the expressions that came up in the game, and then to put them into a sentence to show what they mean.

Word snap: Using word cards – e.g. from the class word bag or word box (see page 51) – students work in small groups, with the aim of collecting as many word 'pairs' as possible. One player 'deals' two word cards, face up, so that everyone can read them. The first player to think of a way the words are connected gets to keep the pair, and two more words are laid down. A connection could be: same part of speech; synonyms or antonyms; same lexical set; or, simply, a meaningful sentence can be made using both words. If no connection can be made, the two cards are shuffled back into the pack. The teacher will need to be available to decide in the case of connections being 'challenged'.

Word race: The class is divided into teams and each team is given a board marker pen (or piece of chalk). The board is divided into as many sections as there are teams. The teacher (or a specially appointed student) says a word in the students' language, and the first team to get the correct English translation on to the board earns a point. The game continues for as many words as it is felt necessary to review. The game is suitable for a monolingual class, but a variation of it, which would be suitable for multilingual classes, would be to read out definitions of words, or give synonyms or show pictures, rather than give translations.

Spelling race: The board is divided in two halves, and a representative from each of two teams stands at the board with a board marker pen or chalk. The teacher shows the rest of the class a word on a card. The teams must simultaneously spell (not say) the word to their representative, who cannot see the word. The first team to get the word on to the board with its correct spelling earns a point. The game continues with different students taking turns to be the team representative. This game is more difficult than it sounds, especially if words are chosen that include letters which are frequently confused – such as *i* and *e*, *v* and *b*, *j* and *g*. Lots of variations of this game are possible. The word could be displayed as a picture, so that the teams have to decide what the word is before spelling it.

The above is by no means an exhaustive list of word games, but is representative of some generic game types, guessing being one of the most favoured. Used with discretion, putting words to play is a valid and enjoyable way of putting words to work.

Conclusions In this chapter we looked at classroom activities designed to integrate newly acquired words into the learner's mental lexicon. Key principles underlying such activities are the importance of:

- making successive decisions about words
- productive as well as receptive tasks
- the judicious use of highly engaging activities such as games

Decision-making tasks include the following types:
- identification
- selecting
- matching
- sorting
- ranking and sequencing

Production tasks can be divided into those that require:
- completion of sentences and texts
- creation of sentences and texts

Games that draw attention to newly learned words often encourage recall through guessing and categorising.

Looking ahead In Chapter 1 we established that words both 'contain' other words (as *head* is contained in *ahead*), and that a word-like unit may in fact consist of several words (as in *head and shoulders* or *a head start*). In fact, there seems to be a continuum of 'wordiness', from individual syllables, up to what are now commonly called lexical chunks. This expanded notion of what a word is – and how it impacts on teaching – is the subject of the next chapter.

7 Teaching word parts and word chunks

- Teaching word formation and word combination
- A lexical approach
- Teaching lexical chunks
- Teaching word grammar
- Teaching phrasal verbs
- Teaching idioms

Teaching word formation and word combination

In Chapter 1 we looked at some of the principles of word formation in English. We noted that words can be formed by the addition of prefixes and suffixes – a process called **affixation**. (The word *affixation* is itself an example of the result of adding affixes to the root *fix*.) We also saw how, by **compounding**, two or more words can join up to make one. Thus: *black + board = blackboard*. Or, new words can be created by a process called **conversion**, when a word that in one context is one part of speech (such as a noun), in another context can be enlisted to serve a different function (such as a verb). Hence, you may have heard the relatively recent term *to board* as in *The teacher boarded the new words and the students wrote them down*.

Then again words can cluster (but not join up) to form **multi-word units** – loosely called **chunks** – that behave as if they were single words. For example, alongside *black*, the *Longman Dictionary of Contemporary English* lists: *black and white, black and blue, black sheep, in the black* and *to black out*. (This last is an example of a **phrasal verb**.) Many chunks have an **idiomatic** meaning – that is to say the meaning of the chunk as a whole is not directly inferrable from the individual words: *He's the **black sheep** of the family; you've introduced a **red herring**,* etc.

The way bits of words combine, and the way words themselves can be combined, is a constant source of difficulty for learners. Errors of the following types are common:

- Affixation errors
  There are *uncountless* ways to bring happiness to my life thanks to the internet.
  After finishing the paragraph and reading it again, I felt *unsatisfy*.
  I think that my real and only *knowledgements* are in the vocabulary.

- Compounding errors
  In London I took a *two floor bus* and of course crossed the city in the highest floor.
  I saw my dog died in a *box's shoes*.

- Errors of multi-word units
  We have also a *buses network*.
  Sometimes dog isn't the *best man's friend*.

- Collocation errors
  I don't like when I *do mistakes*.
  Some teachers are strict they *put us a lot of homework* and exams.

- Phrasal verb errors
  She used to go to school with her maid, and a maid was *picking up* her from school.
  There are some days that the better it's stay in bed and don't *get up* you.

- Idiom errors
  I have no more money. So most of time I just *watch shops' window*.
  I don't like *to blow my own horn*, but my grammar knowledge and my vocabulary are quite good.

In responding to these kinds of problems, there are two possible approaches. You can either

- teach rules, or
- expose learners to lots of correct examples

A rule-based approach starts by isolating and highlighting any relevant patterns or regularities. Take word formation, for example. In a rule-based approach, words can be grouped and presented according to the manner of formation (affixation, compounding, conversion, etc). Within these categories finer distinctions can be made. So, of the words formed by affixation we can select those formed by the addition of prefixes, and this group can be narrowed down further to those that have a negative meaning. The way these words are formed can then be described in general terms in the form of a rule – or 'rule of thumb'. Here is an example of such an explicit rule statement (from Gude K and Duckworth M, *Proficiency Masterclass*, OUP):

B Negative prefixes. The prefixes *mis-*, *dis-*, *ig-*, and *un-* can all be used to give a word a rather negative meaning. The prefix may help you to guess the meaning of the word.

mis- = 'wrongly, badly' or 'not done' (*mismanage*)
dis- = 'away from, the opposite of, lack of' (*distaste*)
ig- = 'not, lacking in' (*ignorant*)
un- = 'not, lack of, the opposite, reversal or removal of' (*undo*)

Here is some advice to help you choose the correct prefix.

- *dis-* can be used to form verbs, eg *dissatisfy*; adjectives, eg *dishonest*; and nouns, eg *disability*.
- The prefix *ig-* appears only before the letter *n*.

Here, on the other hand, is a table which suggests – but doesn't explicitly state – a rule about noun and verb endings:

1 *Now you can* **strengthen** *the thin green line.*

Strengthen is a verb which is formed from the adjective **strong**. Work in pairs and complete this table.

from Naunton J, *Think First Certificate*, Longman

ADJECTIVE	NOUN	VERB
wide		
strong		
deep		
weak		
short		
high		

A similar approach is used with word **collocations** (see page 7), wherever a general tendency can be identified. Here, for example, is a coursebook extract that focuses on the difference between *make* and *do* combinations:

VOCABULARY

from Bell J and Gower R, *Intermediate Matters*, Longman

Make or do?

1 Read the following sentences carefully.
Last night I tried to do my homework. However, I kept making mistakes because the man upstairs was doing his exercises and making a noise.

Make usually means to create, bring into existence, or produce a result.
Do usually means to perform an action. However, there are exceptions to this 'rule', as you will see in Exercise 3.

One problem with a rule-based approach is that the scope of the rule is not always clear. How many, and which, adjectives can be turned into verbs by the addition of *-en*, for example? *Sweet* and *fresh* – yes, but *wet* and *dry*? There is the added problem of the lack of one-to-one match between forms and categories. For example, *in-* and *un-* both express negation (*uncertain*, *inactive*), but *in-* can also be used with the meaning of *in*, or *within* (as in *inclusive*). And when do we use *in-*, as opposed to *un-* or *non-* or *dis-*, to convey negation? How, for example, does the learner know whether to use *unsatisfied, dissatisfied, insatisfied* or *nonsatisfied*?

One advantage of knowing the meanings of different affixes, however, is that they may help the learner unpack the meaning of unfamiliar words when reading and listening. So, a reader coming across *dissatisfied* for the first time should have no trouble understanding it if they know *satisfied* and are familiar with different negative prefixes. However, even when applying the rules to reception there are problems. *Outline* does not mean *out of line*; *research* does not mean *search again*; nor does *inflammable* mean *non-flammable*. Some teachers therefore recommend using word formation as a guide to meaning only if all other means (such as using context clues) fail.

The alternative to a rule-based approach is an **item learning** one. In other words, the learning of complex words (like *indisposed* or *dissatisfied*) would simply involve the same processes as the learning of simple ones (like *sick* or *sad*). That is, it is basically a memory task, with each word learned as an individual item. And, as with any memory task, the quantity of encounters with the items is a critical factor. According to this view, learners need exposure, and plenty of it, rather than rules.

There are good grounds for favouring an item learning approach. For a start, this seems to be the way words are acquired naturally. They are first learned as items, and then gradually re-categorised according to rules. That is, once a critical mass of separate items (such as *widen, strengthen, deepen, weaken*, etc.) has been learned, the mind starts to sort them according to their shared regularities (adjective or noun + *-en* = verb). This seems to be the case not only for the learning of patterns of word formation but for the learning of grammar as well. Learners may have to learn a lot of separate instances of a structure (*I am going … are you coming? … he was saying …*) before these items coalesce into a rule (subject + *to be* + *-ing*). In fact, item learning may be a prerequisite for rule learning generally. (This doesn't mean, of course, that the process always results in correct inferences. Learners can over-generalise from their own rules, so as to produce *He's a good cooker*, for example.)

The main disadvantage of an item learning approach is that it is very gradual and requires a great deal of exposure. But the good news is that the process can be speeded up by **consciousness-raising**. Consciousness-raising means drawing the learners' attention to the patterns and regularities of the language – helping them to **notice** these regularities. In this way, the teacher can facilitate the development of a *feel* (as opposed to a cast-iron rule) for what is the best interpretation of a word, or the most acceptable production of one. This does not necessarily mean teaching rules, but simply making patterns stand out. In a way, it is a compromise position between rule learning and item memorisation.

One writer, Anita Sökmen, provides a good example of how the teacher can guide learners to work out meaning, while at the same time integrating new knowledge with old:

> A less-structured approach to word parts is to sporadically ask students to analyze words. For example, in one course I have taught for several years, the word *innate* routinely comes up and students rarely know the meaning of the word, or its root, '*nat*'. However, once we review what the prefix '*in*' means, and I elicit other words containing the root '*nat*' (*native, natural, nation, nationality, pre-natal*), someone in the class can infer the meaning, *birth*, from their understanding of the brainstormed words. In this way, word unit analysis asks learners to compare the new word with

known words in order to get to their core meaning. Because it demands a deeper level of processing and reactivation of old, known words with the new, it has the potential of enhancing long-term storage.

(from Schmitt N and McCarthy M (Eds.), *Vocabulary*, CUP)

Other pattern-highlighting techniques involve the use of texts and include the following:

- learners are given a text and asked to search for and underline all compound nouns, negative prefixes, multi-word units, etc.

- learners find words in a text that are derivations. For example, 'Find three words in the text that are derived from *sense* ...'

- learners classify these derivations according to which part of speech they are

- learners categorise underlined words in a text according to a common affix, or according to the word formation principle they exemplify (compounding, conversion, etc.)

The more of these kinds of operations the learner does the better, since (as we saw in the last chapter) the more decisions the learner makes about a word the greater the depth of processing.

A great advantage of working from texts is that the words that are to be focused on are already in context, hence their meanings may be clearer than if presented as isolated words in a list (see Chapter 4). Also, and perhaps more importantly, the shared context will bring words together that are commonly associated. In the following text, for example, there are a number of words associated with time, crime and the law:

TIME LIMITS
There are strict time limits on the detention of persons without charge. An arrested person may not be detained without charge for more than 24 hours, unless a serious arrestable offence has been committed. If a serious arrestable offence has been committed a superintendent can extend the period to 36 hours to secure or preserve evidence by continued questioning. Where a serious arrestable offence has been committed and the suspect needs to be held in custody beyond the 36 hour period, the police must bring the suspect before a magistrate to extend the time limit to a maximum of 60 hours.

(from McCarrick-Watson, *Essential English Legal System*, Cavendish)

As well as words associated with the legal process (*detention, arrested, charge, offence, commit, superintendent, questioning*, etc.) there are words of the same derivation (*detention, detained; arrested, arrestable; person, persons*). There are also a number of examples of collocation and chunking. Some relate to time: *time limits, extend the period, 36 hours, the 36 hour period*; and others to crime: *commit an offence; without charge; hold in custody*. These words and combinations are found not only in close association, but in their typical grammar contexts. For example, the crime language occurs in passive constructions: *to be detained without charge* and *[an] offence has been committed.* This particular text has the added advantage that a number of key words and phrases are repeated (e.g. *a serious arrestable offence has been committed*) thereby increasing the likelihood of retention in memory.

An approach to focusing on these features might be:

- Ask students to read the text and to answer comprehension questions to gauge level of understanding. For example:

  1 The maximum time you can be detained without charge is:
     a 24 hours   b 36 hours   c 60 hours

  2 You can be detained for 36 hours only if:
     a a serious arrestable offence has been committed.
     b a magistrate gives permission.
     c further questioning is necessary.

- Ask learners (working together and using dictionaries) to underline all words relating to legal processes, and to categorise these according to a) people, b) processes.

- Ask them to use dictionaries to make verbs for these nouns: *limit, detention, charge, offence, questioning, suspect,* and to make nouns of these verbs: *arrest, detain, commit, extend, secure, preserve.* Which of the verb forms can take *-able* to form an adjective?

- Ask them to circle all time expressions with numbers and note the prepositions used in each case.

- Ask learners to identify the verbs that fill these slots: _____ *a person without charge*; _____ *an offence*; _____ *a suspect in custody*; _____ *a suspect before a magistrate*; _____ *a time limit.*

- Ask learners to rewrite the passage in 'plain English', e.g. as if they were explaining it to a friend. Alternatively, ask them to translate it into their own language.

- Learners then use the rewritten (or translated) passage as a basis for reconstructing the original text from memory. They then compare the reconstruction with the original.

- A follow-up activity might be to ask learners to research and summarise this aspect of the legal system in their own country (respecting, of course, their cultural sensitivities).

Note that this text, although short, is difficult and the tasks would be achievable only by quite advanced learners. Nevertheless, the same tasks could be adapted to much easier texts, and used at lower levels.

To summarise, then: the teaching of the grammar of word formation and word combination can be approached from two directions: early instruction in the rules, or the learning of a quantity of vocabulary items from which these rules are slowly distilled. We have looked at the case for a midway position that recognises the need for early exposure but at the same time accepts that consciousness-raising through focused attention can speed up the process of 'getting a feel for it'. Plentiful exposure plus consciousness-raising is a key principle underlying what has come to be known as a **lexical approach**.

A lexical approach

A lexical approach to language teaching foregrounds vocabulary learning, both in the form of individual, high frequency words, and in the form of word combinations (or **chunks**). The impetus for a lexical approach to language teaching derives from the following principles:

- a syllabus should be organised around meanings
- the most frequent words encode the most frequent meanings
  and
- words typically co-occur with other words
- these co-occurrences (or chunks) are an aid to fluency

A syllabus organised around meanings rather than forms (such as grammar structures) is called a **semantic syllabus**. A number of theorists have suggested that a syllabus of meanings – especially those meanings that learners are likely to need to express – would be more useful than a syllabus of structures. For example, most learners will at some time need to express such categories of meaning (or **notions**) as *possession* or *frequency* or *regret* or *manner*. Simply teaching learners a variety of structures, such as the *present simple* or the *second conditional*, is no guarantee that their communicative needs will be met. The present simple, for example, supports a wide range of meanings (*present habit*, *future itinerary*, *past narrative*, etc), some of which may be less useful than others. Wouldn't it be better to start with the more useful meanings themselves, rather than the structure?

A semantic syllabus – i.e. one based around meanings – is likely to have a strong lexical focus. The following sentences, for example, all involve the present simple, but they express different notions. These notional meanings are signalled by certain key words (underlined):

Does this towel <u>belong</u> to you? (possession)

How <u>often</u> do you go to London? (frequency)

I <u>wish</u> I'd done French. (regret)

Exercise is the best <u>way</u> of losing weight. (manner)

Words like *belong*, *often*, *wish* and *way* carry the lion's share of the meaning in these sentences: the grammar is largely padding. A lexical approach argues that meaning is encoded primarily in words. This view motivated two coursebook writers, Dave and Jane Willis, to propose that a **lexical syllabus** might be the best way of organising a course. The Willises believed that a syllabus based around the most frequent words in the language would cover the most frequent meanings in the language. Accordingly, they based their beginners' course around the 700 most frequent words in English. They used **corpus** data (i.e. computer banks of naturally occurring text – see page 68) to find out how these words 'behaved' – that is, the kinds of words and structures that were associated with these high frequency words.

For example, an extremely common word in English is *way*. According to COBUILD corpus data, it is in fact the third most common noun in English (after *time* and *people*). An analysis of corpus data shows that *way* is used to express a variety of meanings:

1 method or means	It's a useful way of raising revenue. The cheapest way is to hire a van.
2 manner, style, behaviour	He smiles in a superior way. Play soccer Jack Charlton's way.
3 what happens, what is the case	That's the way it goes. We were so pleased with the way things were going.
4 degree, extent, respect	She's very kind and sweet in lots of ways. In no way am I a politically effective person.
5 location, movement, direction, space	A man asked me the way to St Paul's. Get out of the way.

(after Willis D, *The Lexical Syllabus*, Collins)

Using corpus data, they then studied what kinds of grammatical structures *way* was typically found with – i.e. its **syntactic environment**. For example, the first use of *way* in the table above (meaning 'method or means') is commonly found in association with this pattern:

| way + of + -ing | a useful way of raising revenue |
| | the different ways of cooking fish |

The next step was to devise teaching materials that illustrated these meanings and patterns, bearing in mind that the starting point was not the pattern itself, but the meaning (*method*, *means*), and its frequency, as evidenced in the high frequency of the word *way*.

Here, for example, is how Willis and Willis summarise this use of *way* in *The Collins COBUILD English Course 2*.

Similar treatment is given to other high frequency words in the language, such as *thing, so, do, place, get, like, look*, and *would*. Note that some of these words – like *do* and *would* – are traditionally associated with specific grammatical structures, such as the present simple or the second conditional. However, in a lexically organised course, they are dealt with in much the same way as words like *way* and *like*. That is, first their principle meanings, and then their typical syntactic environments, are identified. Interestingly, when the syntactic environment of *would* (to talk about hypothetical situations) was examined, it was found that the combination of *would* and *if*, as in the 'second conditional' (*I'd do an MA if I had the money*) occurred relatively infrequently. Much more common was *would* on its own, as in

> **way**
>
> *There are different ways of writing 'colour' – the American way (color) or the English way (colour).*
> *How many ways are there of saying this number?*
> *Practise these ways of agreeing and disagreeing.*
> *I like the way he sings.*
> *Do it this way. Look.*

It would be nice to keep bees.
Opening the beaches would not be a solution.
'Would she make a deal like that?' she wondered.

The Willises argued that *would* should be dealt with as just another word, rather than as part of a syntactic structure. A lexical view of language, then, starts to dissolve the distinction between function words and lexical words. In so doing, it starts to dissolve the distinction between grammar and vocabulary.

The second major development underlying a lexical approach was the recognition of the important role played by multi-word units, or **chunks** (see page 6). A number of researchers have noticed that a lot of early language learning takes the form of chunks (such as *this-is-mine, give-me*, and *leave-me-alone*). These are acquired as single, unanalysed units. The capacity to use these chunks in conversational exchanges seems to be an important factor in developing fluency. Using 'pre-fabricated' language, rather than using grammar rules to fabricate language from scratch, saves valuable processing time. These chunks are then stored away and only at a later stage of development are they analysed into their component parts. So, *this-is-mine* is eventually broken down into:

determiner (*this/that*, etc.) + *to be* + possessive pronoun (*mine, yours*, etc.)

This analysis allows the production of other combinations using the same pattern, such as *That is yours* or *Those are hers*.

This 'chunking' process serves two purposes in early language production: it enables the child to have chunks of language available for immediate use, while at the same time it provides the child with language patterns to hold in reserve for later analysis. Not only that, some of the new creations (e.g. *that is yours, those are hers*) can in turn be 're-chunked' – i.e. memorised as wholes, and stored for later retrieval. The researchers Pawley and Syder proposed that adult language users have at their command a repertoire of literally hundreds of thousands of these memorised chunks. For example:

How are you?
Long time no see.
So anyway …
Don't mention it.
There you are, you see.
Speak of the devil.
It's got nothing to do with me.
Hang on a minute.
If you ask me …

It seems that the mental lexicon is not so much a dictionary as a phrase book.

It is this 'phrase book' view of language that prompted Michael Lewis to propose his version of a lexical approach (called *the* Lexical Approach). Lewis argues that 'language consists of grammaticalised lexis, not lexicalised grammar'. In other words, he challenges the traditional view that language competence consists of having a foundation of grammatical structures into which we slot individual words. Instead, we store a huge assortment of memorised words, phrases and collocations, along with their associated 'grammar'. In order to maintain conversational fluency, we select from this vast phrase book the chunks we need, and then fine-tune for grammar. Thus, to make a request, we might select the chunk *D'you think you could …* and tack on to it another chunk – *turn the volume down?* – while at the same time making any appropriate grammatical adjustments to ensure the two chunks stick together neatly. (Compare that with: *Would you mind + turnING the volume down?*) According to a lexical approach, language learning is essentially a process of item learning, as opposed to rule learning. In fact, Lewis is very sceptical about the value of studying traditional grammar rules at all.

It should be clear that the lexical syllabus of Dave and Jane Willis and Michael Lewis's Lexical Approach share a number of features. Both acknowledge the important meaning-making function of vocabulary, and both question the traditional distinction between vocabulary and grammar. In their view, words are really 'small grammar' and grammar is 'big words'. Where these writers differ is in their classroom approach, the Willises favouring a **task-based approach** to learning the semantic syllabus, while Lewis argues for a more analytic, text-based approach, in which texts are examined for the kinds of chunks embedded in them.

Teaching lexical chunks

So far we have been talking about lexical chunks as if they were a single undifferentiated category. But, as we saw in Chapter 1 (page 6), there are different types of chunks and different degrees of 'chunkiness'. Of the different types, the following are the most important for teaching purposes:

- collocations – such as *widely travelled; rich and famous; make do with; set the table*
- phrasal verbs – such as *get up; log on; run out of; go on about*
- idioms, catchphrases and sayings – such as *hell for leather; get cold feet; as old as the hills; mind your own business; takes one to know one*
- sentence frames – such as *would you mind if …?; the thing is …; I'd … if I were you; what really gets me is …*
- social formulae – such as *see you later; have a nice day; yours sincerely*
- discourse markers – such as *frankly speaking; on the other hand; I take your point; once upon a time; to cut a long story short …*

Within these categories further distinctions can be made in terms of **fixedness** and **idiomaticity**. Fixed chunks are those that don't allow any variation: you can say *over the moon* (to mean *ecstatic*) but not *under the moon* (to mean *not ecstatic*). Nor *over the full moon, over the sun*, etc. Many chunks are semi-fixed, in that they allow some degree of variation. *Nice to see you* is semi-fixed in that it allows *lovely, good, wonderful*, etc. in the *nice* slot, and *meet, talk to, hear from*, etc. in the *see* slot.

Some chunks are transparent in that the meaning of the whole is clear from their parts, as in the case of *as old as the hills* and *to knock down*. Others are much more idiomatic: *to spill the beans* and *to knock off* (meaning *to steal*). Neither fixedness nor idiomaticity are absolute values, however. Rather there is a cline from very fixed to very free, and from very idiomatic to very transparent. Phrasal verbs are a case in point. Some phrasal verbs are syntactically flexible: *I'll bring up the paper* or *I'll bring the paper up*. Others are not: *I can't tell the twins apart* but not *I can't tell apart the twins*. Moreover, the combination *bring up* has a range of meanings, some literal (*I'll bring up the paper*), some semi-idiomatic (*Don't bring that subject up again*) and some very idiomatic (*They brought their children up to speak Italian*).

The ability to deploy a wide range of lexical chunks both accurately and appropriately is probably what most distinguishes advanced learners from intermediate ones. How is this capacity developed? Probably not by learning rules – as we saw with word formation, the rules (if there are any) are difficult to learn and apply. A lexical approach is based on the belief that lexical competence comes simply from:

* frequent exposure, and
* consciousness-raising

To which we could perhaps add a third factor:

* memorising

Classroom language provides plentiful opportunities for exposure to lexical chunks. Many learners are familiar with expressions like *I don't understand* and *I don't know* long before they have been presented with the 'rules' of present simple negation. By increasing the stock of classroom phrases, teachers can exploit the capacity of chunks to provide the raw material for the later acquisition of grammar. Many teachers cover their classroom walls with useful phrases and insist on their use whenever an appropriate opportunity arises. A sampling of phrases I have noticed on classroom walls includes:

> What does X mean?
> How do you say X?
> What's the (past/plural/opposite, etc.) of X?
> Can you say that again?
> Can you write it up?
> How do you spell it?
> I'm not sure.
> I've forgotten.
> I left it at home.
> I haven't finished yet.
> It's (your/my/his) turn.
> You go first.
> Here you are.
> Pass me the …
> Let's have a break.
> etc.

The repetitive nature of classroom activity ensures plentiful exposure to these chunks. This is vital, because occasional and random exposure is insufficient. Many learners simply aren't aware if a combination is one that occurs frequently (and is therefore a chunk) or if it is a 'one-off'. Nevertheless, there is more chance of encountering instances of chunking in authentic text than in text that has been 'doctored' for teaching purposes.

This is yet another argument for using authentic texts in the classroom, despite the difficulties often associated with them.

Here, for example, is an extract from a fairly well-known authentic text:

Yo, I'll tell you what I want what I really really want,
So tell me what you want what you really really want
I'll tell you what I want what I really really want,
So tell me what you want what you really really want
I wanna I wanna I wanna I wanna I wanna really really really wanna zigazig ha
If you want my future, forget my past,
If you wanna get with me, better make it fast
Now don't go wasting my precious time
Get your act together we could be just fine …

If you wannabe my lover, you gotta get with my friends
Make it last forever, Friendship never ends
If you wannabe my lover, you have got to give,
Taking is too easy but that's the way it is.
What d'ya think about that? Now you know how I feel.
Say you can handle my love, are you for real?
I won't be hasty, I'll give you a try
If you really bug me then I'll say goodbye

(from *Wannabe* by the Spice Girls)

Like many pop songs, the lyrics of this song are rich in lexical chunks, including sentence frames (*I'll tell you what I …; what I really [really] want [is …]; If you wanna … better …; If you really, then I'll …*), collocations (*wasting my precious time; last forever; taking it … easy; give you a try*), and catchphrases (*better make it fast; get your act together; that's the way it is; are you for real?*).

How could you use the above song text? Essentially, the approach need not be very different from the approach to the legal English text on page 110. That is:

- check understanding of text (for example, by eliciting a paraphrase or translation of the text)
- using transcript, set tasks focusing on features of words in combination

Examples of such tasks might be:

- Underline all contractions. Decontract them (i.e. *wanna = want to*)
- Find examples of these sentence patterns in the song:
  … tell … what …
  If you … imperative …
  If you … you have got to …
  If you … then I'll …
- Write some more examples, using these patterns, that would fit the theme of the song.
- Use examples from the song to show the difference between *tell* and *say*.

117

- Find the verbs that fill these slots: ____ *it fast*; _____ *my precious time*; ___ *your act together*; ___ *forever*; ____ *it easy*; ____ *goodbye*.

Their repetitiveness, combined with their tendency to incorporate a lot of spoken chunk-type language, make pop songs a useful resource for vocabulary work. And not only do they recycle many current idioms and catchphrases, they are often responsible for introducing new ones into the language, such as *What I really really want …* Advertising has a similar effect: think of *finger-licking good*, *it's the real thing* and *it reaches parts that other […]s don't reach*.

But it is not just informal language that is rich in lexical chunks. As we saw earlier, legalistic language is richly patterned in this way. And so is the language of business. In fact, increasingly the teaching of business English recognises the importance of raising awareness about collocation.

Here, for example, is an exercise on collocations related to the word *sales*:

The word in the centre of the diagram is the **keyword**. There are different kinds of words in the **background** words. Use different coloured pens to underline the background words so that you divide them into groups. Find some two-word and three-word partnerships. Look for some partnerships which include **the keyword** and **a verb** from the background words. Write four sentences about your own situation. Use coloured pens or highlight the word partnerships so you can check them easily later.

from Wilberg P and Lewis M, *Business English: An Individual Learning Programme*, LTP

Notice that the focus is not just on noun + noun collocations (*sales volume*) but on verb + noun + noun combinations (e.g. *boost our sales volume*). Chunks of this size require the addition of only a little real grammar to provide much of the substance of typical business text: *We need to boost our sales volume.*

Here are some more ideas for teaching **collocation**:

- Learners sort words on cards into their collocational pairs (e.g. *warm + welcome, slim + chance, golden + opportunity, lucky + break, mixed + reception*, etc.). Use the same cards to play pelmanism (see page 97). Or they sort them into **binomial pairs** (pairs of words that follow a fixed sequence and often have idiomatic meaning such as *hot and cold, to and fro, out and about, sick and tired*). Or into groups, according to whether they collocate with particular 'headwords': e.g. *trip* (*business, day, round, return, boat*), *holiday* (*summer, family, public, one month, working*) and *weekend* (*long, every, last, next, holiday*). Follow up by asking learners to write sentences using these combinations.

- Read out a list of words: learners in groups think of as many collocations or related expressions as they can. Set a time limit – the group with the most collocations wins a point. Good words for this include parts of the body (*face, head, back, foot, hand*), colours (*red, green, blue, black*, etc.) and opposites, such as *weak/strong, narrow/wide, safe/dangerous, old/young*, etc.

- Fill in a collocational grid, using dictionaries, to show common collocations. For example, here's a very simple (and completed) one for *wide* and *broad*:

wide	broad	
•		door
•	•	street
•	•	river
	•	smile
	•	shoulders
	•	nose
•		gap
	•	accent
•		world
•	•	range
•		variety
•		apart
•		awake

In preparation for writing or speaking activities, learners can spend some time searching databases for useful collocations. Ask them first to brainstorm any nouns and verbs they are likely to need, and then to check for common collocates, using a concordance program (see Chapter 5) such as the COBUILD corpus on the Internet or a collocation dictionary (such as the *LTP Dictionary of Selected Collocations*), or simply a good learners' dictionary. Here, for example, are collocates and compound words for keywords selected in preparation for a composition on the subject of *flying*. They were all found using entries in the *Longman Dictionary of Contemporary English*:

fly: fly direct, fly on to, fly economy class, fear of flying
flight: an hour's flight, my flight's been called, charter flight, flight attendant, flight path, flight recorder
air: by air, airborne, airbus, aircraft, aircrew, airfare, air hostess, airline, airplane, airport, airsick, air traffic controller
travel: travel by train, car etc, travel widely, travel around, travel light, travel the world; well-travelled, widely travelled

 Ask learners to prepare 'collocation maps' of high frequency words and their collocates. Words like *have, take, give, make* and *get* lend themselves to this kind of treatment. They are often used in combination with nouns to form an expression which has a meaning of its own, as in *have a look, take a break, give advice, make an appointment*, so that the verb itself has little or no independent meaning. For this reason, they are called **delexical verbs**. Here, for example, is a collocation map for *have*, which shows its range of collocations organised into meaning categories:

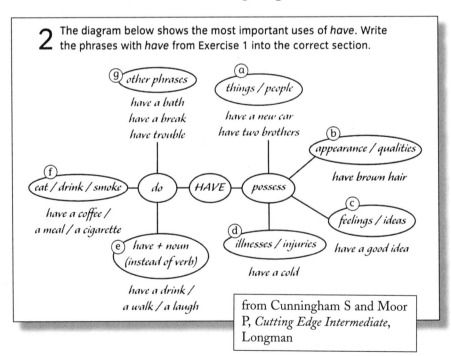

2 The diagram below shows the most important uses of *have*. Write the phrases with *have* from Exercise 1 into the correct section.

from Cunningham S and Moor P, *Cutting Edge Intermediate*, Longman

Learners can either create their own maps using dictionaries (or concordance programs – see page 70), or add to an existing map, as this task (also from *Cutting Edge Intermediate*) suggests:

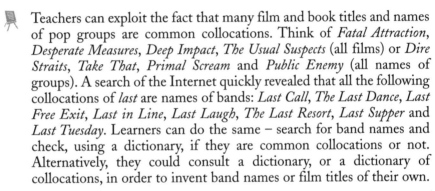

3 **a)** Add the phrases below to the correct section of the diagram.

| have a broken leg have a party have fun have a lot of energy |
| have a holiday have a meeting have a strange feeling have a wash |

b) With which uses can you also use *have got*? What do you notice?

Teachers can exploit the fact that many film and book titles and names of pop groups are common collocations. Think of *Fatal Attraction, Desperate Measures, Deep Impact, The Usual Suspects* (all films) or *Dire Straits, Take That, Primal Scream* and *Public Enemy* (all names of groups). A search of the Internet quickly revealed that all the following collocations of *last* are names of bands: *Last Call, The Last Dance, Last Free Exit, Last in Line, Last Laugh, The Last Resort, Last Supper* and *Last Tuesday*. Learners can do the same – search for band names and check, using a dictionary, if they are common collocations or not. Alternatively, they could consult a dictionary, or a dictionary of collocations, in order to invent band names or film titles of their own.

Because of the two-part nature of collocations, any matching activities lend themselves to work on them (see page 97). Similarly, odd one out tasks are useful. For example:

What is the one word in each row that does *not* usually go with the word on the left?

win	*match war salary election race lottery*
earn	*money degree living salary interest place*
gain	*weight advantage access support wages experience*

But there is a limit to the number of collocations that can be dealt with in activities like the ones above. The amount of time spent on targeting particular isolated collocations has to be balanced against time spent engaged in real language use, such as reading and speaking. It may, in fact, be in the context of real language use that the best learning opportunities will occur. A lot of work on collocation (and vocabulary generally) may happen in response to learners' errors. This reactive approach is described by Morgan Lewis:

Imagine a student produces *He's a strong smoker*. You could simply supply the student with the standard collocate – *heavy* – and move on. But an ideal opportunity to activate language on the edge of the student's lexicon has been missed. It requires very little extra time or explaining to add: *occasional, chain* and *non* as more collocates of *smoker*.

(from Morgan Lewis in *Teaching Collocation*, LTP)

Finally, as a general approach to the teaching of lexical phrases and collocation, the following advice is sound:

*   Become more aware of phrases and collocations yourself.
*   Make your students aware of phrases and collocations.
*   Keep an eye on usefulness and be aware of overloading students.
*   Feed in phrases on a 'little but often' basis.
*   Introduce phrases in context, but drill them as short chunks.
*   Point out patterns in phrases.
*   Be ready to answer students' questions briefly.
*   Keep written records of phrases as phrases.
*   Reinforce and recycle the phrases as much as you can.

(from *Cutting Edge Intermediate Teachers' Book*, Longman)

Teaching word grammar

It may seem out of place to be talking about grammar in a book on vocabulary. However, there is only a thin line – if indeed there is a line at all – between these two areas of language. As we saw in Chapter 2, knowing a word means knowing its associated grammar. What exactly is the associated grammar of a word? It is those patterns of words that typically co-occur with it. For example, a word like *say* has a different grammar from a word like *tell*. You can *tell someone something* but you can't *say someone something*. The grammar of *say* and *tell* can be represented like this (where *V* means verb, and *n* means noun group):

say: V that (as in *She says (that) she is cold*)
tell: V n that (as in *He told me (that) he was broke*)

Words that are related in meaning to either *say* or *tell* tend to fall into one of these two patterns. Thus, verbs following the *V that* pattern and having a similar meaning to *say* include *admit, explain, report, state* and *suggest*. Verbs like *tell*, on the other hand, which follow a *V n that* pattern, include: *convince, inform, persuade, promise, remind* and *warn*. Confusing the two patterns results in errors like the following:

My friend suggested me to go to Madrid for a weekend.
The agency said me it wasn't their problem.
I want to explain you something about the tour.

Helping learners identify word grammar is basically the same as helping them identify collocations: a case of providing them with rich data and focusing their attention on the patterns. As an aid to teachers, reference books are now appearing which organise words according to their grammatical characteristics. Here, for example, is an extract from one such book:

2 Some verbs are followed by a noun group and a that-clause. For example, in *I told her that there had been an accident*, the verb *tell* is followed by the noun group *her* and the that-clause *that there had been an accident*. This pattern is **V n that**.

After most of these verbs, the word *that* is often left out, especially in speech.

Active pattern

from *Verbs: Patterns and Practice*, *Classroom Edition*, Collins COBUILD

	Verb group	noun group	that-clause
He	told	me	he loved me.
They	had warned	me	that it would hurt.

Passive pattern

	Verb group	that-clause
He	was informed	that he had been disqualified.
He	was told	that it could never happen.

Verbs with this pattern are concerned with causing someone to know or think something.

assure	guarantee	promise	satisfy	tell
bet	inform	reassure	show	warn
convince	persuade	remind	teach	

*We are pleased to **inform** you that we have been able to accept your application.*

*I **reminded** her that on several occasions she had **remarked** on the boy's improvement.*

Teaching phrasal verbs

Phrasal verbs are another instance of the fuzziness at the boundary between words and grammar. They are particularly problematic for learners both because of their lexical meanings (which are often idiomatic) and their grammatical form. Here is how phrasal verbs are often grouped, according to their grammar:

2 There are four types of phrasal verb.

Type 1: intransitive e.g. *come to* (recover consciousness)
These don't take an object.

Type 2: transitive inseparable e.g. *look into* (investigate)
These must take an object which always comes after the verb.

Type 3: transitive separable e.g. *put off* (postpone)
The object can either come between the verb and the particle or after the verb. If we use a pronoun then it must go between.

Type 4: three-part, e.g. *put up with* (endure)
These are always transitive inseparable.

from Naunton J, *Think Ahead to First Certificate*, Longman

Traditional approaches to the teaching of phrasal verbs have tended to focus on these rules. Hence, when phrasal verbs are presented they are categorised according to whether they are Type 1, Type 2, etc. They are also often grouped according to their lexical verb (that is, the word that carries the major share of the meaning): *get up*, *get back*, *get off*, *get over*, etc, and exercises are designed to test the learner's knowledge of the difference. For example:

Use phrasal verbs with *get* to complete these sentences:
1 I can't _____ how much Julia has changed: it's amazing!
2 Excuse me, I want to _____ at the next stop.
3 The concert was cancelled so I'm going to see if I can _____ my money _____.

Typical exercise types used in the teaching of phrasal verbs include:

- sentence gap-fills (as the example above)
- re-phrasing: e.g. changing the verb in the sentence (e.g. *depart*) to a phrasal verb that has a similar meaning (e.g. *set off*)
- matching: e.g. matching the phrasal verb with its synonym

More recently, exercise types have focused on the meanings of the **particles** – a particle being the adverb or preposition component of the phrasal verb (*in*, *back*, *off*, *around*, etc). A focus on particles aims to sensitise learners to the shared meanings of a group such as *carry on*, *drive on*, *hang on*, *go on* and *come on*. Here, for example, is an exercise sequence that deals with the particle *down*:

Phrasal verb study

Down

Down is an adverb and a preposition. The basic meaning of down is to do with movement from a higher position or level to a lower one. In the text on page 36 of the Students' Book you read:

In 1948 Tennessee Williams and I *drove down* in his jeep from Rome to Naples ...

1 a Match these descriptions of *down* phrasal verbs with the sentences below.

1 Movement and position
2 Decreasing, lowering and reducing
3 Fastening and fixing
4 Collapsing and attacking
5 Completeness, ending and change
6 Eating and drinking
7 Writing and recording

I drank down my double Scotch eagerly. _____

The lid of the box was nailed down. _____

The water floods their homes or breaks down the walls. _____

Go and lie down on your bed. _____

If the firms failed to make enough money, they would close down. _____

They ask me the date and flight number: I always write it down so I'll remember. _____

It's a bit hot in here – turn it down. _____

b Here are five more *down* phrasal verbs. Check their meaning in your dictionary and write a sentence for each one.

drive down –
cool down –
stick down –
kick down –
note down

from Radley P and Millerchip C, *Workout Upper Intermediate*, Longman

---

The systematic approach to the teaching of p⸻
driven approach to the teaching of word form⸻
to believe that a rule-driven approach is any⸻
verbs than it is with composite words. Often th⸻
learners tend to avoid using phrasal verbs for fear⸻
a good basis for mastering an important area of lan⸻
that phrasal verbs are best learned on an item-by-i⸻
in short contexts that demonstrate their syntactic b⸻
passage, which comes from a guide to the Cambric⸻
English examination, offers some good advice to stud⸻

1 Whenever you read a book, newspaper or text in ⸻, get into the
   habit of *identifying* and underlining phrasal verbs ...
2 Write down in a special notebook the sentences in which they appear.
3 Use your English–English dictionary to look up the meaning, and
   write this after your sentence.
4 Try to write your own sentence using the same phrasal verb in a
   different context.
5 Get an English teacher or friend to check that your sentences are
   correct.
6 Limit the number of new phrasal verbs you collect to, say, two or three
   each day; if you do five or ten minutes' good work with each, you will
   quickly build up a useful stock of words which you have actually seen
   used in the English you have read.

(from Naylor H and Hagger S, *First Certificate Handbook*, Hulton Educational)

This approach is self-directed and text-based, and, admittedly, assumes a
high degree of motivation on the part of the learner. Nevertheless, the
approach can be adapted to the classroom. For a start, the teacher can
increase the probability of learners coming across phrasal verbs by providing
texts that are likely to have a high frequency of phrasal verbs in them.
Because phrasal verbs are often idiomatic they tend, like other idioms, to
cluster together – where you find one, you are likely to find others. Here, for
example, is a short text from a magazine with the phrasal verbs underlined:

Next time you go rushing off to sign up for an exercise class, consider first
what you want to get out of it. […] If you really want to de-stress, set an
hour or so aside afterwards to go home, listen to music and have a
leisurely shower or bath. Working out, having a shower and then dashing
back to work or rushing on to meet friends just doesn't allow you enough
time to benefit fully from the relaxing after-effects of exercise.

(from *New Woman* magazine)

Some books on phrasal verbs present theme-related sets of verbs in specially
written texts. Thus, a text about relationships may include such phrasal
verbs as *go out with*, *get on with*, *fall out*, *split up*, *make up*, *get back together*,
etc. As with lexical sets (see page 37), however, there is a danger that words
of too similar a meaning will interfere with each other – especially if they

have a similar form (e.g. *go out with, get on with*). A looser and more natural relationship may be more effective, such as the way words occur in a text, as in this example:

---

1 In the listening exercise on page 31 you will hear six new phrasal verbs. They are in **bold type** in this paragraph. From their context, work out which ones mean:

to leave   to recover consciousness   to finish
to arrive   to begin suddenly   to escape

War had **broken out** in the desert kingdom and we realized that we had to **get away**. Amanda **turned up** at my apartment three hours late, so we immediately got the car and **set off** across the desert. Soon, our petrol supply **ran out**, but we managed to beg some from a passing lorry. We were within sight of the border, when there was a sudden, loud bang and everything went black. When I **came round**, night had fallen and Amanda was watching over me with a worried expression. It was then that I realized we had driven over a landmine.

2 Complete these sentences by using each phrasal verb once.

1 He is still unconscious; I'll call you when he ....
2 She was so unhappy at home that she just had to ....
3 If you .... late, you won't be allowed into the concert.
4 We'll have to .... really early to catch the ferry.
5 Just use a cheque if your cash ....
6 A flu epidemic has .... at work; I hope I don't catch it.

---

from Naunton J, *Think Ahead to First Certificate*, Longman

Note that the occurrence of phrasal verbs in the text is fairly natural and that they are highlighted in order to promote noticing. Moreover, the tasks in this sequence move from recognition to production and the exercise is not encumbered with complex explanation or categorisation. All of these ingredients are conducive to successful vocabulary learning.

Finally, teachers should also try and include phrasal verbs in their classroom language as much as possible – and draw attention to these from time to time. Common classroom expressions incorporating phrasal verbs are *sit down, put your hand up, turn your papers over, write this down, cover the page up, look it up, hurry up* and *calm down!* By this means, exposure to a rich diet of phrasal verbs can begin on Day 1 of the course.

Teaching idioms

We've seen that many phrasal verbs are idiomatic – in that their meanings are not easily unpacked from their component parts. Knowing the meaning of *put* and *up* allows us to interpret the sentence *I put up a shelf in the kitchen.* But this knowledge is not much help in unpacking either *I put Luke up for the weekend* or *I put up with Luke for the weekend.* Both these last examples are idiomatic. Idiomaticity exists at both the single word and multi-word level. Individual words can be used figuratively, as in *This plan doesn't* **grab** *me; The kitchen is a* **pigsty**; *I can't* **unpack** *the meaning of this idiom.* More typically, idioms are formed from collocations, and vary from being both very fixed and very idiomatic (*smell a rat; the coast is clear*) to being both less fixed and less idiomatic (*explode a myth/theory, etc; run a business/theatre, etc*).

Idioms present problems in both understanding and in production. They are difficult to understand because they are not easily unpacked, and they are difficult to produce because they often allow no variation. Few errors sound more comical than an even slightly muddled idiom (e.g. *I don't want to blow my own horn,* instead of *I don't want to blow my own trumpet*). Moreover, many idioms have a very narrow register range, being used only in certain contexts and for certain effects. They therefore need to be approached with a great deal of caution, and most teaching guides recommend teaching them for recognition only.

Traditional teaching approaches tend to group idioms together according to some category, and present them in sets. But, as with phrasal verbs, teaching a set of idioms that are notionally related – such as idioms associated with parts of the body (*down at heel, put your feet up, foot the bill, toe the line,* etc.) – would seem to be a sure recipe for confusion. It's not difficult to imagine what could go wrong: *put your heels up, toe the bill,* etc. More typically, idioms are grouped by theme. For example, the expressions *under the weather, off colour, run down* and *out of sorts* are all synonymous with *ill.* But again, if these are being taught for production, the potential for confusion is high.

As with phrasal verbs, a more effective and less perilous approach might be simply to teach them as they arise, and in their contexts of use. That is, to treat them as individual lexical items in their own right, without making a *song* and *dance* about them. Since idioms tend to cluster together, certain text types are often very rich in them. In this extract (from *Sugar*) idioms (including idiomatic phrasal verbs) are underlined.

Eastenders

Martin gets a big wake-up call this month when Mark is taken seriously ill. How will he cope knowing his big bro's <u>days could be numbered</u> and will Nicky <u>stick by him</u> <u>through thick and thin</u>?

Home and Away

Tom offers to pay for Justine's courses in the city with the money he earned from acting in the commercial. What a sweetie, eh? However, Justine isn't that impressed, and feels that Tom's cramping her style. How can she let him down gently?

Coronation Street

The Mike, Mark and Linda triangle's still going strong, and sparks are beginning to fly between Linda and Mark's new girlie, Claire. Eeek! Things aren't too good over at the Platt's either.

Emmerdale

Mark is annoyed when neither of his parents make it to the parent's evening … how embarrassing! Richie lends Sarah a shoulder to cry on after yet another bust-up with Jack. Will those two ever get on?

To use a text like this in class, learners could be set the task of working out the underlined idioms from either their form or their context. For example, *going strong* is easily unpacked from its components. *Sparks are beginning to fly* is less obvious, but its negative connotation can be deduced from what follows (*Eeek! Things aren't too good …*). Showing learners how to work out idiomatic meaning from these kinds of clues can not only contribute to passive vocabulary knowledge but can improve reading skills as well.

Conclusions

There is more to words than simply 'words'. In this chapter we have seen:

- how parts of words combine in systematic ways to form whole words
- how whole words combine in systematic ways to form chunks

But, the fact that these combinations are systematic does not mean that the teaching of word formation or of word combination should necessarily be rule-based. The systems may be too complicated or too irregular to be of much use to learners, either for receptive or productive purposes.

Instead, an approach that combines frequent and contextualised exposure with consciousness-raising may work best. This is recommended for the teaching of:

- composite words
- collocations
- phrasal verbs
- idioms

Looking ahead

So far we have been concerned with teaching and learning. But, for various reasons and at various stages in the process, the learning of vocabulary needs to be measured. In the next chapter we look at ways of testing vocabulary knowledge – both before, during and at the end of instruction.

8 How to test vocabulary

- Why test vocabulary?
- What to test
- Types of test
- Measuring word knowledge
- Assessing vocabulary size
- Doing action research

Why test vocabulary? Why test anything? The obvious answer is that, without testing, there is no reliable means of knowing how effective a teaching sequence has been. Testing provides a form of feedback, both for learners and teachers. Moreover, testing has a useful **backwash** effect: if learners know they are going to be tested on their vocabulary learning, they may take vocabulary learning more seriously. Testing motivates learners to review vocabulary in preparation for a test. It also provides an excuse for further, post-test, review – when, for example, the teacher goes over the answers in class. In this way, testing can be seen as part of the **recycling** of vocabulary generally. In fact, the only difference between many recycling exercises and tests is that only the latter are scored. Here, for example, is a review activity from a coursebook that could just as well form an item in a test:

---

4 Vocabulary

a) Make six lists of the words in the box: 1 The body; 2 Travel; 3 The country; 4 Illness; 5 Jobs; 6 Food.

> field   hurt   luggage   builder   steak   rice
> electrician   cough   face   delay   wood
> fish   businessman   path   mushrooms   toe
> flight   finger   platform   arm   mountain
> aspirin   backache

from Bell J and Gower R, *Elementary Matters*, Longman

b) Mark the stress on the correct syllable of words of more than one syllable.

Informal testing of this type is best done on a regular basis. Ideally, in fact, vocabulary covered in the previous lesson should be tested at the beginning of the next one. If not, the chances of retaining the new vocabulary are greatly reduced. The principle of **distributed practice** (see page 24) argues that the spacing of these review phases should gradually be increased. This requires a certain discipline on the part of teachers to keep track of their vocabulary input, and to schedule tests at the optimal times. One informal way of testing is to get the learners to test each other, using their vocabulary notebooks (see Chapter 9) or the class word box (see page 51).

More formal testing may be required at certain strategic stages in a course. Tests of vocabulary knowledge sometimes form a part of **placement tests**, or as a component of a **diagnostic test** in advance of planning a course programme. Such tests usually involve some attempt to measure extent of vocabulary knowledge. Tests of **achievement** at the end of a course, and of overall **proficiency**, as measured by external examinations such as the Cambridge First Certificate or TOEFL, typically include a vocabulary testing component. Vocabulary knowledge is sometimes targeted in tests of **reading ability**, since there is a strong correlation between the two. Finally, learners' developing vocabulary knowledge, and their use of vocabulary learning strategies, may be the subject of testing for **research** purposes – especially the kind of research that teachers themselves can carry out in their own classrooms.

What to test

In Chapter 2 we concluded that knowing a word means knowing:

- the word's form – both spoken and written
- the word's meaning (or meanings)
- any connotations the word might have
- whether the word is specific to a certain register or style
- the word's grammatical characteristics – e.g. part of speech
- the word's common collocations
- the word's derivations
- the word's relative frequency

Furthermore, all these aspects of word knowledge can be realised receptively (in listening and reading) or productively (in speaking and writing). Any vocabulary test, therefore, needs to take into account the multi-dimensional character of word knowledge.

Most vocabulary tests target only one or two aspects of word knowledge. For example, the following items (1–3) focus on spelling, meaning and collocation respectively:

| 1 | Teacher: 'Write down these words. Number 1, *confident*. Number 2, *independent*. Number 3, *expectant*. Number 4, *reluctant*', etc. |

| 2 | Write the English word that means: 1 a place where you go to buy meat; 2 the person who repairs your kitchen tap if it leaks; 3 the thing that you buy at a post office if you want to post a letter; etc. |

3 | Choose the best word to complete each sentence:
1 The flight attendant asked the passengers to _____ attention to the safety demonstration.
  a give   b devote   c pay   d lend
2 A severe hurricane in the South Pacific has _____ many lives.
  a claimed   b taken   c killed   d destroyed
3 The delegates blamed each other when the peace talks broke

  _____.
  a off   b up   c on   d down
etc.

Note that in tests 1 and 2 no context is provided, whereas in the third the targeted language is (minimally) **contextualised**. Of course, contexts can be added. In the case of test 1, the teacher could dictate whole sentences. In the case of test 2, learners could be asked to put the words into sentences.

Note also that tests 1 and 2 require learners to **produce** the correct form – i.e. to recall them from long-term memory. On the other hand, the collocation test (test 3) is receptive in that it simply tests the learner's ability to **recognise** the correct form. This is a limitation if the aim is also to test a learner's ability to produce these forms. However, it could be made productive if the multiple choice answers were removed:

Choose the best word to complete each sentence:
1 The flight attendant asked the passengers to _____ attention to the safety demonstration.
2 A severe hurricane in the South Pacific has _____ many lives.
3 The delegates blamed each other when the peace talks broke _____.
etc.

Whether to test with or without a context, or to test for recognition or for production, are issues that are best resolved by taking into account the purpose of the test and also its likely effect on teaching. If the purpose of the test is to predict the learner's reading ability, for example, then a receptive test will be sufficient. But it should also be a contextualised text, because reading involves using context clues to help work out word meaning. A de-contextualised word test might not be a valid test of reading ability. Moreover, it has been argued that de-contextualised tests encourage learners simply to learn long lists of words. On the plus side, de-contexualised tests are usually easy to compile and mark, so they are therefore very practicable.

To sum up, there is bound to be a trade-off between issues of **validity** (does the test assess what I want it to assess?), of **practicality** (is it easy to administer?), and of **backwash** (will the test have a positive effect on learning?). Also at issue is the question of the test's **reliability**. For example, will it give consistent results, regardless of who marks it, and will it give the same result for students of the same ability? The following test task assesses productive, contextualised word knowledge, so it is a valid test of the learner's command of vocabulary for a 'real life' purpose. But, since it is scored somewhat impressionistically, it may not be a very reliable test:

> Write a letter of about 200 words to a friend, explaining that you have recently moved house and why, and inviting the friend to a housewarming party.
>
> Scoring: Rate the range and accuracy of the writer's vocabulary knowledge on a scale from 4 (excellent) to 1 (very poor).

The reliability of the test can be improved by providing more explicit criteria for marking (see page 135). Nevertheless, applying such criteria effectively is liable to slow marking down, and thus reduce the test's practicality.

Considerations of validity and reliability are less of an issue in informal testing, however, where the main objective is to motivate review and recycling. More important, perhaps, is that the learners accept it as being a valid test – that it has what is called **face validity**. Beyond that, it doesn't really matter what the test is like, so long as it encourages review.

Types of test
We have already seen an example of a **multiple choice** test (in the collocation example at the top of page 131). Multiple choice tests are a popular way of testing in that they are easy to score (a computer can do it), and they are easy to design (or seem to be). Moreover, the multiple choice format can be used with isolated words, words in a sentence context, or words in whole texts. Here, for example is a 'word only' example:

> *tangle*   means
> a a type of dance
> b a tropical forest
> c a confused mass
> d a kind of fruit

Here, on the other hand, is a contextualised multiple choice test:

> CANCER 22 June–22 July
> Someone else is [a playing; b calling; c singing] the tune and for the moment you're quite happy to go [a along; b around; c away] with what seems like a reasonable idea. Hobbies [a make; b use; c take] up far too much time and children could need support with a new activity. Feelings are [a going; b running; c climbing] high so ensure you're getting the affection you need …

(from *ME* magazine)

On the negative side, multiple choice tests have been criticised because

- learners may choose the answer by a process of elimination, which hardly constitutes 'knowing' the right answer
- depending on the number of possible answers (called **distractors**), there is a one-in-three (or one-in-four) chance of getting the answer right
- they test recognition only – not the ability to produce the word

• they are not as easy to design as might appear. On what basis are the distractors chosen, for example? Synonyms? Words commonly confused? Words of a similar sound or spelling? False friends?

An alternative to multiple choice is some form of **gap-fill**. Gap-fill tests require learners to recall the word from memory in order to complete a sentence or text. Thus they test the ability to produce a word rather than simply recognise it. The best-known example of this test type is the **cloze test**. In a cloze test, the gaps are regularly spaced – e.g. every seventh, eighth, or ninth word. In this way, knowledge of a wide range of word types – including grammar words as well as content words – is tested. Moreover, the ability to complete the gaps depends on understanding the context, as in this example, in which every sixth word has been deleted:

Tumbu fly

In Africa south of the Sahara, another (1) _____ the traveller may encounter is (2) _____ tumbu or mango fly, which (3) _____ its eggs on clothing laid (4) _____ on the ground to dry. (5) _____ larvae hatch and burrow their (6) _____ into the skin, causing boil-like (7) _____. These can be avoided by (8) _____ that clothes, bedding, etc., are (9) _____ spread on the ground to dry.

(from Dawood R, *Travellers' Health*, OUP)

The succesful answer to item (9) above depends on learners having understood the gist of the passage. Is it *always* or *never*, for example? In fact, cloze tests were originally designed as tests of reading. It is arguable, therefore, whether they are really vocabulary tests at all.

A variant of the cloze test is one in which, rather than every *n*th word, specifically chosen words are deleted. In this way, the test can be steered more towards content words, and hence become a more valid test of vocabulary. Most teachers will be familiar with tests of this **selective** (or **open**) **cloze** type, although it is more often used to test grammar than vocabulary. The problem with gap-fills, however, is that there is often more than one possible correct answer, which makes scoring difficult. Thus, for item (1) above, the words *problem, parasite, danger* or even *thing* are all acceptable. One way of controlling this is to provide the first letters of the word:

Tumbu fly

In Africa south of the Sahara, another problem the traveller may e_____ is the tumbu or mango fly, which l_____ its eggs on clothing laid out on the ground to dry. The larvae h_____ and burrow their way into the s_____, causing boil-like s_____. These can be a_____ by ensuring that clothes, bedding, etc., are not s_____ on the ground to dry.

A variety of this approach is called the **C-test**. In a C-test, the second half of every second word is deleted as shown overleaf:

> **Tumbu fly**
>
> In Africa south of the Sahara, another prob____ the trav____ may
> encou____ is t____ tumbu o____ mango fl____, which la____ its
> eg____ on cloth____ laid o____ on t____ ground t____ dry. T____
> larvae hat____ and bur____ their w____ into t____ skin, caus____
> boil-like swel____. These c____ be avoi____ by ensu____ that clot____,
> bedding, et____, are n____ spread o____ the gro____ to dr____.

At first sight, this looks even less like a vocabulary test than does a cloze test. However, researchers have shown that success at doing C-tests correlates with success at other kinds of vocabulary test. Hence, it has been argued that C-tests are valid tests of overall vocabulary knowledge, and thus can usefully serve as placement tests. They are not, however, of much use to teachers as informal tests of progress, since they cannot be tailored to test specifically targeted words.

Another variety of gap-fill tests learners' knowledge of word formation, by asking them to convert words from one form to another so as to fit a context. Here is an example:

> Change the word on the left into a suitable form to fill the gap:
> 1 *compose*   On one occasion the opera was conducted by the _____.
> 2 *place*   Have you seen my keys? I seem to have _____ them.

This kind of task tests learners' knowledge of derivations (*composer* and *misplaced* as opposed to, say, the incorrect *compositor* or *deplaced*). It also tests their ability to interpret the surrounding context, in order to make the correct choice among several possible derivations (not *composure* or *displaced*, for example).

Even if sometimes the contexts are only a single sentence, one of the strengths of gap-fills is that they provide contexts for the words that are being targeted. This is consistent with the view that language should be both taught and tested in context. In fact, words like *compose* or *place* would be difficult to test out of context, given that they have multiple meanings. However, gap-fills require only minimal production on the part of the learner, and so it is arguable whether they really test the learner's ability to use the targeted words in contexts of their own creation. The following test types attempt to remedy this weakness.

One way is simply to ask learners to write sentences of their own that show the meaning of targeted words. However, as experienced teachers know, it is often difficult to assess learners' word knowledge on the basis of their own sentences. For example, while three of the following five sentences are well-formed, only the last displays a sound grasp of both the form and meaning of the word *sleep*:

Tony sleeped.
Tony slept.
Tony slept for ten hours.
Tony was so tired he was slept for ten hours.
Tony was so tired he slept for ten hours.

A more revealing test of productive vocabulary knowledge is to set learners the task of writing a whole text that includes the selected vocabulary items. This is feasible only if the words themselves are likely to co-occur. Here is an example where this is the case:

> Write a paragraph of about 100 words to include at least six of the following ten words. You can change the form of the word, if necessary – e.g. *work* → *worked* :
>
> | | | | |
> |---|---|---|---|
> | voucher | stain | sale | unwrap |
> | store | rug | couch | refund |
> | torn | complain | | |

When scoring such a test, marks can be allocated for both correct form and appropriate use of each of the selected words.

The above tasks target pre-selected words – words that may have been covered in preceding lessons, for example. A more global assessment of learners' vocabulary knowledge can be gained from an evaluation of their writing and speaking overall. Many tests of learners' production, such as the writing component of the Cambridge First Certificate examination, include an assessment of the candidate's vocabulary knowledge, both its range and its accuracy. Usually this is assessed **qualitatively** – that is, a general impression is made of the learner's vocabulary knowledge according to criteria such as the following:

Wide range of words appropriately and accurately used; good use of idiom and collocation; appropriate style	4
Adequate range, with only occasional errors of spelling, word form, style, collocation, or word choice; meaning clear overall	3
Limited range of words, with some repetition; frequent errors of spelling, style, collocation, or word choice, leading to occasional difficulties in understanding meaning	2
Very narrow range, highly repetitive; frequent spelling and word form errors; little or no awareness of collocation or style; meaning frequently obscure	1

However, without considerable standardisation, such criteria are often difficult to apply. Different examiners will have different opinions as to what constitutes an 'adequate range' of words, for example.

Measuring word knowledge

An alternative approach is to evaluate the data **quantitatively** – that is, using objective and measurable criteria. Three aspects of vocabulary knowledge that are measurable quantitatively are:

- lexical density
- lexical variety
- lexical sophistication

Lexical density is a measure of the proportion of **content words** in a text. Content words – as opposed to function words – are words that carry a high information load, such as nouns, adjectives and verbs (see page 4). Written text that contains a high proportion of such words is characteristic of proficient writers. **Lexical variety**, on the other hand, is a measure of the different words in the text. Again, a high proportion of different words is an indicator of an extensive vocabulary knowledge – what is often called **range**. Finally, **lexical sophistication** is assessed by counting the number of relatively infrequent words in a text – such as the number of words that fall outside of a list of the top 2,000 most frequent words.

Here, for example, is a text written in response to the task on page 132:

> I'm writting to you as I have just finished moving to a new house, it was very tiring days. I left my old house because there were some things I didn't like, such as it had quite so little rooms. Not only were there little and dark rooms but there were also little sunlight; it was always in the shade. Moreover, I asked to the owner of the house to paint it, as it was very dirty, but he turned down what I had asked so I decided to leave the house.
>
> I have moved to a brand-new building so there are no problems with the painting and other things at all. That house is very comfortable and it has also large windows to pass through the sunlight. By the way, my new neighbours are very nice, they helped me with moving my furniture and all my things.
>
> I have moved to an area near lots of parks, it is a beautiful place.
>
> Well, to sum up I'd like you to come to my housewarming party to open that pretty place I've got. So wishing to hear from you soon

The lexical density of this text – i.e. the number of content words as a percentage of the total number of words – is something like 35 per cent. For the purposes of this calculation, content words are considered to be nouns, verbs (but not auxiliary or modal verbs), adjectives, and adverbs derived from adjectives (e.g. *quickly*). The lexical variety – the number of different words as a proportion of the total number of words – is almost exactly 50 per cent (94 out of 189). For this calculation, the different forms of a verb, such as *left* and *to leave*, are counted as one word type, while lexical chunks, such as phrasal verbs (*turned down*) and discourse markers (*to sum up*) are counted as single items.

Finally, the number of words falling outside the top two frequency bands, as indicated in the *Collins COBUILD English Dictionary*, is exactly ten: *tiring, sunlight, shade, moreover, dirty, brand-new, comfortable, neighbour, furniture* and *housewarming*. This represents about 10 per cent of the total number of different word types, and provides a measure of the lexical sophistication. To sum up, the student has a score of 35, 50 and 10 for lexical density, variety and sophistication respectively.

Of course, such a calculation needs to be balanced against a measure of the **accuracy** of vocabulary use. However, this is notoriously difficult to measure using quantitative means. Some errors are less serious than others (is *my old house* an error?). Others spread over more than one word (e.g. *to pass through the sunlight*). Still others are difficult to distinguish from grammar mistakes (*quite so little rooms*). An assessment of accuracy is likely to be somewhat impressionistic, therefore.

By contrast, here is how a native speaker responded to the same task:

Just a note to let you know that at last I've moved (see address above). You probably remember that I was having a miserable time in my last flat because of the noise, particularly from the bar downstairs which used to stay open to three in the morning. I tried all sorts of things, including lodging a formal complaint with the local council, but nothing worked, so finally I decided to quit. I never really liked that neighbourhood much anyway. It was also a long way from work.

Through a friend of a friend I was lucky enough to find something almost straightaway. It's in a much quieter area, only ten minutes from the office and there's even a view of the river from the terrace. It's more expensive than the other place, and it needs quite a lot of work but it's going to be lovely. I've already met the neighbours and they seem pleasant enough – no dogs or loud music so far! Anyway, once I've had it done up, I'm planning to throw a little housewarming party, so this is by way of an invitation. I'll let you know the details nearer the event.

In this case, the lexical density was 42 per cent and the lexical variety roughly 65 per cent. The number of low frequency words was 16, representing 13 per cent of the different word types. This provides a point of comparison with the 35 per cent, 50 per cent and 10 per cent of the student composition.

Clearly, this is a fairly laborious way of going about assessing vocabulary knowledge. Moreover, any assessment of the density, variety and sophistication of a learner's use of vocabulary in a text needs to take account of the kind of text it is. For example, academic writing is usually considerably more lexically dense than fiction. Spoken text is a lot less dense than written text. But at least these three measures provide an objective way of assessing vocabulary knowledge, and may be helpful as a means of evaluating a learner's progress over time. And, with practice, teachers can become fairly proficient at making an impressionistic but reasonably accurate assessment of these criteria without the necessity of totting up every word.

Assessing vocabulary size

Sometimes it is useful to assess the size of a learner's vocabulary. For example, as a factor in determining a learner's readiness to sit a public examination, the number of words they know may be crucial. It is estimated that a recognition vocabulary of at least 4,500 words is necessary for the Cambridge First Certificate examination. There is little point in a learner entering for the exam if his or her vocabulary size is barely 2,000. How, then, do you go about assessing vocabulary size?

One fairly crude measure is to use a dictionary and choose a random selection of words – say every tenth word on every tenth page – and incorporate these into a test. The test could take the form of multiple choice questions, or a multiple matching task, such as the following (which has the advantage of testing several words at once):

	Match the following words with their meaning (there are more meanings than words):
	1 tall narrow building
crowd	2 annoy
gull	3 type of artist
pester	4 small sailing boat
sculptor	5 sea bird
	6 a lot of people

Or learners could simply be asked to translate the words into their first language. The proportion of words correctly known represents the proportion of words in the whole dictionary. So, if the learner knows thirty out of a hundred words randomly chosen (i.e. 30 per cent), and there are 10,000 headwords in the dictionary, then a very rough estimate of the learner's vocabulary size is 30 per cent of 10,000, or 3,000 words.

Another approach is to ask learners themselves to assess the number of words they know by giving them a representative sample of words in the form of a list and asking them to tick the words they are familiar with. A more sophisticated self-assessment test takes into account the fact that word knowledge involves varying degrees of depth. Rather than *I know this word* vs *I don't know this word*, candidates can be asked to rate their knowledge according to the following categories:

I don't remember seeing this word before.
I recognise this word but I don't know what it means.
I think this word means _____.
I can use this word in a sentence. For example: _____.

The test can be made more accurate still by selecting the words to be tested from different frequency bands. This can be fairly easily done, using the coding system in the *Collins COBUILD English Dictionary*, for example, which discriminates between five different frequency bands:

- the 700 most frequent words. For example: *other, family, week, start, available*
- the next 1,200 most frequent words. For example: *imagine, justice, reform, cash, agreement*
- the next 1,500 most frequent words. For example: *sensible, fancy, lucky, weigh, beauty*
- the next 3,200 most frequent words. For example: *relevant, intake, neutral, hockey, drawer*
- the next 8,100 most frequent words. For example: *pickled, congregation, jut, craftsman, scourge*

This gives a sample from a total of nearly 15,000 words overall. If, say, thirty words are tested at each level (using, for example, the multiple matching task illustrated above), the results should give a fairly accurate indication of the learner's vocabulary size. Thus, if the test demonstrates that the test taker knows twenty-eight first band words, eighteen second band words but only four third band words, it is safe to assume that their vocabulary size is within the first two bands, that is to say, within 1,900 words.

Other, often ingenious, ways of assessing vocabulary size have been devised. However, given the complexity and intricacy of the mental lexicon, and the difficulty of establishing what exactly constitutes a word, any estimate of vocabulary size is only ever going to be approximate, at best. Nevertheless, even an approximate measure may be better than none, when it comes to deciding, for example, how much preparation may be necessary for an exam.

Doing action research

Testing, we have said, is a way of getting feedback on the teaching–learning process. In that sense, it is a form of small-scale research. Research itself is part of a cycle of inquiry and experiment that characterises the working life of professional practitioners. Most teachers are in a constant state of 'trying something out', to see if it has any noticeable effect on learning outcomes. It may be a new book, or a new technique, or simply a new way of organising the classroom furniture. Vocabulary teaching lends itself to this kind of experimentation, since, unlike grammar, vocabulary knowledge is more readily itemised, and hence more easily measurable. It is easier, for example, to assess whether twenty words can be recalled a week after they have been introduced, than assess a learner's command of the present perfect over the same period of time.

Small-scale classroom research implemented by teachers and directed at improving learning outcomes is called **action research**. Action research does not need to meet the same rigorous standards as, for example, the more elaborate 'scientific' research carried out by academics. This does not mean that it lacks rigour entirely. The same principles that relate to effective testing – such as validity and reliability – apply equally to action research. But above all, action research should be practicable – it should not place undue demands on either teachers or students, and it should have practical outcomes.

Below are detailed some possible lines of inquiry regarding the teaching of vocabulary that practising teachers could pursue in their own classrooms. They are directed not so much at measuring learners against each other (as in an examination), as assessing the effectiveness of the learning–teaching process in general. They all involve some kind of experimental teaching and/or learning activity (the **treatment**) and then a **post-test** of vocabulary recall. Strictly speaking, the results of the post-test are only valid if some kind of **pre-test** has been conducted in advance of the treatment, although this is not always practicable.

- **To investigate different learning styles**: Some learners prefer to see new words instantly, others are happy simply to hear them and run them through their articulatory loop (see page 23). To find out what works best with your own learners, teach the class ten new words by repeating and drilling, but not writing, them. In a subsequent lesson, teach another ten words, by writing them on the board, and repeating them, but not drilling them. Allow the same time interval (e.g. a week) between each presentation before testing each batch of ten words to see which batch is recalled best. Note any major differences between different learners. You can vary this procedure by adjusting the order and combination of hearing, seeing, and repeating the words. You could also combine this experiment with a short questionnaire about learning styles: *Do you prefer to see a new word instantly? Do you prefer to hear a new word before you see it?* etc. Note any correlations between learners' preferred styles and the results of the experiment.

- **To investigate the effectiveness of different mnemonic techniques**: Explain to learners that you are going to present, say, twenty new words, and that you will test them on their recall of these words in a week's time. Suggest that they think of ways of remembering these words. Present the words – using any of the approaches suggested in Chapter 5. Test the learners a week later – using any of the testing methods suggested in this chapter. Compare results and then ask learners to report on the way that they went about remembering the words, paying particular attention to any memory techniques that the more successful students used. Then present another set of new words, asking learners to apply the memory techniques used by the successful learners. Test again in a week's time, and see if there is any overall improvement in recall. A variation of this experiment might be to teach one half of the class a mnemonic technique, such as the **keyword technique** (see page 145), teach all the class a set of words, and see if the experimental group (i.e. those instructed in the keyword technique) show noticeably better recall. They can then explain to their classmates how they applied this technique.

- **To investigate different ways of selecting words for presentation**: In Chapter 3 it was suggested that presenting words in closely related lexical sets might be counterproductive, as the similarities in meaning might cause cross-interference. To test this view, teach three batches of, say, ten words in successive lessons, and in subsequent lessons test for recall. The first batch of words should all belong to the same lexical set; the second should be randomly chosen; and the third should have a loose relationship – e.g. words that might co-occur in the same text. (One way of compiling this last batch is simply to select ten words from one or two paragraphs of an authentic text.)

- **To investigate the effect of extensive reading on vocabulary acquisition**: Provide learners with a graded reader or, at an advanced level, an authentic novel or book of short stories. Set regular tasks to encourage out-of-class reading, and programme discussions of the reading material during class time. Meanwhile, select words from the material that are likely to be unfamiliar to learners. If possible, try to note how many times the selected words are repeated in the reading material. Do not draw any special attention to these words before the testing stage. At the end of the reading phase, test learners on their recall of the words by, for example, using the four 'word familarity' categories mentioned earlier in this chapter (see page 138). See if the results of this test correlate in any way with the number of times the words were repeated in the text.

- **To investigate vocabulary recording strategies**: Ask learners to let you borrow their vocabulary notebooks overnight. Note down the way they record vocabulary – whether they simply list words randomly, whether they gloss them with translations, or definitions, whether they include contextualised examples, etc. Choose a selection of words that are common to all notebooks (if possible) and test the class on these words in a subsequent lesson. Compare individual results to determine whether there is any correlation between vocabulary recording strategies and recall. Use the results of this experiment to discuss the best ways of recording vocabulary (see the next chapter for more on ways of recording vocabulary).

- **To investigate the effect of guessing-from-context**: Prepare a reading text for the class that includes a number of words known to be (or likely to be) unfamiliar. For one half of the class, provide a gloss of these difficult words, e.g. in the form of a translation or definition. For example, here is part of a text with glosses in Spanish:

A DAY IN THE LIFE OF CABIN CREW

4.00am

I'm on early shift[1] today, so it's still dark when the alarm[2] goes off. When you're getting up at the crack of dawn[3], you need to be organised, so I checked my rosters[4] and prepared my uniform and cabin[5] bag last night. Today I'm doing what's known in the trade[6] as 'a double Amsterdam' …

1 turno
2 despertador
3 al romper el alba
4 listas, programas
5 cabina
6 oficio

(from *EasyJet In Flight* magazine)

The other half of the class have no such help, and have to guess the meaning of the unfamiliar words from context. Ask comprehension questions about the text that require learners to engage with the unfamiliar words. Allow them to collaborate on answering the questions, but avoid giving any definition or translation of the unfamiliar words. Simply encourage them to try to work out the meaning from the context. In a subsequent lesson, test recall of the words in the text. See if there is any difference between the two halves of the class – those that did not have to do much cognitive 'work', and those that did.

- **To investigate the effect of dictionary use**: Follow the same steps as in the previous experiment, but this time allow the group with no glosses to consult dictionaries (rather than relying on context). Again, see if recall is enhanced by the decision-making involved in consulting a dictionary. A further variant of this experiment would be to allow one half of the class to look up unfamiliar words in a dictionary, while restricting the other half to using context clues, and then comparing the results of a recall test.

The above list of research ideas by no means exhausts the possible lines of inquiry open to the teacher when exploring the teaching of vocabulary. Even if the results of these experiments are inconclusive, sharing your findings with the class can generate discussion of different vocabulary learning strategies. This in turn will raise awareness as to how vocabulary might best be learned and this can only be of benefit to all.

Conclusions

In this chapter we have looked at different ways vocabulary learning can be tested. Testing needs to take account of factors such as:
- validity – are you testing what you want to test?
- reliability – will the test give consistent results?
- practicality – is it easy to administer and mark?
- face validity – will the learners take it seriously?

Testing can be both informal (as in regular progress tests) or formal (as in end-of-course achievement tests). Sometimes, e.g. for placement purposes, it is useful to test for vocabulary size.

Good tests have a positive backwash effect – for example, they encourage good learning strategies.

Vocabulary tests can be divided into tests of:
- recognition
- production

They also divide between tests where words are tested:
- out of context
- in context

Finally, vocabulary knowledge can be assessed:
- qualitatively – by using assessment scales, for example
- quantitatively – by doing word counts to test for lexical density, for example

Testing is one way of assessing learning outcomes – the products of learning. One way of assessing the processes of learning is by means of action research. An action research cycle typically includes:
- a pre-test
- an experimental treatment
- a post-test

Looking ahead   One of the benefits of action research is that it can help raise awareness, on the part of both teacher and learner, of the best ways of going about learning vocabulary. In the next and final chapter, we explore the subject of vocabulary learning strategies in more depth.

How to train good vocabulary learners

- **Learner training**
- **Using mnemonics**
- **Word cards**
- **Guessing from context**
- **Coping strategies for production**
- **Using dictionaries**
- **Spelling rules**
- **Keeping records**
- **Motivation**

Learner training

Some years ago a leading authority on second language learning, Wilga Rivers, wrote:

> *Vocabulary cannot be taught.* It can be presented, explained, included in all kinds of activities, and experienced in all manner of associations ... but ultimately it is learned by the individual. As language teachers, *we must arouse interest in words* and a certain excitement in personal development in this area ... We can help our students by giving them ideas on how to learn, but each will finally learn a very personal selection of items, organized into relationships in an individual way.
>
> (from *Communicating Naturally in a Second Language*, CUP)

The unique quality of each person's mental lexicon, and the idiosyncratic way it is acquired, have been recurring themes in this book. This does not mean, however, that the teacher is redundant. On the contrary, the teacher can play a major role in motivating learners to take vocabulary seriously, and in 'giving them ideas on how to learn'. That is the theme of this chapter: learner training.

Learner training – i.e. training learners to learn effectively – has been informed by research into the strategies that successful learners use. Studies have shown that good learners do the following things:

- They pay attention to form – which, in vocabulary terms, means paying attention to the constituents of words, to their spelling, to their pronunciation and to the way they are stressed.

- They pay attention to meaning – which means they pay attention to the way words are similar or different in meaning, to the connotations of words, to their style and to their associations.
- They are good guessers – which means they work out the meanings of unfamiliar words from their form and from contextual clues.
- They take risks and are not afraid of making mistakes – which means they make the most of limited resources, and they adopt strategies to cope when the right words simply don't come forth.
- They know how to organise their own learning – by, for example, keeping a systematic record of new words, using dictionaries and other study aids resourcefully, using memorising techniques, and putting time aside for the 'spade work' in language learning, such as repetitive practice.

This last point suggests that good language learners have achieved a measure of autonomy and have developed their own techniques – that they don't need to be trained how to learn. Nevertheless, less self-directed learners might benefit from guidance – by, for example, being shown a range of vocabulary learning techniques, and choosing those which best suit their preferred learning style. Particularly useful are techniques for remembering words, since, as we saw in Chapter 2, a great deal of what is involved in acquiring a functioning lexicon is simply a memory task.

Using mnemonics

Techniques for remembering things are called **mnemonics**. In Chapter 2 (page 25) we saw that the best mnemonics are those that:

- have a visual element
- are self-generated – i.e. not 'borrowed' from another learner or the teacher

The best-known mnemonic technique is called the **keyword technique**. This involves devising an image that typically connects the pronunciation of the second language word with the meaning of a first language word. For example, when I was learning the Maori word *te aroha (love)* the word sounded a little like the English word *arrow* + *-er,* so I pictured Cupid with a bow and arrow.

Devising keywords takes time, and a certain amount of training. Indeed, it can take more time and training than some practitioners think it is worth. However, the research evidence is compelling: there seems to be no other single technique that works as well. Therefore, when teaching new vocabulary items, it may be a good idea to allow learners a few minutes to silently and individually devise keywords. Then, if you ask them to tell their neighbours about their keywords it will not only reinforce them, but it may help train learners who are having trouble adopting this technique.

Word cards

Apart from the keyword technique, there is probably no vocabulary learning technique more rewarding than the use of word cards. In fact, it is arguably more effective than the keyword technique, since there are some learners who find 'imaging' difficult, but all learners can be trained to prepare and use sets of word cards.

The word card technique involves these steps:

- Learners write a word to be learned on one side of a small card (about the size of a business card) and its mother tongue translation on the other.

- Depending on the difficulty of the words (see page 27) a full set at any one time should consist of between 20 and 50 cards.
- Words do not have to belong to lexical sets – in fact it is probably better that they don't, so as to avoid the interference effect of words of similar meaning being learned together (see page 37).
- Learners test themselves on the words by first recalling the meaning of the new words – i.e. looking at each new word and then checking their understanding of each one by looking at the word's translation.
- They then reverse the process, using the translation to trigger the form of the new word.
- Words that cause difficulty should be moved to the top of the pile. In any case, the cards should be shuffled periodically to avoid 'serial effects' – that is, remembering words because of the order they come in and not for any other reason.
- The sequence of learning and review should become increasingly spaced (according to the principle of spacing – see page 24).
- As words are learned they should be discarded, and new word cards made and added to the set.

To train learners to adopt this technique – and to always carry around with them a set of cards – it pays at first to supply students with blank cards until they get into the habit of obtaining their own. Hand out the cards after a vocabulary-rich stage of a lesson and demonstrate how to prepare half a dozen cards, letting individuals choose which words they want to learn. (Discourage learners from making cards of words they are already familiar with.) It helps if you have a set of cards of your own as examples, with which you can demonstrate a simple sequence of activities. It is not important what language you choose for your own L2. The purpose is simply to demonstrate the method. This is the basic procedure:

1 Look at the L2 word first (*te aroha*) and then check the meaning (*love*). Repeat this with the whole set.

2 Look at the L1 word first (*love*) and try to recall the L2 word (*te aroha*); check and continue through the whole set.
3 Repeat this sequence two or three times.
4 Shuffle the cards so that they are in a different order, and repeat steps 1 to 3.

In subsequent lessons, ask learners to produce their word card sets, and invite them to comment on their usefulness, how many words they have learned, and how often they reviewed them. Some learners, of course, will not have used their cards at all. Others will already be in the habit. Continue incorporating word card activities into lessons, until the majority of learners are using them on a regular basis.

Here are some other activities that can be done in class to encourage the independent use of word cards. Note that some of them depend on learners sharing the same L1:

Peer teaching and testing: At the beginning of the lesson, pair students off, and ask them to compare their current word card sets. Encourage them to teach each other the words in their sets that they do not share, and to test each other.

Association games: For example, each learner lays down one card at the same time, with the L2 word face up. The first to make a coherent sentence incorporating both words gets a point. (The teacher may have to adjudicate the coherence of some of the sentences.) If no association can be made by either player, put the cards aside and deal two more. Continue in this way until all the cards are used.

Guess my word: When learners are already familiar with each other's word cards, each takes a word at random, and the other has to guess which word it is by asking yes/no questions, such as *Is it a noun/ verb/adjective ...? Does it begin with ...? Has it got one/two/three syllables ...?* etc.

De-vowelled words: Each of a pair selects a word from their word cards and writes it down without its vowels – their partner has to work out what the word is.

Ghost writing: Each of a pair takes turns to write the word in the air, or on their partner's back. Their partner has to work out what the word is.

Categories: In pairs or small groups, learners organise their words into categories, e.g. according to whether the words have hot or cold, or masculine or feminine, or good or bad, or sweet or sour, associations.

Learners can use the cards as material for other word games such as Word Race, Back to Board, and Pictionary® (see Chapter 6).

Guessing from context In Chapter 2 it was argued that learners need a threshold vocabulary of at least 2,000 word families, and that this would provide familiarity with roughly nine out of ten words in a non-specialist text. Increasing the core vocabulary to 3,000 or even 5,000 would further reduce the ratio of unknown to known words in a non-specialist text, but not greatly. In fact, no matter how many words learners acquire, they will always be coming across unfamiliar words in their reading and listening. This is why they will always need to be able to make intelligent guesses as to the meaning of unknown words. Guessing from context is probably one of the most useful skills learners can acquire and apply both inside and outside the classroom. What's more, it seems to be one that can be taught and implemented relatively easily. It is also one that we all already use – perhaps unconsciously – when reading and listening in our mother tongue. So it is probably less a case of learning a new skill than transferring an existing one. The problem for most learners when guessing the meaning of words in a second language is that they are less confident about their understanding of the context than they would be in their L1. They therefore tend to rely on the context less. For this reason, vocabulary 'guesswork' should be integrated as often as possible into text-based activities, such as reading or listening for comprehension, and will be most effective after a global or gist understanding of the text has been established.

Recommended steps for guessing from context are these:

- Decide the part of speech of the unknown word – whether, for example, it is a noun, verb, adjective, etc. Its position in the sentence may be a guide, as might its ending (e.g. an -ed or -ing ending might indicate it is a verb).
- Look for further clues in the word's immediate collocates – if it is a noun, does it have an article (which might suggest whether it is countable or not)? If it is a verb, does it have an object?
- Look at the wider context, including the surrounding clauses and sentences – especially if there are 'signposting' words, such as *but, and, however, so*, that might give a clue as to how the new word is connected to its context. For example: *We got home, tired but **elated***: the presence of *but* suggests that *elated* is not similar in meaning to *tired*. Compare: *We got home, tired and **downhearted***.
- Look at the form of the word for any clues as to meaning. For example: *downhearted* is made up of *down* + *heart* + a participle affix (-*ed*).
- Make a guess as to the meaning of the word, on the basis of the above strategies.
- Read on and see if the guess is confirmed; if not – and if the word seems critical to the understanding of the text – go back and repeat the above steps. If the word does not seem critical, carry on reading. Maybe the meaning will become clearer later on.
- When all else fails, consult a dictionary.

Many useful exercise types have been devised to train learners in these strategies. It is a particular focus of instruction for students preparing for examinations, where they will not have access to dictionaries. Here are two coursebook exercises which target guessing from context strategies:

Guessing vocabulary in context

Part A

Look at the sentences below. All the words in *italics* are nonsense words. Work out what those words mean from the context of the sentence. Example:
Tribbet must mean scarf, because it is something you put round your neck when it's cold.

a) It was a very cold day so I put a *tribbet* round my neck.
b) I was so *fliglive* that I drank a whole bottle of Coke.
c) I did three *tralets* yesterday but I failed them all because I hadn't studied enough.
d) I did the exam very *trodly* because I had a headache.
e) I *sarked* very late at work because I overslept.

Part B

In the sentences above decide whether the nonsense words are: adverbs; verbs (past tense); nouns; adjectives.
Example: *Tribbet must be a noun, because a comes before it.*

from Bell J and Gower R,
Intermediate Matters, Longman

Exercise 6

Read the following text once, and then look carefully at each of the words printed in italics. Remember when looking at each word (if its meaning is unknown to you) that you should decide:

(a) what kind of word it is
(b) what information is given in the sentence or the whole passage which can help you to work out the meaning.

We got in a little blue car heavily decorated with shining *brass* and upholstered in deep red plush: we were the only ones in a car made to take six. As we waited to start, I tried to make myself comfortable on the seats, but they were so high and *vast* that I could only sit on the edge with my legs *dangling* and my hands tightly *clutching* the brass safety *rail* in front: I felt like a pea in a pod (...)
(from *The Only Child* by James Kirkup)

When you have done this, look at the questions which follow and in each case write down from the four choices given, the word which seems closest in meaning to the word quoted from the passage.

1 brass
A cloth   B wood   C paper   D metal
2 vast
A small   B hard   C big   D soft
3 dangling
A running   B hanging   C moving   D standing
(etc.)

from Naylor H and Haggar S, *First Certificate Handbook*, Hulton Educational

Coping strategies for production

Guessing the meaning of unknown words from context is a strategy that helps learners cope when reading and listening. But how can they make up for gaps in their word knowledge when speaking or writing? Do coping strategies exist for production?

Even in our first language we use strategies to get round the problem of not knowing a word, or not being able to recall it in time. Vague terms such as *thingy*, *thingummy* and *whatsit* are enlisted to fill the gap, as in this example (from a conversation):

> Oh the whole glass is blue I thought it was the liquid that was blue (laughter). I thought it was erm that whatsit piña colada or whatever it is – it's bright blue – curaçao or something.

Vague language is equally useful for learners of a second language. Words and phrases like *a sort of*, *a kind of*, *stuff*, *thing*, etc. can be usefully taught at even quite low levels. Here, for example, is a coursebook extract that targets vague language and is directed at low intermediate learners:

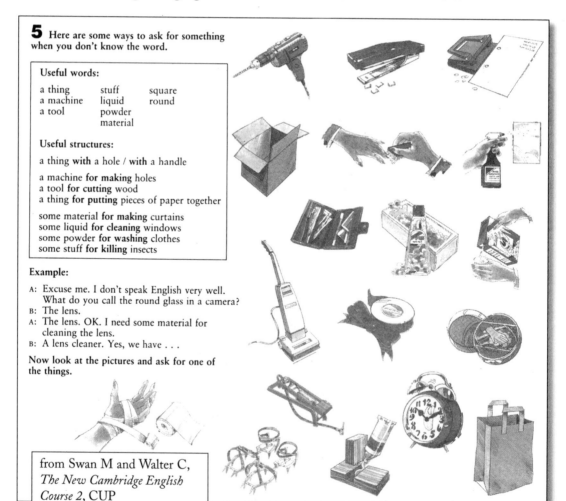

5 Here are some ways to ask for something when you don't know the word.

Useful words:

a thing	stuff	square
a machine	liquid	round
a tool	powder	
	material	

Useful structures:

a thing **with** a hole / **with** a handle

a machine **for making** holes
a tool **for cutting** wood
a thing **for putting** pieces of paper together

some material **for making** curtains
some liquid **for cleaning** windows
some powder **for washing** clothes
some stuff **for killing** insects

Example:

A: Excuse me. I don't speak English very well. What do you call the round glass in a camera?
B: The lens.
A: The lens. OK. I need some material for cleaning the lens.
B: A lens cleaner. Yes, we have . . .

Now look at the pictures and ask for one of the things.

from Swan M and Walter C, *The New Cambridge English Course 2*, CUP

Other ways of getting round gaps in vocabulary knowledge include:

- paraphrasing – as in 'a bed for carrying sick people' (for *stretcher*)
- describing – as in 'it's like a chair, it's got four legs, you sit on it, but it hasn't got a back' (for *stool*)
- using a rough synonym - as in 'the car is broken' (for *the car won't start*)
- 'foreignising' the equivalent L1 word – as when a Spanish speaker correctly omits the final *-o* in *tranquillo* to produce *tranquil*, or, less successfully when a student of mine asked for 'carpet' in an English stationery shop, reasoning (incorrectly) that the word for *folder* might be the Spanish word (*carpeta*) minus the *-a*.
- using gesture and mime – for example, if trying to buy a saw or a hammer.
- using the L1 word – in the hope that the listener will know it, or that it won't be very different in the L2.

Learners can first be exposed to these strategies (on tape, for example) and then apply them – through role plays. Buying tools and gadgets from a hardware store is a productive scenario. When talking with learners, it sometimes pays to resist supplying them with the words they are looking for, in order to encourage them to integrate coping strategies into their talk. Reminding learners that proficient speakers also suffer from gaps in their vocabulary knowledge can be helpful: teachers can draw attention to the language they themselves use when experiencing word retrieval difficulties.

Exposing learners to 'defining' language, as used in dictionaries, is another way of providing them with the means to cope with vocabulary gaps. Some learner dictionaries deliberately use an informal, spoken style in their definitions, as in this example (from the *Collins COBUILD English Dictionary*):

> A **corkscrew** is a device for pulling corks out of bottles. It has a spiral-shaped metal rod with a point that you push into the cork and a handle which you pull to remove the cork.

Examples like these can serve as useful models for learners to write their own definitions – using language such as *a device for -ing*; *it has ...*; *X-shaped*; *... that/which you ...* etc. As well as trying to learn the names of relatively infrequent items (as in the example from *Test your Vocabulary 1* on page 45), learners might also write definitions of them. As further practice, they can then exchange their definitions and guess which definition matches which picture.

Using dictionaries

Dictionaries – as we have seen – can be used as a last resort when 'guessing from context' strategies fail. But they can also be used productively, both for generating text and as resources for vocabulary acquisition. Their usefulness depends on learners being able to access the information they contain both speedily and accurately. Training learners in effective dictionary use is particularly important since many learners may not be familiar with dictionary conventions, even in their own language. Such training also provides them with the means to continue vocabulary acquisition long after their course of formal study has been completed.

Key skills involved in effective dictionary use are the following:

- Recognising features of dictionary layout, such as use of alphabetical order, headwords, grammar and pronunciation information, definitions, etc.
- Understanding the way dictionary entries are coded – particularly the use of abbreviations such as *adj* (adjective), *sth* (something), *ScotE* (Scottish English), etc.
- Discriminating between the different meanings of a word, especially a word with many **polysemes** (see page 8) such as *course* or *fair*, or words that are **homonyms** such as *bill, bat* and *shed* or **homographs** such as *windy, live* and *lead* (see page 8).
- Cross-checking (when using a bilingual dictionary) that the translation equivalent that is offered is the best choice for the meaning that is required. For example, a French learner wishing to express *embrasser* (as in *je t'embrasse*) in English may find several different equivalents in their dictionary: *1 embrace. 2 hug. 3 kiss. 4 include.* Only by checking 'backwards' (e.g. by looking up the entry for *kiss*) will they discover that some of the English words may have a more restricted meaning and may not be appropriate for their purpose.
- Using synonyms, antonyms and other information to narrow the choice of best word for the meaning intended. For example, a learner wanting to convey the meaning *carefree* but knowing only *careless* could use this as the starting point in a dictionary search. Similarly, the learner who wants to correct the sentence '*They told everyone their engaged*' will find both the noun *engagement* and the correct verb *announced* under the entries alongside *engaged* in any good learners' dictionary. Or a learner wondering if *steed* substitutes for *horse* will find that it has poetic connotations and is generally only used in a literary context.
- Inferring the spelling of an unfamiliar word from only having heard it, in order to check its meaning in the dictionary.

Ways of training learners in the above skills include the following:

 Direct attention to the dictionary's layout information, as displayed in a typical entry. Such example entries can usually be found in the introductory matter at the front of the dictionary. You could prepare a wallchart or overhead transparency that displays this information. Then prepare a quiz that learners can answer in groups, using their dictionaries. The words should be obscure because, if the learners already know the words, there would be no incentive to use their dictionaries. For example:

1 Which one in each of the following lists are not English words?
   a *terrapin*   b *termagant*   c *terkle*   d *tern*
   a *wede*   b *wedlock*   c *weenie*   d *wedge*
   a *caterpillar*   b *cattery*   c *catism*   d *caterwaul*

2 What part of speech are
   a *gaggle*   b *parch*   c *barring*   d *peaky*

3 What is the past tense of
   a *abide*   b *rend*   c *rid*   d *strive*

4 Find the words from which these words are derived:
   a *shies*   b *racily*   c *begotten*   d *gravelly*

5 What preposition usually follows each of these words?
   a *believe*   b *ashamed*   c *opposed*   d *consist*

6 In terms of pronunciation, which is the odd one out in each group?
   a *incise*   b *concise*   c *precise*
   a *death*   b *breath*   c *sheath*
   a *rude*   b *feud*   c *lewd*

7 What is the American equivalent of
   a *dinner jacket*
   b *pavement artist*
   c *holiday maker*
   d *spare tyre*

Design a similar set of activities based on just one page of a learners' dictionary.

Set learners the task of identifying which of different **headwords** matches a given meaning. A headword is any word which has an entry of its own. In the case of homonyms and homographs, most dictionaries give separate entries, and number the headwords accordingly. Thus:

spar[1] to practise boxing with someone
spar[2] a thick pole, especially one on a ship to support sails or ropes

(adapted from the *Longman Dictionary of Contemporary English*)

Here is an exercise aimed at sensitising learners to this dictionary feature:

1. Find the entries for **post** in your dictionary.
2. Notice that there are 5 separate entries, each with a numbered headword.
3. Write the number of the headword used in these sentences.

e g *I'll post the letter tomorrow*	Headword number
post has the meaning of headword number	4
a The soldier stood at his post.	
b There are two large gateposts in front of the house.	
c At sunset, bugles blew the last post.	
d Is the post delivered to each house?	

from Underhill A, *Use Your Dictionary*, OUP

📋 Set similar tasks that require learners to discriminate between the different meanings (or **polysemes**) under one headword, or the different phrasal verbs associated with one headword (e.g. *get up, get on, get over*).

📋 With groups of students speaking the same mother tongue and using bilingual dictionaries, set translation tasks involving words with multiple meanings in both the L1 and L2. Encourage them to cross-check the words to ensure that the translation matches the meaning required by the context. English words which could be targeted in such exercises because their translation is problematic include: *country, to meet, way, to spend, to stay, to stand, to get, trip, home, fun, to join, mind*, and virtually all common prepositions.

📋 Set learners the task of devising word chains using dictionary entries. Different pairs can be given a starting word, and then ten minutes to produce as long a chain as possible, choosing only words that are related in some meaningful way with the immediately preceding word. They can then explain their word chains to other pairs. Here, for example, is a word chain that started from the word *horrid* in the *Longman Dictionary of Contemporary English*:

> horrid → unpleasant → (not) enjoyable → pleasure → happiness → feelings → anger → offensive → insulting → rude → annoy → unhappy → worried → anxious

📋 Encourage dictionary use when learners are self-correcting their written work. Indicate, for example, where a mistake is due to the wrong spelling (*wich* for *which*), the wrong choice of word (*nervous* for *angry*), or the wrong form of the word chosen (*argues* for *arguments*). As preparation, distribute examples of vocabulary errors collected from homework, and ask learners to work in pairs or small groups, using dictionaries, to correct them.

📋 Encourage learners to guess the spelling of unknown words that occur when they are listening to a recorded cassette, for example. Pause the cassette after words known to be unfamiliar, and allow learners time to work in pairs to work out the spelling. They may then check the spelling in the dictionary, looking up the meaning at the same time.

It was pointed out (on page 148) that the first line of attack on meeting unfamiliar words in a text is to use 'guessing from context' strategies and that dictionaries should only be consulted as a last resort. If learners are shortcutting the guessing stage, one way of reducing their dependence on dictionaries is the following:

📋 Hand out a text that has a number of words in it that you expect will be unfamiliar to learners. Ask them individually to choose just five words that they are allowed to look up. Before handing out dictionaries, ask them to compare and revise their 'shortlists' in pairs. If one student thinks they know a word on their partner's list (through having worked it out from context, for example) they can explain it to them and delete that word from their list. They continue in the same way in successively larger groups, before submitting the words to a class vote. Only when the class agrees on a definitive short-list of five words can the dictionaries be consulted. In this way, learners can negotiate which words are most important for an understanding of the text, and which cannot be deduced from context. The activity also requires learners to make repeated decisions about words, which – as we have seen – is an aid to memorisation.

Spelling rules

Dictionaries are often used to check spelling, and spelling in English is somewhat problematic. This is because there is often more than one way of spelling a sound, and more than one way of pronouncing a letter (or combination of letters). Think of the way the /i:/ sound can be spelt in words such as *me, flea, tree, Pete, ceiling* and *believe*. Or (famously) the different pronunciations of the letters *ough* as in *rough, though, thorough* and *bough*. The situation is complicated by the existence of many words that are spelt the same but pronounced differently (**homographs**), and many that are pronounced the same but spelt differently (**homophones** – see page 8). On top of which, there is a small set of words that have alternative spellings: *gaol/jail; judgement/judgment; skillful/skilful; alright/all right;* etc. This can give the impression that English spelling is totally capricious.

However, if English spelling really is so irregular, how is it that competent speakers of the language can usually make a reasonably good guess as to how to spell an unknown word? In fact, English spelling is surprisingly regular. Research studies have shown that as many as eight out of every ten words are spelt according to a regular pattern and that only three per cent of words are so unpredictable that they have to be learned by rote. This three per cent includes many of the most common words in English – such as *one, two, you, were, would, said* – which, because of their frequency, don't cause learners many problems.

This suggests that it may be worthwhile teaching some of the more productive rules of English spelling. These rules will equip learners with a handy tool when writing. Familiarity with spelling regularities will also help them predict the pronunciation of a new word when they meet it in their reading. It is yet another way of making learners less dependent on either their teacher or their dictionary.

Four such highly productive rules have been identified by researchers. They are:

- Use *i* before *e* except after *c* or when pronounced like the *e* in *bed*. This rule accounts for: *chief, piece, relieve, receipt, ceiling, their* and *heir.*
- If the word ends in a consonant + *y*, then you change the *y* to *i* when adding a suffix. This accounts for: *happier, relies, beautiful, pitiless* and *married.*
- If the word ends in a syllable formed by a combination of a single consonant, a single vowel and a single consonant, such as *wet, run, travel, stop,* you double the final consonant when adding an ending that begins

with a vowel, such as *-er, -ing, -est*, giving *wetter, running, traveller, stopped, beginner* and *biggest*.
- If there is an unpronounced *e* at the end of the word, and if the suffix begins with a vowel, then you drop the *e*: *loving, liked, nudist, writer*.

These rules can be taught and practised **deductively** – that is, the rule is given and then it is applied to examples. Or the rules can be discovered **inductively** – that is, learners can study examples and work out the rules for themselves. One such way of guiding learners to discover for themselves rules of spelling, including sound–spelling regularities, is the following:

- Dictate a number of words that have a common sound – such as /ai/ as in *fly*. Alternatively, if learners are familiar with it, write up the words in phonemic script. Try to include only words that learners are likely to be familiar with. For example (at elementary level): *fly, my, drive, high, like, sky, night, fine, try, white, fight, nine ...* Encourage them to have a guess at the spelling, if they are not sure.
- Allow them to use dictionaries to check the spellings.
- Ask them to group the words into three different patterns, according to spelling. They should be able to identify the patterns: *-y, i_e,* and *-igh*. Ask them to see if they can see any possible rules for choosing any of these spellings. (The *-y* spelling occurs only at the end of words.)
- Point out that these are the three commonest spellings of the /ai/ sound, and that by far the most frequent is *i_e.* (In fact, this spelling is used in nearly 75 per cent of words that contain this sound.) Less common are *-y* and *-igh*.
- Dictate some more words – this time words that are likely to be unfamiliar to the learners, e.g. *sty, flight, hive, chime, blight, pry, dime, spite, dine.* Ask them to try to write these words, to compare their attempts, and then to check their dictionaries. If they can't find their first guess (e.g. *blite*), suggest they try another spelling (*blight*).
- Ask learners to write sentences using as many /ai/ words as possible. Give them an example: e.g. *My shy bride likes nice white wine.* Ask them to read their sentences aloud. This will help reinforce the sound–spelling relationships.

Keeping records

The point has been made that the learning of a new word is not instantaneous, but that it requires repeated visits and conscious study. Much of this revisiting and studying of words will have to take place outside class time, since there simply isn't time enough in class for review and recycling. This means that learners will have to depend to a large extent on their own vocabulary records. However, few students are so organised that they automatically record the content of vocabulary lessons in a way that will provide a useful reference for later study. As an example of how not to record vocabulary, here is how one student took notes on a lesson on the theme of description:

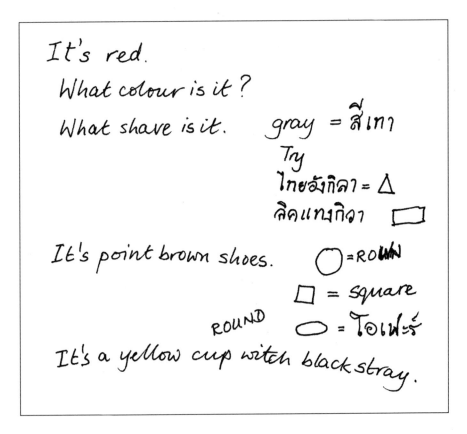

Like other vocabulary learning skills, the keeping of vocabulary notebooks is a skill that usually requires some classroom training. At the same time, as with any mnemonic system, it is probably best if learners develop their own preferred method of recording vocabulary. But some exposure to different systems might help raise their awareness of the options available. Here are some ideas as to how to go about this:

- Advise learners to have a special notebook solely for vocabulary. Ideally, it should be of a size that they can carry round with them. Alternatively, recommend that they keep a part of their class notes separated for the purposes of recording vocabulary only.

- From previous classes, save examples of 'bad' vocabulary records – like the example above – and use these as a springboard for discussion on the best way to organise vocabulary. At the same time, look out for good examples of vocabulary note-keeping, and contrast these with the less effective examples. Many coursebooks now include ideas for organising vocabulary. Here, for example, is advice on making 'mind maps':

1 With another student, put the words below into these different groups.

1 breakfast food and drink   4 family members
2 numbers   5 continents and countries
3 days of the week   6 interests

tea	father	reading	twenty-five	coffee
ham	Monday	sport	hot chocolate	Sunday
cheese	Europe	music	grandmother	two
baby	sugar	toast	Thursday	films
son	Friday	daughter	Wednesday	seventy
butter	eggs	eight	Australia	brother
Asia	Africa	forty-five	Greece	France

2 Add other words you know to each group.

3 Work with another student. Organise the continents and countries like this:

from Mohamed S and Acklam R,
The Beginners' Choice, Longman

 Ask learners regularly to compare and comment on their vocabulary notebooks. Elicit any useful tips. Possible issues that may arise are:

- the organisation of words – are they recorded chronologically, as they came up in class, or are they organised alphabetically, or into themes?
- the forms of words – is there any indication as to pronunciation, for example? Are derivations included?
- the meanings of words – is translation used to supply the meaning, or are definitions, synonyms, and/or examples given?
- chunks – are multi-word units and idioms recorded separately?
- mnemonics – is any mnemonic information included, e.g. using the keyword technique (see page 145)?

Set an example yourself, by planning board work in such a way that it is easy for learners to copy and organise their own vocabulary record. If possible, reserve one section of the board for new words. Mark word stress and any other problematic features of pronunciation, e.g. using phonemic script. Here is an example of well-organised board work:

Clothes

What's he/she wearing?

A striped	cotton	shirt
checked	woollen	pullover
plain	leather	jacket

patterns:

checked /tʃekt/

striped /straɪpt/

plain /pleɪn/

materials:

cotton

woollen

leather

synthetic

Allow time in the lesson for learners to record vocabulary and to devise mnemonics. Often the disorganised nature of learners' notebooks is simply the result of being rushed. Use the beginning of subsequent lessons for a period of quiet review.

Check students' vocabulary notebooks from time to time. This provides an incentive to learners to maintain a record of their vocabulary learning, and is also a useful resource for choosing words that may need to be reviewed and recycled later on.

Motivation   At the beginning of this chapter, we quoted Wilga Rivers, to the effect that: 'As language teachers, *we must arouse interest in words* and a certain excitement in personal development in this area'. How is this worthy aim to be achieved? One way is simply to timetable plenty of time for vocabulary-focused activities. Teachers can take heart from recent developments in research that seem to suggest that a heavy concentration on vocabulary acquisition, especially in the early stages of learning, is a prerequisite for later proficiency in the language. It may be the case that mastery of the grammar system depends on there being a critical mass of vocabulary to work with. Teachers need not fear, therefore, that they are 'wasting time' teaching vocabulary.

It is also important not to short-change learners by depriving them of vocabulary learning activities that arise during the course of the lesson, even if these might seem to be peripheral to the main focus of the lesson. A lot of the vocabulary that surfaces during teacher–student, and student–student conversation may in fact be more useful – and more memorable – simply because it has arisen out of the students' own needs and interests. Similarly, classroom texts, whether in the coursebook or prepared by the teacher, offer a rich source of words. There has been a tendency in recent classroom practice, in dealing with texts, to focus on superficial reading skills such as skimming and scanning. Students are cautioned 'not to try and understand every word'. It seems a wasted opportunity, though, not to exploit such texts to the full, especially since many students feel that they would like to 'understand every word' in a text. To deny them this satisfaction may be counterproductive.

As a teacher, possibly a learner, and definitely a user of words yourself, you should share your sense of the excitement and fascination of words with your students. Vocabulary learning never stops, even long after the grammar system is firmly in place. New words are being coined daily, and old words are assuming new meanings. Here are just a few of the thousands of words and phrases that have entered the lexicon in the last ten years: *bad hair day, canyoning, cone off, dadrock, dumb down, internaut* and *spamming*. Talking about words like these, and even coining new ones, can sensitise learners not only to the rules governing word formation, but also offer an insight into aspects of the cultures that produce such coinages.

Finally, share your own learning experiences – and those of other learners, both successful and unsuccessful – with your learners. Here, for example, is how one successful language learner – the nineteenth-century explorer Sir Richard Burton – describes the learning strategies he developed. Burton is alleged to have mastered around 30 languages, and could learn a new one in just two months. This is an annotated description of his technique, in his own words. (The numbers refer to the strategies listed below.)

I got a simple grammar and vocabulary, marked out the forms and words which I knew were absolutely necessary[1], and learnt them by heart[2] by carrying them in my pocket and looking over them at spare moments during the day[3]. I never worked for more than a quarter of an hour at a time, for after that the brain lost its freshness[4]. After learning some three hundred words[5], easily done in a week, I stumbled through some easy book-work (one of the Gospels is the most come-atable[6]), and underlined every word that I wished to recollect[7], in order to read over my pencillings at least once a day[8] ... If I came across a new sound like the Arabic *Ghayn*, I trained my tongue to it by repeating it so many thousand times a day[9]. When I read, I invariably read out loud, so that the ear might aid memory[10] ... whenever I conversed with anybody in a language I was learning, I took the trouble to repeat their words inaudibly after them, and so to learn the trick of pronunciation and emphasis[11].

These are the strategies Burton seems to have employed:

1 He concentrated initially on what was necessary – presumably in order to achieve a minimum level of effective communication.
2 He used item memorisation, at least at the early stages of learning, rather than the learning of rules.
3 He constantly reviewed what he had learned, perhaps using the principle of distributed practice.
4 He reviewed in short bursts, taking advantage of periods of optimal attention.
5 He acquired a critical mass of words to start with, sufficient to provide a core vocabulary for the reading of texts.
6 To reduce the strain on this limited vocabulary, he chose texts whose content he was already familiar with in his own language. He seems to have recognised the need for comprehensible input.
7 He made conscious decisions about which words he would intentionally learn, and highlighted these on the page.
8 Again, he constantly reviewed the targeted words.
9 He drilled spoken features of the language that required neuro-physiological (as opposed to cognitive) control.
10 He exploited the sound of words to facilitate storage in memory.
11 He used subvocalisation techniques to assist memory.

All of these techniques have been vindicated in subsequent research into vocabulary acquisition. What is significant, though, about Burton's account, is the determination with which he went about learning languages, a determination driven by his fascination for other peoples and other cultures. If something of this fascination can rub off in the classroom, maybe vocabulary learning will assume a momentum of its own.

Task File

Introduction

- The exercises in this section all relate to topics discussed in the chapter to which the exercises refer. Some expect definite answers, while others only ask for the reader's ideas and opinions.

- Tutors can decide when it is appropriate to use the tasks in this section. Readers working on their own can do the tasks at any stage in their reading of the book.

- An answer key (pages 178 to 182) is provided after the Task File for those tasks where it is possible to provide specific or suggested answers. The symbol ☞ beside an exercise indicates that answers are given for that exercise in the answer key.

- The material in the Task File can be photocopied for use in limited circumstances. Please see the note on the back of the title page for the restrictions on photocopying.

**TASK FILE
Chapter
1**

What's in a word?

A Lexical relations   Pages 3–10

What is the relationship between the words in the following groups?

1 a big loud oval green sensitive involuntary
  b make surrender understand grab belong
2 a feminine femininity feminist feminism
  b ease easy easily easiness uneasy uneasily
3 a strange odd funny peculiar weird
  b help assist aid lend a hand
4 a like dislike
  b freezing boiling
  c turn on turn off
  d friend enemy
5 a goldfish trout sole eel shark
  b boil fry bake roast grill braise
6 lean bank tender tap plain mean flounder
7 a log on monitor download browser
  b hand luggage gate number check in boarding pass

B Lexical relations   Pages 3–10

In the text below, find examples of the following:

1 two synonyms
2 two antonyms
3 two co-hyponyms
4 a hyponym and its superordinate term
5 three words belonging to the same lexical field
6 a root word and its derivative
7 two words derived from the same root

Sculpture
Making models and figures, or statues, is a form of art called sculpture. Sculpture is done in two ways: by *carving* and *moulding*. In carving, the sculptor cuts into a block of wood or stone with sharp tools. In moulding, he makes a model in soft clay, then bakes the clay to harden it. From the hard model he makes a mould, and pours into it wet concrete or hot, liquid metal (such as bronze). When this hardens, a perfect 'casting' of the model is left.
  Today sculptors also use materials such as pieces of glass, metal and cloth, as well as wood and stone.

(from Jack A, *Pocket Encyclopedia*, Kingfisher Books)

C Word formation   Page 5

The following words are recent coinages in English. Match each with its definition – and then decide what principle(s) of word formation each one is an example of.

twigloo	sport that involves descending mountain streams at high speed
internaut	freely distributed computer software
dumb down	a small computer application
canyoning	very large place serving alcoholic drinks and food
applet	make something less intellectually demanding
trainspotter	habitual user of the Internet
decluttering	a tree-house made of branches
shareware	getting rid of unnecessary things
superpub	a collector of information about train movements

How words are learned

☞ A Knowing a word   Pages 15–16

This dictionary entry for the words *occur* and *occurrence* comprises different aspects of what knowing these words means. Identify the different aspects of word knowledge and match them with these categories: *meaning, spoken form, grammar, derived forms, collocations, register, frequency.*

(from the *Longman Dictionary of Contemporary English*)

> **S1**
> **W1** **oc·cur** /əˈkɜː‖əˈkɜːr/ *v* **occurred, occurring** [I] *formal* **1** to happen: *Many accidents occur in the home.* | *Climatic changes have occurred at intervals throughout the millennium.* **2** [always + adv/prep] to happen or exist in a particular place or situation: [+ **in/among** etc] *Whooping cough occurs mainly in young children.*
>   **occur to** sb *phr v* [T not in passive] if an idea or thought occurs to you, it suddenly comes into your mind: **it occurs to sb that** *Didn't it occur to you that your husband might be late?* | *The possibility that she might be wrong never occurred to her.* | **it occurs to sb to do sth** *I suppose it never occurred to you to phone the police?*
>
>   **oc·cur·rence** /əˈkʌrəns‖əˈkɜːr-/ *n* **1** [C] something that happens: **a common/rare/regular occurrence**: *Flooding under this bridge is a common occurrence.* | *Laughter was a rare occurrence in his classroom.* **2** [U] the fact of something happening: *the frequent occurrence of violent storms in the area*

☞ B First language vocabulary learning   Page 18

Here are two extracts of mother and child talk. In the first, the child, Kathryn (C), is aged one year and nine months; in the second she is a year older. What evidence can you find of the development of her lexicon?

1   C: (picks up red bean bag in shape of a bicycle) Santa Claus.
    M: Santa Claus? that's a bicycle, honey. that's not Santa Claus. that's a bicycle. red bicycle.
    C: bicycle. (puts bicycle on car) sits.
    M: yes, he's sitting down. that's right.

2   C: (looking under her skirt) I just have see. I'm gonna get some rubber pants.
    A: why?
    C: because then I won't go tinkle in these pants so I'll get some rubber pants … I have to go get some of those rubber pants. (going into her bedroom) I'll be right back. the door is open so I can get in.

(from Peccei J, *Child Language*, Routledge)

☞ C Learners' vocabulary errors   Pages 28–29

In this extract of student writing, identify the lexical errors according to whether they are *form-related* (e.g. mis-selections, misformations, spelling mistakes), or *meaning-related* (e.g. wrong word choice).

I never have done para-gliding in my life, because I have a little of giddness. Consequently I like the sports that I stay at the floor. For example, I has been skating for many years from I was eight years old until threeten. During this time I went to the club all Saturdays morning, but I never have participated in competitions. One day when I was skating I falled and I did hurt my uncle. This falled didn't permit me to return at the skate.

List the errors:

mis-selection	
misformation	
wrong spelling	
wrong word choice	

TASK FILE
Chapter
3

Classroom sources of words

🔑 **A Selecting words to teach**   Pages 34–35

The following words are introduced for active study in three successive levels of a coursebook series (Bell J and Gower R, *Elementary Matters*, *Intermediate Matters*, *Upper Intermediate Matters*, Longman). Can you group them according to the level at which they were introduced, i.e. Elementary, Intermediate, Upper Intermediate? (Ten words have been selected from each level.) On what grounds did you make your choice? For example, usefulness, frequency, learnability, teachability?

stylish	cheque	glimpse	uneventful
afford	intelligent	coat	windscreen
run out of	awful	crocodile	village
flight	be fond of	incredibly	fantastic
plead guilty	split up with	terrified	tissues
carrots	squeak	stockbroker	overtake
showers	try on	September	balding
strenuous	heart attack		

B Exploiting coursebook material   Pages 38–42

Here are two vocabulary exercises from a coursebook. Can you devise ways of extending the exercises, so that learners make several decisions about both the form and meaning of the words?

Build your vocabulary

Word field: biography

What is the usual order of these events in your country?

You retire.
You get engaged.
You graduate.
You are born.

You study.
You get divorced.
You do military service.
You die.
You get married.
You find a job.
You have children.
You leave home.

7 Match the verbs with the pictures:
swim   run   ride   jog
walk   exercise   dive

(from Thornbury S, *Highlight Pre-Intermediate*, Heinemann)

C Dealing with words in coursebook texts   Page 40

The following text comes from Unit 17 of a 20-unit beginners' course (Mohamed S and Acklam R, *The Beginners' Choice*, Longman). Students have to read the text and complete the chart. What words are likely to be unfamiliar to learners? Which of these are necessary in order to do the task? How would you deal with these words? For example, would you pre-teach them? If so, how?

Jamaica

The history of Jamaica is one of colonialism. English is the official language, but there is also a Jamaican patois.

The weather is generally sunny and warm, the temperature varies by only three or four degrees whatever the season.

Reggae music is everywhere and nearly always has a political and/or religious message. Different Christian religions exist, but Rastafarianism is particularly popular with young people. It stresses the spiritual unity of Africa and looks for political change.

There is parliamentary democracy in Jamaica but the country is right of centre due to economic pressures. The main export is sugar and tourism is important, but very little money reaches the poor.

However, more than 55% of the 2.5 million Jamaicans now live in towns and, on average, people live until they are seventy-three.

Harvesting sugar cane

POPULATION	
LANGUAGES	
RELIGIONS	
POLITICS	
CLIMATE	
LIFE EXPECTANCY	

Texts, dictionaries and corpora

☞ **A Short texts**   Page 53

Identify and list any lexical chains of three or more words in the following text. Give each list a title. A lexical chain can consist of repeated words, synonyms and antonyms, hyponyms, or simply words that belong to the same lexical field.

Squeaky Clean

Birds caught in oil spills could soon be cleaned using iron powder and magnets. Unlike detergents, the technique removes oil without destroying the waterproof properties of feathers.

   John Orbell and his colleagues at the Victoria University of Technology in Melbourne, Australia, found that oil sticks to fine iron powder in preference to birds' feathers. Combing the feathers with a magnet removes the oil as well as the iron. 'We were quite amazed by the efficiency of the cleansing process,' says Orbell.

   Magnetic cleaning is also much quicker than existing treatments, which involve gently scrubbing feathers before rinsing and drying. 'The dry cleaning process takes a matter of minutes,' says Orbell. As less handling is required, the procedure should be less stressful for the birds and allow more to be treated per hour.

(by Jon Copley, from *New Scientist*)

☞ **B Literary texts**   Page 57

Identify any lexical features of the following poem that you could guide your learners to notice and manipulate:

Wild Iron

Sea go dark, dark with wind
Feet go heavy, heavy with sand
Thoughts go wild, wild with the sound
Of iron on the old shed swinging, clanging:
Go dark, go heavy, go wild, go round,
        Dark with the wind
        Heavy with the sand
Wild with the iron that tears at the nail
And the foundering shriek of the gale.

(Allen Curnow, *Collected Poems*, Carcarnet Press)

☞ **C Corpora**   Pages 68–70

What grammatical and semantic information about the word *iron* is revealed by this extract from the *COBUILD* corpus? For example, what different parts of speech does *iron* function as? What different meanings does it have?

```
             I mean the Earth is made mainly of iron and silicon and things like that
        a super-family of enzymes that use iron and oxygen to do interesting
                as well as plenty of vitamins, iron and potassium, and lots of fibre.
    There's a coin laundry, complete with iron and ironing board, in the pool area
    being beaten over the head with a 3ft iron bar by a boy outside the school, who
           he learned two things: the value of iron discipline, and the inequities and
       building materials, such as steel and iron, in shortage, Iran may have to turn
            to hold a preliminary meeting to iron out their differences and present a
        calls for ruthlessness, hardness, and iron resolution, the behavior of an
     and 127 tonnes of granite. No steel or iron was used; the slabs and pieces of
              [p] [h] Daly produces display of iron will Golf Heineken Classic [/h] [b]
       the green. If you normally hit a 3-iron 180 yards, take a 4-iron, or even a
```

TASK FILE
Chapter
5

How to present vocabulary

☞ A Ways of presenting words   Page 77

Consider how you would present each of the following six sets of words. What do you think would be the most appropriate means of presenting them? (E.g. visual aids, a situation, real objects, etc.)

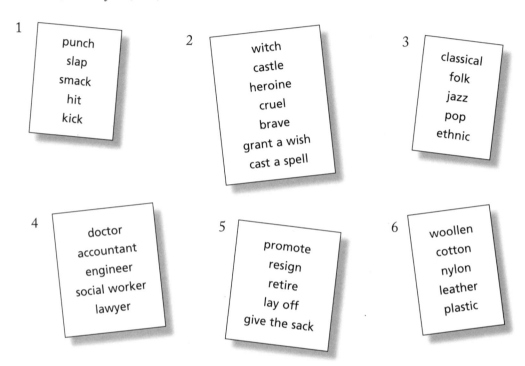

1
punch
slap
smack
hit
kick

2
witch
castle
heroine
cruel
brave
grant a wish
cast a spell

3
classical
folk
jazz
pop
ethnic

4
doctor
accountant
engineer
social worker
lawyer

5
promote
resign
retire
lay off
give the sack

6
woollen
cotton
nylon
leather
plastic

☞ B Anticipating problems   Pages 75–76

Look at the following words. What problems of meaning (including style and use) or form (either spoken or written) might they present to learners? Discuss what you could do in class to help learners with these problems.

stomachache	actually
lawyer	gentleman
thorough	crisps
comfortable	remind
furniture	invaluable
get on with	chuffed

☞ **C Presenting a lexical set** Pages 75–76

The following activities come from a coursebook presentation (Bell J and Gower R, *Elementary Matters*, Longman) but they are out of sequence. Can you organise them into a logical sequence? What factors did you consider when ordering the activities? Note that some of the activities refer to the photograph (in colour in the original) and the box of words below.

> cap   socks   coat   jacket   jeans   sweater   trousers   skirt   hat
> cardigan   trainers   dress   T-shirt   shoes

1   What are Alex and Jim wearing?
2   Match the words in the box with the clothes in the photograph.
3   Work with a partner and sit back to back. What's your partner wearing? If you can't remember, ask a question. Example: *Are you wearing black (socks) or blue socks?*
4   Match the words in the box with the parts of the body (A or B or A and B). Use a dictionary to help you. Example: *cap = A, socks = B, coat = A and B.*
5   Correct these sentences:
    1   Steve's wearing black jeans, a white T-shirt and a grey sweater. He's got red socks and green trainers. He's wearing a black cap.
    2   Pauline's wearing a short red skirt, a blue cardigan and a black hat.
6   Which clothes are red, yellow, white, black, brown, blue, green or grey? Examples: *Alex's dress is green. Steve's jeans are blue. Jim's wearing grey trousers.*

How to put words to work

A Exploiting coursebook material   Pages 93–101

Here is a vocabulary activity from a beginners' course (Mohamed S and Acklam R, *The Beginners' Choice*, Longman), consisting of two stages. Devise at least three further stages which would require learners to 'put the words to work' – both receptively and productively.

> **2 Look at the picture below and number the parts of the body.**
>
> hair **2**   head ...   foot ...   nose ...   eye ...
> leg ...   knee ...   finger ...   mouth ...   hand ...
> toe ...   shoulder ...   face ...   arm ...   back ...
> ear ...   stomach ...
>
> **3** 📼 **Listen and check your answers.**

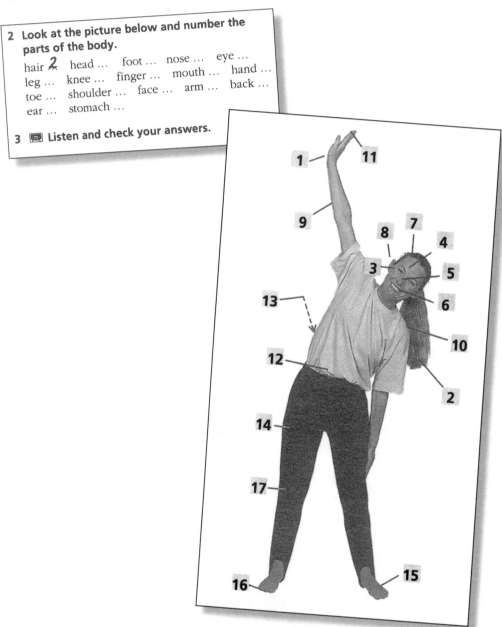

☞ B Cognitive and affective depth   Pages 93–101

Research suggests that tasks with depth have a greater learning pay-off than tasks that lack depth. Rate the following tasks according to the amount of depth – either affective (emotional) depth or cognitive (intellectual) depth. For example: cognitively demanding vs cognitively undemanding; affectively engaging vs affectively unengaging. Place the number of each task on this grid:

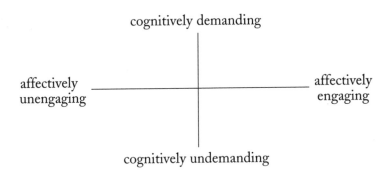

cognitively demanding

affectively unengaging

affectively engaging

cognitively undemanding

All eight tasks relate to the following set of words:

doing housework
babysitting
eating out
working out
going shopping
redecorating

watching TV
going for a drink
reading
gardening
going for a drive
surfing the net

playing music
going for a walk
swimming
going to the movies

1 Put the words in alphabetical order.
2 Listen and repeat the words.
3 Prepare questions using at least six of these words, and ask your classmates. Report their answers to the class.
4 Rank these words in the order of personal preference.
5 Categorise these words into three groups. Then identify the odd one out in each group.
6 Make true and false sentences about yourself using eight of these words, beginning *I really like* … or *I don't like* … *very much*. Can your partner guess which are true and which are false?
7 Look these words up in the dictionary and check you know their meaning.
8 Translate these words into your language.

C Word games   Pages 102–104

There have been a number of popular television programmes based around word games, such as (in the UK) *Call my Bluff* and *Blankety-Blank*. What TV and radio word games are you familiar with – and how might these be adapted for classroom purposes?

TASK FILE
Chapter
7

Teaching word parts and word chunks

☞ **A Combinations** Pages 106–107

Look at coursebook extracts 1–5 below. What combining principle (e.g. compounding, affixation, collocation) does each of these coursebook activities target?

1

> **a** You can make *hair* and *eye* into adjectives, e.g. *dark-haired*, *blue-eyed*. **Can you make more adjectives like this?**
>
> left-   fair-   green-   hot-   narrow-   broad-   short-
>
> blooded   shouldered   haired   sighted   handed   eyed   minded
>
> **b Check the meaning. Which adjectives describe personality? Which ones describe you or someone you know?**

(from McGowen B and Richardson V, *Clockwise Pre–Intermediate*, OUP)

2

> **1 Work with another student. Put the opposites of the adjectives below in one of the columns. Are the words in the columns generally negative or positive in meaning?**
>
> | un | dis | im | in |
> |----|-----|-----|-----|
> | | | | |
>
> attractive   friendly   sensitive   loyal
> experienced   caring   ambitious   adaptable
> reliable   obedient   polite   tolerant
> patient   selfish   decisive   faithful
> romantic   lucky   fair   intelligent

(from Mohamed S and Acklam R, *Intermediate Choice*, Longman)

3

> **2** How many sports can you make by using words from column 1 and column 2?
>
> | 1 | 2 |
> |------|--------|
> | hand | polo |
> | horse | skiing |
> | water | ball |
> | ice | racing |
> | basket | hockey |
> | motor | skating |
> | net | |
> | base | |

(from Thornbury S, *Highlight Pre–Intermediate*, Heinemann)

4

> **1** Complete the text.
>
> in a small village   ourselves   retiring
> in different countries   travelling   golf
>
> > My parents are diplomats, and they've worked all over the world. It was strange for me and my sister growing up ¹ _____ , but it made us very independent – we can look after ² _____ . My father's looking forward to ³ _____ now. I think he's had enough of living abroad, and he wants to settle down ⁴ _____ and take up ⁵ _____ ! It'll be harder for my mum, I don't think she'll ever give up ⁶ _____ .
>
> **2** Write sentences about yourself with the multi-word verbs in the text.

(from McGowen B and Richardson V, *Clockwise Pre–Intermediate*, OUP)

5

> **Walk around the classroom and find one person who:**
>
> a   sometimes goes on holiday alone.
> b   hates going shopping.
> c   usually goes for a drink / coffee after class.
> d   usually goes home as soon as the lesson finishes.
> e   is going out on Saturday night.
> f   is going away next weekend.
> g   goes jogging regularly.
> h   likes going for a walk in the countryside.

(from Cunningham S and Moor P, *Cutting Edge Intermediate*, Longman)

B Word grammar   Page 122

Sort these verbs into three groups according to their associated grammatical patterns. Can you find any similarities of meaning within each group?

manage	develop	proceed	show
disappear	advise	fail	emerge
teach	attempt	ask	arrive

C Idioms   Pages 127–128

Identify any idioms – including phrasal verbs used idiomatically – in this text.

1.40 Neighbours
Navy girl Janine finally comes clean and admits to her mother Cheryl that she has been the victim of domestic violence. No wonder she was so terrified when her ex-boyfriend Ross turned up in Ramsay Street.

7.30 Coronation Street
Behind-the-scenes investigations mean things look grim for Vicky and Steve. The syndicate looks forward to its first race. Reg's flat goes up for sale – is he finally moving on? And Don has an idea that could put the garage back on its feet. Teenage sweethearts Kelly and Ashley are going great guns with their romance, and it continues apace. And at last, Judy gets the job she wanted.

(from the *Radio Times*)

**TASK FILE
Chapter
8**

How to test vocabulary

A Vocabulary tests   Pages 129–132

Here are two tests of vocabulary. Discuss and evaluate them according to criteria of validity, reliability, practicality and backwash. Tick the categories in the box for each test.

1 Put more words in these lists.
   Example: uncle, aunt, cousin, father
   1 arm, nose, ……… ……… ……… ……… ………
   2 breakfast, dinner, ………
   3 triangle, cross, ……… ………
   4 knife, cup, ……… ………
   5 fly, walk, ……… ……… ………
   etc.

   (from Swan M and Walter C, *The Cambridge English Course 1*, CUP)

validity	low		medium		high	
reliability	low		medium		high	
practicality	little		average		a lot	
backwash	negative		average		positive	

2 Read the following text and use the word given in capitals at the end of each line to form a word that fits in the gap in the same line. There is an example at the beginning (0). Write your answers on the answer sheet.

Media career opportunities

Nowadays there is a (0) ..*variety*.. of career opportunities	VARY
in the media. It is possible to study (1) …………… at	JOURNALIST
most universities, many of which offer (2) ……………	OPTION
courses in reporting on sports and (3) …………… . Newer	ENTERTAIN
degrees in media studies, which were (4) …………… as	AVAILABLE
recently as ten years ago, attract (5) ……………	ENTHUSIASM
students from all over the country.	
Some graduates prefer to work in (6) …………… as it	ADVERTISE
etc.	

validity	low		medium		high	
reliability	low		medium		high	
practicality	little		average		a lot	
backwash	negative		average		positive	

☞ B Measuring word knowledge   Pages 135–137

Read the following piece of student writing and rate it in terms of the word knowledge the writer displays, using the scale on page 135. Check your intuition against a more quantitative measure, by evaluating the text's lexical density, variety and sophistication (see page 136). (To measure its lexical sophistication, you will need access to a dictionary that provides word frequency information, e.g. the *Longman Dictionary of Contemporary English*.)

> Living longer is the dream of many people because they don't want to separate from their family and friends. But scientists are making researches to increase the life span. Technology is used to extend life span. For example, ten years ago the average span of life in Turkey was fifty to sixty but today it increases to sixty to seventy with the help of technological improvements. Many people believe that this is very big advantage for human life. They believe that it prevent many illness and by this way improves the quality of life. But I don't agree with them because technology has many negative effects such as human's nature, environment and human's health. To sum up, we are damaging lots of things including human being while trying to lengthen life span. So that we must think twice before doing something to human being whether it is useful or harmful.

TASK FILE
Chapter
9

How to train good vocabulary learners

A Learner training   Page 144

Here is some advice for learners from coursebooks. Discuss and assess it in terms of the principles outlined in Chapter 9. Is it good advice? Is it practical? Is it likely to give results?

(from Palencia R and Thornbury S, *Over to Us! 4, Students' Book*, Longman)

• Develop an efficient means of storing vocabulary which you can easily refer to later. Experiment with the following.
- Alphabetical card indexes with definitions or translations of words.
- A special note-book with new words listed by topic area.
- An alphabetical note-book (e.g. an address book) which you can keep with you at all times.
- An alphabetical list on your home computer. (This has the advantage over the others as it will be easier to update.)

(from Radley P and Millerchip C, *Workout Upper Intermediate*, Longman)

Expression Organiser

This section helps you to record and translate some of the most important expressions from each unit. It is always best to record words in phrases, rather than individual words. Sometimes you can translate very easily. Sometimes you must think of an equivalent expression in your own language.

1a

What do your parents do? ....
He runs his own business. ....
She works in advertising. ....
To be honest, ...
He sounds really interesting. ....
She looks really friendly. ....

2a

What shall we do tonight? ....
So what kind of things are you interested in? ....
Well, I'm really into music. ....
Jazz and blues and that sort of thing. ....
I'm really interested in art. ....
I quite like reading too. ....

(from Dellar H and Hocking D, *Innovations*, LTP)

☞ B Self-correction   Page 154

Read this text written by a student and identify lexical errors. Devise a coded marking scheme that will encourage the learner to self-correct, using a dictionary, for example. What general advice would you give this learner?

During thanksgiving day, I went to American family for 4 days. It was very interesting. First, I was amazed about my host and hostness they have 7 children. In my country, most of families have 2 children. Then I went to my hostness's parents had thanksgiving dinner. This was another surprised. There were 42 people in this family. This is real big family. I also did something that I never did it before. I rode a horse, made pizza, baked cookies, and decorated Christmas's tree. Finally, my home stay made a big chocolate cake that is my favorite cake for me to give a farewell dinner. I was really missed them, and I hope I can go home stay again.

Task File Key

Chapter 1

A 1 same word class, i.e. all adjectives (a), all verbs (b)
2 same word family, i.e. a root (*femin-*) and its derivatives
3 synonyms, i.e. words or phrases of similar meaning
4 antonyms, i.e. words of opposite meaning
5 co-hyponyms, i.e. kinds of fish (a), ways of cooking (b)
6 homonyms, i.e. all of these are words that have at least two totally different meanings
7 words belonging to the same lexical field, i.e. computers (a), air travel (b)

B 1 synonyms: *models, figures*
2 antonyms: *soft, hard*
3 co-hyponyms: *wood, stone, concrete, clay, glass, metal, cloth* (all *materials*)
4 hyponym and superordinate term: *wood* etc. and *material*; *bronze* and *metal*; *sculpture* and *art*
5 lexical field: virtually all the content words belong to the lexical field of sculpture, e.g. *art, carving, cuts, block, tools, clay, bakes, mould, casting, sculptor*
6 a root and its derivative: *hard* and *harden*; *mould* and *moulding*
7 two words derived from the same root: *sculpture* and *sculptor* (from *sculpt*)

C *twigloo*: a tree-house made of branches – a blend of *twig* and *igloo*
internaut: habitual user of the Internet – a blend of *Internet* and *astronaut*
dumb down: make something less intellectually demanding – conversion of *dumb* (from adjective to verb) plus adverb particle (*down*) to form, by compounding, a phrasal verb
canyoning: sport that involves descending mountain streams at high speed – formed by conversion from noun to verb and affixation: *canyon* + *-ing*
applet: a small computer application – formed by a combination of clipping and affixation: *application* + *-let*
trainspotter: a collector of information about train movements – formed by compounding of *train* + *spotter*, *spotter* being formed by affixation: *spot* + *-er*
decluttering: getting rid of unnecessary things – formed by conversion from noun to verb (*clutter*) and affixation: *de-* + *clutter* + *-ing*
shareware: freely distributed computer software – formed by affixation: *share* + *-ware* (by analogy with *hardware, software*)
superpub: very large place serving alcoholic drinks and food – formed by affixation: *super* + *pub*. *Pub* itself is a clipping of *public house*.

Chapter 2

A

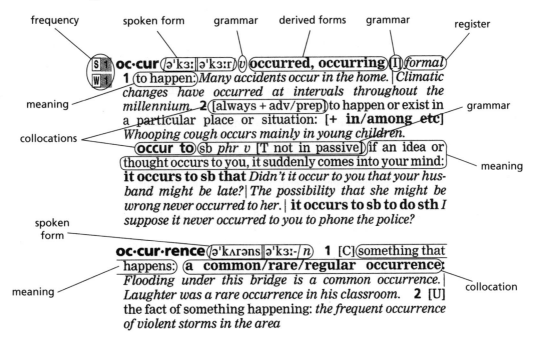

frequency · spoken form · grammar · derived forms · grammar · register · meaning · collocations · spoken form · meaning · grammar · meaning · collocation

oc·cur /əˈkɜː, əˈkɜːr/ v **occurred, occurring** [I] formal
1 to happen: *Many accidents occur in the home.* | *Climatic changes have occurred at intervals throughout the millennium.* **2** [always + adv/prep] to happen or exist in a particular place or situation: [+ in/among etc] *Whooping cough occurs mainly in young children.*
occur to sb phr v [T not in passive] if an idea or thought occurs to you, it suddenly comes into your mind: **it occurs to sb that** *Didn't it occur to you that your husband might be late?* | *The possibility that she might be wrong never occurred to her.* | **it occurs to sb to do sth** *I suppose it never occurred to you to phone the police?*

oc·cur·rence /əˈkʌrəns, əˈkɜː-/ n **1** [C] something that happens: **a common/rare/regular occurrence** *Flooding under this bridge is a common occurrence.* | *Laughter was a rare occurrence in his classroom.* **2** [U] the fact of something happening: *the frequent occurrence of violent storms in the area*

B   Apart from her very limited vocabulary at age 1:9, the child over-generalises the meaning of words, so that *Santa Claus* refers to anything large, red and rounded, perhaps. A year later, however, words are used precisely (*pants*) and modified so as to match exactly what is being referred to (*rubber pants*). Words are also used in their correct combinations (*go get, right back, get in*). There is also evidence of some 'chunk' learning: *gonna, some of those* and *I'll be right back.* Notice, also, the use of linkers (*because, so*) to make logical connections across utterances.

C   Mis-selection: *uncle* (for *ankle*). Misformations: *threeten, Saturdays, (I) falled, (this) falled, (the) skate.* Wrong spelling: *giddness, permite.* Wrong word choice: *floor* (for *ground*), *from* (for *since*), *all* (for *every*), (*return*) *at* (for *to*).

Chapter 3

A   The words were presented at these levels:
Elementary: *cheque, intelligent, coat, awful, village, flight, tissues, carrots, try on, September*
Intermediate: *stylish, afford, crocodile, be fond of, incredibly, fantastic, terrified, showers, balding, heart attack*
Upper Intermediate: *glimpse, uneventful, windscreen, run out of, plead guilty, split up with, squeak, stockbroker, overtake, strenuous*

Note that this is how one coursebook series graded the words. Other books might introduce them at different levels (or not at all), according to factors such as the choice of coursebook themes and texts.

Chapter 4

A   There are at least four main lexical chains running through this text: *birds, oil, iron* and *cleaning*. (Unsurprisingly, these four themes sum up the gist of the text: *Iron cleans birds of oil*.) Words in the *bird* chain are *birds* and *feathers* (repeated frequently). *Oil* chain words are *oil* (repeated) and *spill*; *iron*-related words include *magnet* and *(iron) powder*; *cleaning* words include *cleaned, detergents, combing, cleansing, scrubbing, rinsing, drying, dry cleaning*. There are also a number of words connected to the theme of *process* (*process, treatments, procedure*).

B   Salient features of the poem include:
adjectives (many repeated): *dark, heavy, wild*
go + the above adjectives: *go wild*, etc.
adjective + *with* + noun: *wild with the sound*, etc.
and the larger pattern: noun + *go* + adjective, adjective + *with* + noun
participles: *swinging, clanging, foundering*
onomatopoeic words (words that sound like the thing they are describing):
   clanging, shriek
preponderance of one-syllable, Anglo-Saxon (as opposed to Latinate) words:
   dark, feet, sand, shed, etc.

C   The corpus data reveals that *iron* can be used as both a countable and uncountable noun (*a 3-iron* and *no steel or iron*, respectively), that it can modify other nouns (e.g. *iron bar*), that it can be used figuratively with nouns like *discipline, resolution*, and *will* (meaning *very strong*), and it forms a phrasal verb with *out* (*to iron out*).

Chapter 5

A   Some appropriate ways of presenting these groups of words might be:
1 through mime; 2 through a story; 3 through recorded examples of music, or by reference to known musicians; 4 by means of visual aids, or definitions; 5 through a situation, or a number of situations, related to work; 6 through realia (i.e. real examples of materials).

Note that – according to the available visual or technological aids, the ingenuity of the teacher, the learning styles of the students – other means of presentation might be just as effective.

B   *stomachache:* pronunciation and spelling
lawyer: pronunciation and spelling; meaning (different cultures classify people who work in law differently)
thorough: spelling and pronunciation; meaning (confusion with *through*)
comfortable: pronunciation (specifically a tendency to stress the second syllable)
furniture: meaning (the fact that *furniture* is uncountable – *some furniture*, not *furnitures*) also pronunciation
get on with: meaning (idiomatic phrasal verb)
actually: meaning (in many languages the equivalent words mean 'at the moment')
gentleman: meaning (its use is restricted to certain contexts – e.g. *ladies and gentlemen*; it has connotations associated with class); form (the plural is irregular)
crisps: pronunciation; meaning (confusion with *chips*)

remind: the form of the grammar that accompanies it (*remind someone to do something, remind someone of something*); meaning (confusion with *remember*)

invaluable: meaning (the negative prefix suggests it means 'not valuable')

chuffed: meaning (colloquial, typically spoken, style); pronunciation

C   The actual coursebook order is the following: 4, 2, 6, 5, 1, 3.

Chapter 6

B

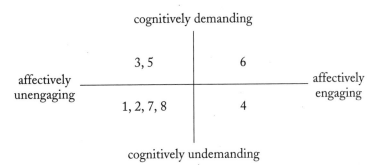

A 1 compounding; 2 affixation; 3 compounding; 4 multi-word compounds (phrasal verbs); 5 collocation.

Chapter 7

A   1 compounding; 2 affixation; 3 compounding; 4 multi-word compounds (phrasal verbs); 5 collocation.

B   Group 1: *manage, proceed, fail, attempt*: all are followed by *to*-infinitive and are associated with actions and processes.

Group 2: *develop, disappear, emerge, arrive*: all are verbs that take no object (i.e. intransitive verbs) and their shared meaning is one of things changing state or moving.

Group 3: *show, advise, teach, ask*: all these verbs can be followed by a direct object and *to*-infinitive (as in *I advised her to see a doctor*). Note that only three (*show, teach, ask*) can be used with an indirect object: *I showed him the way.* All four verbs imply that someone influences someone else, often through words.

C   Idioms are underlined:

1.40 Neighbours

Navy girl Janine finally <u>comes clean</u> and admits to her mother Cheryl that she has been the victim of domestic violence. <u>No wonder</u> she was so terrified when her ex-boyfriend Ross <u>turned up</u> in Ramsay Street.

7.30 Coronation Street

<u>Behind-the-scenes</u> investigations mean <u>things look grim</u> for Vicky and Steve. The syndicate <u>looks forward</u> to its first race. Reg's flat goes <u>up for sale</u> – is he finally <u>moving on</u>? And Don has an idea that could put the garage <u>back on its feet</u>. Teenage sweethearts Kelly and Ashley are <u>going great guns</u> with their romance, and it <u>continues apace</u>. And <u>at last</u>, Judy gets the job she wanted.

Chapter 8

B   A pencil-and-paper count of the text's lexical density gives a figure of 47% (71 content words out of 150); its lexical variety is 61% (92 different words out of 150), and its sophistication is 4% – the relatively infrequent words being *span, improvements, illness, negative, lengthen, harmful.*

Chapter 9

B   One simple way of coding lexical errors might be to use the abbreviations: WF (for wrong form), WC (for wrong collocation), and WW (for wrong word). WF and WC errors are relatively easily corrected by reference to a good dictionary. WW errors are less easily self-corrected, unless the learner has access to a thesaurus-type lexicon. Here is the student's text, coded for the three types of errors:

During (WW) thanksgiving day, I went to American family for 4 days. It was very interesting.First, I was amazed about (WC) my host and hostness (WF) they have 7 children. In my country, most of families have 2 children.Then I went to my hostness's (WF) parents had thanksgiving dinner. This was another surprised (WF). There were 42 people in this family. This is real big family. I also did something that I never did it before. I rode a horse, made pizza, baked cookies, and decorated Christmas's tree (WF). Finally, my home stay made a big chocolate cake that is my favorite cake for me to give a farewell dinner. I was really missed them, and I hope I can go home stay (WC) again.

Further reading

The following books are recommended if you would like to follow up some of the topics discussed in this book:

Aitchison J (1994) *Words in the Mind: An Introduction to the Mental Lexicon*. Blackwell.
Carter R (1998) *Vocabulary: Applied Linguistic Perspectives (2nd edition)*. Routledge.
Gairns R and Redman S (1986) *Working with Words*. Cambridge University Press.
Lewis M (1993) *The Lexical Approach*. Language Teaching Publications.
Lewis M (1997) *Implementing the Lexical Approach*. Language Teaching Publications.
Lewis M (Ed.) (2000) *Teaching Collocation*. Language Teaching Publications.
McCarthy M (1990) *Vocabulary*. Oxford University Press.
Nation I S P (2001) *Learning Vocabulary in Another Language*. Cambridge University Press.
Read J (2000) *Assessing Vocabulary*. Cambridge University Press.
Schmitt N (2000) *Vocabulary in Language Teaching*. Cambridge University Press.
Schmitt N and McCarthy M (Eds.) (1997) *Vocabulary: Description, Acquisition and Pedagogy*. Cambridge University Press.
Sinclair J (1991) *Corpus, Concordance, Collocation*. Oxford University Press.
Stevick E W (1996) *Memory, Meaning and Method (2nd edition)*. Heinle and Heinle.
Willis D (1990) *The Lexical Syllabus*. Collins COBUILD.

The following reference books, CD-ROMs and websites are also useful:

Cambridge Word Selector. (1995) Cambridge University Press.
Collins COBUILD Grammar Patterns: 1 Verbs. (1996) HarperCollins.
Collins COBUILD Grammar Patterns: 1 Nouns and Adjectives. (1998) HarperCollins.
Collins COBUILD English Dictionary. (1995) HarperCollins.
Longman Dictionary of Contemporary English (3rd edition). (1978, 1995) Longman.
Longman Language Activator. (1993) Longman.
WordSmith Tools [concordancing software] (Version 3.0, 2001) Oxford University Press.
British National Corpus Sampler CD-Rom (1999) BNC Consortium.
British National Corpus: http://sara.natcorp.ox.ac.uk/lookup.html
COBUILD Corpus: http://titania.cobuild.collins.co.uk/form.html

Index